Implementing
City Sustainability

RACHEL M. KRAUSE AND CHRISTOPHER V. HAWKINS

Implementing City Sustainability

OVERCOMING ADMINISTRATIVE SILOS
TO ACHIEVE FUNCTIONAL COLLECTIVE ACTION

TEMPLE UNIVERSITY PRESS
Philadelphia • *Rome* • *Tokyo*

TEMPLE UNIVERSITY PRESS
Philadelphia, Pennsylvania 19122
tupress.temple.edu

Library of Congress Cataloging-in-Publication Data

Names: Krause, Rachel Marie, author. | Hawkins, Christopher V. (Christopher Vincent), author.
Title: Implementing city sustainability : overcoming administrative silos to achieve functional collective action / Rachel M. Krause and Christopher V. Hawkins.
Description: Philadelphia : Temple University Press, 2021. | Includes bibliographical references and index. | Summary: "Implementing City Sustainability examines how local governments are organizing to carry out sustainability initiatives. It provides insights into urban sustainability and public management through examination of the mechanisms cities are using to overcome the functional collective action challenges that inevitably arise during the administration of sustainability"—Provided by publisher.
Identifiers: LCCN 2019057718 (print) | LCCN 2019057719 (ebook) | ISBN 9781439919200 (cloth) | ISBN 9781439919217 (paperback) | ISBN 9781439919224 (pdf)
Subjects: LCSH: Municipal government—United States—Case studies. | Interagency coordination—United States—Case studies. | Local government and environmental policy—United States—Case studies. | Sustainability—United States—Case studies.
Classification: LCC JS331 .K734 2021 (print) | LCC JS331 (ebook) | DDC 307.1/4160973—dc23
LC record available at https://lccn.loc.gov/2019057718
LC ebook record available at https://lccn.loc.gov/2019057719

Printed in the United States of America

9 8 7 6 5 4 3 2 1

To our families and partners for their love and support:
Joe and Jean Krause and John White
Maureen, Avery, and Mackenzie Hawkins

Contents

Acknowledgments

We owe a debt of gratitude to the fantastic team of student research assistants who helped with this project: Angela Y. S. Park, Vanessa Balta-Cook, and Serena Kim. We are so happy to have worked with them and to have them now as colleagues and friends!

We thank the local government staff across the country who are dedicated to making their cities more sustainable and took the time to share stories of their successes and struggles by answering our surveys or participating in our interviews. Special thanks go to Chris Castro, Daniel Hamilton, Dennis Murphey, Jackie Kozak Thiel, Leah Bamberger, and Matthew Naud.

We sincerely appreciate the guidance and coordination provided by Aaron Javsicas and Ashley Petrucci and the rest of the team at Temple University Press during the writing and development of this book.

Finally, thanks go to the National Science Foundation Science of Organizations program (grant number 1461526/1461506/1461460) for funding the research that resulted in this book. Any opinions, findings, and conclusions expressed are ours and do not necessarily reflect the views of the National Science Foundation.

Implementing
City Sustainability

1

Introduction to Local Sustainability
and Functional Collective Action

Sustainability is one of those intractable challenges that is simultaneously everyone's responsibility and no one's responsibility. This enables all levels of government, private organizations, communities, and individuals to pass the buck when making the necessary but often difficult changes that would help move sustainability forward. Like climate change, it poses a quintessential collective action problem. Given this context, it is somewhat surprising that local governments have risen to the position of sustainability leaders in the United States and much of the rest of the world. Given the important role they play, this book addresses fundamental questions about how cities organize to design and implement sustainability. Rather than focus exclusively on *what* they are doing, it explores the *processes* and *organizational arrangements* that city governments are employing to pursue sustainability within their communities.

Even within jurisdictions that have adopted sustainability as an explicit goal, the dynamic created by it being "everyone's responsibility and no one's responsibility" hinders its implementation. Cities, like most multipurpose governments, are traditionally organized around their distinct functional responsibilities—for example, planning, public works, community development, parks and recreation, and transportation, to name a few. In this context, we explore the question of which entity is (or should be) responsible for sustainability? And, if multiple units share responsibility, how are the subsequent fuzzy boundaries managed to prevent free-riding and mission shirking by the various partner agencies? This book advances a theory of functional collective action (FCA) and applies it to local sustainability as part of our effort to explain how cities can—and in some cases do—organize to successfully administer complex and functionally transboundary sustainability objectives in a manner that is comprehensive and durable.

To provide a window into the coordination challenges that inherently accompany, and frequently inhibit, cities' sustainability ambitions, as well as to better introduce the idea of FCA, we pull an initial example from the experience of Kansas City, Missouri.

Sustainability Coordination in the Heartland

The Missouri River, about nine hundred feet wide at this point in its journey east, divides Kansas City, Missouri, in two. The area south of the river developed first; its infrastructure is older and its population less affluent. Like in many old cities in the Midwest and Northeast United States, in the older part of Kansas City, stormwater and raw waste share the same sewage system. After hard rain, stormwater runoff overwhelms the pipes and basins meant to manage it, causing it to mix with the city's raw sewage and enter the river and other surface waters untreated—a problem called combined sewer overflow. The U.S. Environmental Protection Agency (EPA) found Kansas City in violation of the federal Clean Water Act and, following the usual course of action, the two governments negotiated a consent decree, which laid out a specific plan for how the city would resolve the problem.

The typical solution to combined sewer overflow involves installing new pipes and other "gray infrastructure" to separate the stormwater and sewage systems, enabling both to handle more water. It is a major financial and engineering undertaking but solves the problem. Kansas City may have pursued this conventional gray approach when confronted by the EPA in the early 2000s; instead, changes that were taking place in the city government at that time led to a greener approach. In 2005, the then mayor, to the surprise of many, signed the U.S. Conference of Mayors' Climate Protection Agreement, committing the city to work to reduce local greenhouse gas (GHG) emissions. Also, around this time, the city created a new position of chief environmental officer and relocated its Office of Environmental Quality from a subunit in a line department to the City Manager's Office, where it had more visibility and authority. These changes, plus the presence of a citizen group that actively pushed for sustainable solutions and later formed the Wet Weather Advisory Board, helped shape a different response. Rather than relying solely on traditional gray infrastructure, the city committed to using "green infrastructure" as a major component of its consent decree with the EPA to control stormwater flows. It was one of the first such agreements to do this and was, at the time, the largest municipal green infrastructure project planned in the country (Whitley 2010). The consent decree was approved in 2010 and gave the city twenty-five years—five years more than the length of time typically agreed on—to fully eliminate the overflow problem at an estimated cost of between $3 billion and $4 billion (Whitley 2010).

With its turn toward green infrastructure, Kansas City embarked on an initiative that not only has the potential to provide broad sustainability benefits but also ushers in a host of new complexities and requires input from a larger and more varied set of actors. Green infrastructure uses vegetation and other natural processes to slow, store, and clean rainwater runoff in urban environments. It often includes elements such as rain gardens, green roofs, bioretention ponds, and permeable pavement. Despite it often being lauded as a "best practice" and yielding multiple co-benefits that contribute to overall community sustainability (e.g., improved air and water quality, reduced energy needs, more green space, improved aesthetics, and climate resiliency), a U.S. city had never before committed to pursuing green infrastructure on such a large scale (Whitley 2010). This commitment required city staff to make a considerable effort to figure out the specifics of the new approach, overcome general resistance to change, and manage the complications and fuzzy boundaries that arose when multiple city departments needed to work together.

As frequently happens when initiatives with broad sustainability benefits are pursued, the city's transition to green infrastructure increased the scope of its stormwater management efforts well beyond the traditional set of actors. The city manager, the city's law department, and the city's water services led consent decree negotiation with the EPA. Water services—a rate-based line department in the city government that jointly houses drinking water, wastewater, and stormwater divisions and functions as the city's water utility—has primary responsibility for the consent decree's implementation. The above units would have been involved regardless of the consent decree's nature. However, the inclusion of green infrastructure as a major component of the compliance plan necessitated the input and cooperation of several additional city departments on various aspects of its design, implementation, and maintenance (Laughlin 2013). For example, Parks and Recreation was tapped to identify native plants with deep root structures appropriate for rain gardens and may be asked to assist with their long-term maintenance. Neighborhood and Housing Services, which is responsible for residential waste collection, was asked to adjust its operations to help ensure that neither trash nor organic material collects and inhibits water flow into the green infrastructure systems. Public Works, which manages parking and streets, became relevant because certain collection basins

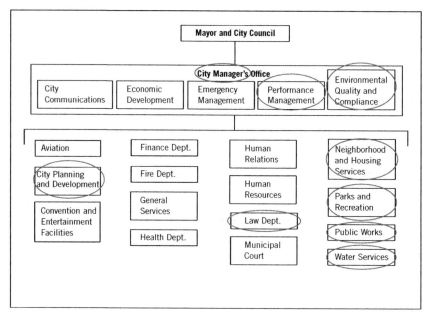

Figure 1.1 Kansas City organizational chart, including the city units relevant to its green infrastructure efforts (circled)

require sidewalk extensions and a reconfiguration of the right-of-way, affecting existing parking and traffic flows. As Figure 1.1 shows, cooperation from a minimum of seven city departments, as well as several of their subunits, is necessary for the long-term success of its green infrastructure initiative.

Kansas City's emphasis on green infrastructure in its 2010 consent decree with the EPA enabled the city to pursue multiple sustainability benefits while also working toward regulatory compliance with the Clean Water Act. Given the breadth of sustainability as a public objective, the use of green infrastructure in stormwater management is relatively narrow and concrete action. Still, to pursue it as an alternative to the traditional approach of using gray infrastructure, action and cooperation were needed from numerous additional city units, not to mention private contractors and community groups. This example illustrates a broader point that is a key theme of this book—namely, that sustainability transcends the typical administrative units organized around distinct functional responsibilities and cannot be successfully pursued without overcoming the obstacles that separate the units and keep them from working cooperatively. We examine the relevant dynamics and questions raised by this example in more detail later in the book, most directly in Chapter 5, which includes an in-depth review of Kansas City's sustainability efforts, as well as in Chapters 4, 6, and

7, which explore other U.S. cities that use different organizational arrangements to support their sustainability initiatives.

The Emergence of Sustainability as a Local Objective

Sustainability bridges human needs with ecological well-being and generally attempts to strike a balance between environmental, economic, and social objectives. It is not a traditional responsibility of local government. For most of their histories, local governments' responsibilities have focused on the provision of tangible services to benefit the residents of their jurisdictions. They have also been highly engaged in the promotion of economic growth (Peterson 1981). Sustainability, particularly its associated environmental and social objectives, is traditionally viewed as outside the wheelhouse of local governments. It has long been thought that cities have neither the incentive nor the ability to effectively achieve these aims.

First, there is a mismatch of scale between local governments and many sustainability challenges. Cities have a relatively small territorial reach and geographically are not large enough to effectively address environmental, social, and economic health problems, which do not adhere to jurisdictional boundaries. For example, air quality, water quality and quantity, transportation, and public health challenges all typically cross city boundaries and require regional solutions. Some sustainability issues, such as climate change, require solutions that are global in scale. These challenges, like the majority of issues related to sustainability, share the fundamental characteristic of being public-goods problems, whereby the benefits from their resolution are public in nature (i.e., they are nonexcludable and shared by all, but the costs of their resolution are private and must be borne by discrete actors) (Olson 1965; Ostrom 1990). This theoretically disincentivizes the pursuit of policy action by making it more advantageous for cities to let others act while free-riding on the benefits. Although public goods pose this type of collective action challenge at all levels of government, they are particularly troublesome for local governments because their jurisdictional reach is smaller, meaning spillovers and incentives to free-ride are typically larger (Feiock 2009).

Second, although it lacks convincing empirical support, the conventional wisdom in the United States holds that economic growth and environmental protection inherently pull in opposite directions. Redistributive social policies, including many of those associated with sustainability, are often also portrayed as being anti-growth (Ostry, Berg, and Tsangarides 2014; Peterson 1981). A large body of literature establishes the primacy of economic development as a local government objective (Molotch 1976; Peterson 1981). Therefore, because they are thought to deter economic growth, traditional perspectives suggest that cities are unlikely to pursue environmental and redistributive policies beyond what is necessary to achieve compliance with basic standards mandated by higher levels of government.

As a result of changing urban economies and demographics, however, this view may no longer match reality. Cities' interests in economic development, cost savings, and improving quality of life are increasingly aligned with sustainability goals (Osgood, Opp, and DeMasters 2017; Portney 2013). For example, cost savings often motivate energy efficiency initiatives, and cities' larger sustainability efforts are often spurred by the desire to secure a "green reputation," which can appeal to mobile residents seeking to live in a place that offers a high quality of life (Feiock and Coutts 2013; Krause 2013; Portney 2013). Quality-of-life amenities, which include aesthetically pleasing natural and built environments and opportunities for outdoor recreation, are widely deemed to be important to the attraction of the highly skilled and educated workforce associated with the "creative class" (Florida 2002, 8; see also Hawkins, Kwon, and Bae 2016). Moreover, election results in the United States consistently demonstrate that people living in cities are more politically liberal than their rural counterparts; and research shows that left-leaning ideologies are more supportive of sustainability, environmental, and climate protection (Heath and Gifford 2006). In this context, by pursuing sustainability goals, urban political actors are simply being politically responsive to their constituents.

The participation of local governments in the pursuit of sustainability is widely recognized as important and considered by some as essential (Clark 2003; Bulkeley and Betsill 2003). Approximately 54 percent of the global population lives in urban areas, which are responsible for an estimated 70 percent of anthropogenic GHG emissions (Seto et al. 2014). Agenda 21, the international blueprint for environmentally sustainable growth signed by 178 nations in 1992, illustrates the critical role of cities. Of the 2,509 actions it identifies for achieving greater sustainability, approximately two-thirds require the active involvement of local government (Keen, Mahanty, and Sauvage 2006). Cities and urban areas are key contributors to problems of unsustainability; they experience concentrated suffering from them, and they often have the legal authority and the operational expertise to address them (Krause 2011a). These perspectives counter some of the previously described logic and suggest that local governments have both control over important policy levers to mitigate unsustainability and the incentive to use it.

In the early 2000s, cities in the United States and around the world began to emerge as leaders and innovators in sustainability policy. By 2005, large numbers of cities had made voluntary, public commitments to reduce their GHG emissions and improve their overall sustainability. Figure 1.2

shows the number of U.S. cities that were members of influential sustainability networks between 2000 and 2017. Although cities can clearly engage in sustainability efforts without any larger affiliation, membership in the group ICLEI–Local Governments for Sustainability and being a signatory of the U.S. Conference of Mayors' Climate Protection Agreement have served as common proxies indicating cities' involvement in sustainability and climate protection (Brody et al. 2008; Krause, Yi, and Feiock 2015; Zahran et al. 2008). Initially very influential, these two networks have lost some of their clout in recent years due in part to targeted political opposition (in the case of ICLEI) and in part to the emergence of numerous alternative organizations, including the Urban Sustainability Directors Network, C40 Cities, and STAR Communities.

Nonetheless, observing these organizations' membership statistics gives insight into the larger pattern of U.S. cities adopting, and dropping, sustainability and climate protection as explicit objectives. As shown in Figure 1.2, the number of U.S. cities actively involved with these issues accelerated rapidly beginning in 2005—the year that the Kyoto Protocol took effect. This was part of a coordinated response on the part of cities protesting the United States' withdrawal from the treaty. Local climate action peaked in 2010, which was one year after municipalities received a large influx of federal money in the form of Energy Efficiency and Conservation Block Grants (EECBGs). EECBG money was part of the 2009 American Recovery and Reinvestment Act passed to stimulate the economy out of recession, and was

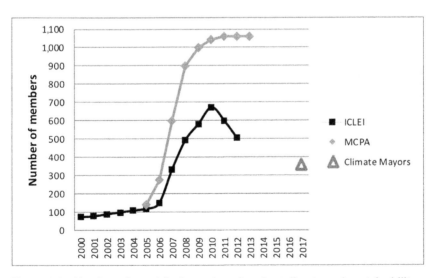

Figure 1.2 Number of municipal members in select climate and sustainability networks, 2000–2017

intended to quickly be spent on local energy and climate improvements. The years since have seen a leveling off and a modest decline in the number of cities with explicit efforts. This has been attributed to political backlash, programmatic cutbacks because of local financial hardships, and the absence of federal funds equivalent to the EECBG (Krause, Yi, and Feiock 2016). Still, cities remain among the most consistent and explicit supporters of climate protection and sustainability in the United States, and may be experiencing a new sense of urgency under the Trump Administration. For example, when, in 2017, President Donald Trump withdrew the United States from the Paris Agreement on climate change, cities took up the mantle as key actors in "the resistance." Within one month of the president's announcement, leaders of over 365 local governments, representing 67 million Americans, had made a pledge, committing to continue reducing their GHG emissions in a manner consistent with the Paris Agreement (Climate Mayors 2019).

Globally, the first portion of this general pattern also seems to hold: a post-Kyoto acceleration of local efforts peaking around 2010. In the years since, some countries—New Zealand, for example—have similarly experienced a decline in the number of committed communities (Birchall 2014). However, in other countries, commitments have remained stable or increased, albeit generally at a slower pace.

The idea that local governments would voluntarily adopt any sort of climate or sustainability initiative initially surprised political and urban scholars—many of whom are trained in theories of public goods and collective action and/or view cities as "growth machines" (Molotch 1976, 310). This seemingly irrational behavior on the part of cities initiated a new line of research to examine why some were eschewing free-rider tendencies and acting counter to established theories (Krause 2010; Portney 2013; Sharp, Daley, and Lynch 2011). Although general feelings of altruism and global responsibility—fueled by concerns about the lack of national-level climate policy—have played a significant role motivating cities, studies have shown that there are numerous local co-benefits associated with sustainability and climate actions, which minimize the perceived irrationality of their pursuit (Kousky and Schneider 2003; Krause 2013; Puppim de Oliveira et al. 2013; Spencer et al. 2017).

We identify three categories of co-benefits that often accompany municipal climate and environmental sustainability initiatives: those that yield fiscal benefits, public health improvements, and local economic advantage. First, efficiency efforts, particularly those focused on energy and water, are frequent components of cities' sustainability portfolios. Although their primary sustainability benefits are, respectively, reducing GHGs and other emissions and forestalling water shortages, they also often result in cost savings for the city government and/or members of the community at large.

This is an important motivating factor as illustrated by a survey of "climate-active" local governments in the United States in which almost one-third identified cost savings for the city government as the "single most important" reason behind their decision to pursue climate protection (Krause 2013, 130). A related financial motivation is the increased ability that cities with established sustainability initiatives often have in obtaining grant money for specific projects from the federal government or philanthropic organizations. Second, public health improvements result from, among other things, better local air and water quality and the healthier lifestyles enabled by walkable communities and easy access to parks and green space (Wolch, Byrne, and Newell 2014; Mendez 2015). Third, having a green reputation and offering residents a high quality of life can provide cities with an economic advantage. This is particularly important when cities compete with each other to attract "creative class industries" (i.e., those in the technology, health, information, and arts sectors), whose highly skilled, educated, and mobile workforces tend to place a high value on environmental quality (Florida 2002, 8; Hawkins, Kwon, and Bae 2016). Proponents of local sustainability often emphasize the occurrence of co-benefits to illustrate the breadth of positive impact and the "buy one, get one free" dynamic that investments in sustainability can generate (see, for example, Hunter 2009 and Floater et al. 2016).

In this context, cities simultaneously face incentives to free-ride on sustainability along with incentives to actively work toward achieving it and its co-benefits. These competing pressures have spurred numerous studies examining why some cities pursue sustainability and others do not (Portney 2013). A political market framework, which presents policy decisions as the outcome of the exchange between government supply and stakeholder demands, is helpful to organize the findings of the extant literature (Feiock, Tavares, and Lubell 2008). On the supply side, high governmental capacity, in terms of both fiscal and human resources, is consistently found to be a key factor enabling cities to pursue climate and sustainability initiatives (Wang et al. 2012; Ryan 2015; Hawkins, Kwon, and Bae 2016; Terman and Feiock 2015). Human resources are particularly important; communities that have at least one staff person dedicated to sustainability issues have notably broader and more ambitious efforts in place (Homsy and Warner 2015; Krause 2012). Empirical studies also find that institutional characteristics, specifically cities' form of government, influence the type and extent of sustainability actions that they pursue. For example, council-manager cities are more likely to pursue energy sustainability actions that increase the efficiency of city government operations, whereas mayor-council cities are more likely to pursue community-focused initiatives (Bae and Feiock 2013). Form of government also has a mediating effect on citizen support, notably increasing its influence in mayoral cities (Sharp, Daley, and Lynch 2011).

On the demand side, support from citizen and community interest groups is a primary factor that explains local involvement (Wang et al. 2012; Portney and Berry 2016; Levesque, Bell, and Calhoun 2016). Community characteristics known to correlate with environmental support, such as a liberal political leaning and high education levels, are commonly employed proxies and consistently show positive impact on city efforts. When controlling for these general indicators of support, studies show that cities' commitments to sustainability are strongly linked to the advocacy of organized interests—such as environmental, neighborhood, or business groups—in the policy-making process (Portney and Berry 2016; Levesque, Bell, and Calhoun 2016). Kent Portney (2013) observes that would-be opposition to city initiatives has been reduced in recent years as a result of a general decline in the importance of the manufacturing sector in local economies.

In addition to this political market supply-demand dynamic occurring within cities, several external factors, including state-level policies and environmental pressures and vulnerabilities, can influence local decisions to pursue climate and sustainability policies. On the whole, however, the impact of these external pressures is generally modest and less consistent than internal ones (Krause 2011a; Lee and Koski 2015).

With questions of why cities show differential commitment to sustainability at least somewhat illuminated, scholars have recommended that the literature shift its focus to issues of implementation and management to better understand the conditions for efficient and effective administration of local initiatives (Wang et al. 2012). Heeding this advice, this book focuses on approaches to overcoming the fuzzy-boundary, coordination, and collective action challenges that are inherent to the implementation of sustainability initiatives. Given its environmental, social, and economic dimensions, sustainability does not fit neatly into the administrative silos that typically characterize city governments. Using this observation as a starting point, we take an institutional approach to examining how administrative structure enables, and inhibits, cities to overcome functional divides and achieve successful outcomes. Although the subject matter of this book is local sustainability, we posit that many of its findings are transferable to any complex problem that requires the cooperation of multiple independent or semi-independent units within an organization to effectively address.

Organizational Form in Local Sustainability

Two decades ago Susan Hanson and Robert Lake observed that "the greatest barrier to sustainability lies in the absence of institutional designs for defining and implementing sustainable practices in local contexts" (2000, 2). Little progress has been made since then. The organizational structures and administrative mechanisms available to resolve FCA problems and support effective sustainability implementation remain largely unexamined. As a result, we know little about the way sustainability functions are (or should be) organized in cities (Portney 2013). It is thus difficult to assess, a priori, whether local governments have established the administrative and institutional arrangements necessary to facilitate the success of their sustainability efforts. The implications of this extend to issues of policy design, implementation, and eventual outcomes that lie at the heart of local policy and public administration research.

The handful of existing studies that consider the role of organizational factors in local sustainability have a narrow focus. Lucie Laurian and Jan Crawford (2016) find that relatively flat city hierarchies inhibit sustainability implementation and point to the value of mid-level managers as intermediaries between elected officials and implementing staff. Eric Zeemering (2017) suggests that sustainability should become a key part of cities' strategic planning processes integrated into, rather than bolted onto, local government systems. Our previous work (Krause, Feiock, and Hawkins 2016; Feiock, Krause, and Hawkins 2017) lays a foundation for the FCA approach advanced here by directing attention to the importance of which agency in local government provides the headquarters for sustainability efforts.

The Role of Institutions in Local Governance

In the late 1980s, the social sciences began to rediscover institutions. Led by Douglass North's (1990) elucidation of how political institutions that secure property rights and reduce transaction costs generate innovation and economic growth, institutional studies have informed our understanding of many governance outcomes including budgeting, political participation, policy choice, and collective action institutions (Ostrom 2005). For example, in the political market approach described in the preceding pages, local government institutions facilitate or impede the influence of specific demands and community interests on policy choices (Lubell, Feiock, and Ramírez de la Cruz 2009; Carr 2015). Institutions encompass formal and informal governing rules. By delineating what is required, prohibited, or permitted, institutions shape behavior individually and collectively (Ostrom 2005).

At the highest level, constitutional rules are embodied in municipal charters and form the basis of local governance by delineating the power, authority, and roles of participants in decision making. The form of municipal government, for example, is established in the local charter and specifies the nature of executive leadership; it establishes the legal basis for who makes decisions related to local government operations—a mayor or city manager (Clingermayer and Feiock 2001). An extensive body of literature investigates how executive powers centralized in the hands of a mayor who is elected by a popular vote of the city's residents may constrain or incentivize decisions on policy. As a result of electoral incentives, cities in which a mayor serves as the chief executive are thought to be more responsive to organized and well-resourced constituencies. Council-manager systems, conversely, minimize the political interference of elected officials in the daily operation of local government and lead to different policy outcomes (Carr 2015). Different forms of government have been shown to systematically favor the implementation of different types of sustainability activities (Bae and Feiock 2013). The urban environmental policy literature also examines legislative structures and rules, demonstrating that district-based representation systems lead to stronger environmental sustainability actions (Lubell, Feiock, and Ramírez de la Cruz 2009; Krause, Feiock, and Hawkins 2016).

Today there is little debate that institutions matter in local governance, but not all are given equal attention. The preoccupation of the literature on formal political institutions, such as form of government and legislative structure, works to the exclusion of informal institutions and formal bureaucratic institutions that organize city administration. This neglect severely limits our understanding of local governance systems.

Like formal rules, informal norms and conventions can constrain or facilitate certain behaviors (North 1990). These norms, conventions, operating practices, and patterns of interactions are sometime constructed in a social network and provide order and predictability to complex situations. Networks reflect the behavior of individuals and define the roles and positions of government units involved in decision making. The observable patterns of social/policy networks provide clues to how, for example, units influence policies that span administrative boundaries. Network patterns can also illustrate the degree of expansiveness and the diversity of administrative units involved in policy design and implementation. Studies of regional collaborative governance suggest that informal networks serve as a complement to formal rules in guiding collective action (Feiock 2013; Feiock and Sholz 2010). Together they determine basic operating parameters such as who will be involved in decision making and how information or resources will be shared among participants within the network. The characteristics of networks thus provide a window to view the informal rules or guideposts that shape interactions among units or agencies within an organization.

Although scholarship on networks has undoubtedly advanced how features of local governance and institutions are measured and tested, identifying and measuring informal institutions remains a challenge. The dos and don'ts that are socialized into behavior are often learned on the ground through repeated interactions. Authority rules, for example, have informal components to the degree that they involve a shared understanding of what is mandatory, authorized, or forbidden in the planning process. Over time, participants consciously become aware of (and habitually apply) informal rules to order their relationships. The working rules that are established are what participants reference if asked to explain and justify their actions to fellow participants in a collaborative effort (Ostrom 1990, 2007). For example, during the implementation of a project, whom to contact and when to contact them may be driven by expectations and procedural norms that are understood implicitly by participants, rather than by formal administrative structures.

Although there is insufficient knowledge about how informal institutions operate in cities, they are likely as important in explaining collective action as formal institutions are. Support for this perspective is presented later in the book, where we review case studies of the sustainability operations of eight U.S. cities and focus on both the formal and informal mechanisms they employ. In these case studies, the degree of influence that sustainability leaders have on other units emerges as fundamentally important. "Influence" here is distinct from "authority," with the latter being a product of formal institutional structures and the former additionally being derived from informal rules, norms, and expected interactions. In the specific case of Kansas City, collaborative activities were guided in part through a set of working rules that governed the relationships among individuals and the units they represent. Informal institutional structures helped shape city decisions in its move toward a green infrastructure solution for stormwater management. They helped determine, for example, what should be pursued (best practices in green infrastructure), the set of participants engaged in collaborative activities (which and how many units should be involved in the new operations), the positions of the relative units in the green infrastructure plan (what unit, for example, will chair the task force or manage the interdepartmental meetings), and the extent and manner of information sharing about the project with the public and collaborating partners. Informal rules such as these provided structure and predictability and reduced uncertainty in the process of designing and implementing the green infrastructure plan.

Bureaucratic institutions, which contain both formal and informal elements and structure how agencies within a single government interact with each other, are likewise not well understood. Our understanding of the institutions that shape intragovernmental interactions at the local level are primarily based on the traditional principles of hierarchy that have defined the formal administrative structures of cities since the Progressive Era. A city organizational chart, much like Kansas City's organizational structure previously presented, is perhaps the most ubiquitous visualization of the hierarchical administrative structure of functional and administrative units within a city. In this typical structure, policy makers, who are elected by citizens, delegate authority to top-level administrators, who then work within a hierarchy to organize and manage the daily affairs of city government. Administrative units in lower positions within the hierarchy are presumed to have less authority compared to the units above them, which likely have more-direct access to the elected officials who sit atop the administrative structure. In short, formal bureaucratic structures routinize organizational activities and define authority relations, connections among subunits, and decision-making structures (March, Schulz, and Zhou 2000).

Although cities share this general type of hierarchical governing arrangement, there is great variation across cities in the scope of authority delegated to different administrative levels and in the procedures imposed on administrative decision making. Institutions, many of which are informal, specify the participation and decision rights of various parties within city government, how much authority is delegated to officials across functional units, and the administrative procedures that determine coordination among units as well as the participation of private interests in the administrative decision-making process. Institutional choices that determine the character of administrative organization are important because they influence who gets what out of the political process—both within city government and with external stakeholders. They also determine the extent of decision making that occurs at the administrative level, the ability of various functional units to influence these decisions, and the incentives that these different actors face in collective action (Horn 1995).

Sustainability as a Functional Collective Action Dilemma

Institutional collective action (ICA) dilemmas result from divided or partitioned authority and arise when decisions made by one governmental actor in a specific jurisdiction or functional area affect other jurisdictions, actors, or functions (Feiock 2013). ICA dilemmas occur *horizontally* between independent governments at the same level as the consequences of one unit's actions spill over to another's jurisdiction—such as when one city in a metro area makes a policy decision that affects neighboring municipalities. They manifest *vertically* as a governmental unit at one level pursues complementary or conflicting actions to those pursued at a higher or lower level—such as when city and state policies interact. ICA dilemmas also arise *functionally* between subunits of a unitary authority—such as when the programmatic decisions of two departments in the same city affect each other's operations (Feiock 2013). Although there is an expanding body of literature devoted to the study of ICA dilemmas and how they can be overcome, little attention has been given to FCA problems among decentralized agencies within a single government (Kim et al. 2020).

FCA dilemmas focus on the fragmentation of bureaucratic responsibilities related to the expressed objective of a single government. Fragmentation of responsibility across multiple units often produces collective dilemmas because of the connectedness of services, objectives, and resource systems (Feiock and Scholz 2010; Feiock 2013; Scott and Thomas 2017). Similar to the interdependencies of cities within a region, the actions of functionally defined departments and agencies within a city can produce positive and negative spillovers. Moreover, "fuzzy boundaries," where clear lines of responsibility for tackling complex policy issues are lacking, remain a frequent challenge (Kettl 2002, 59). As a simple illustration, a potentially problematic FCA dynamic may occur around a city's efforts to acquire public infrastructure for electric vehicle charging if, for example, technical input is needed from its planning, streets, public works, and utility departments. Because it is a new and functionally transboundary objective, there is likely some ambiguity around the nature and extent of each unit's responsibility, including how much of its employees' time and budgetary resources should be devoted to the project. In the absence of intentional coordination, overall action may stall as each unit hesitates to devote more of its own limited resources than necessary or undertake work it may view as another's responsibility.

To resolve FCA dilemmas, some mechanism for functional integration must be employed. As a complex public policy issue, sustainability encompasses a wide range of governmental services and functions, and thus often involves the actions of many city government departments or agencies (Feiock, Krause, and Hawkins 2017). Sustainability is both complex and new to the local agenda. Thus, cities have not coalesced around a single best management approach, and the administrative arrangements they use to develop and implement sustainability initiatives vary considerably (Krause, Feiock, and Hawkins 2016; Hawkins et al. 2015; Feiock, Krause, and Hawkins 2017).

Coordination or collective action dilemmas arise in situations where policy to address complex issues encompasses multiple service functions, and separate bureaucratic agencies are therefore charged with sharing responsibility for these functions. For instance, as described in the Kansas City example, seven different city units are active players in its green infrastructure program. Collective action dilemmas may be more prone to arise where centralized authority is limited or constrained and the administrative units themselves have the task of developing formal and informal mechanisms to collaborate on sustainability. Moreover, regardless of the interdependencies across units, there remain the expectations from appointed and elected officials, as well as from the consumers of services, that individual departmental units will continue to carry out the day-to-day operations and functions that they have historically overseen. These and other dilemmas pose barriers to FCA.

Intentional institutional design can help structure and manage interactions, thereby increasing the ability to bridge fuzzy boundaries and facilitate collective action. This can be achieved, for example, by restructuring hierarchical authority or consolidating administrative agencies to create new entities with authority over comprehensive functional areas. The Kansas City experience offers an illustration of the first approach, when its Office of Environmental Quality was relocated from being a subunit in a line department, where it was buried deep within the hierarchical structure, into the City Manager's Office. This move increased its clout over the numerous departments throughout the city government whose cooperation on sustainability is needed.

In the following chapters, we build on nascent FCA conceptualizations by identifying four general types of administrative arrangements that institutions can use to integrate sustainability across administrative units: consolidated agencies, lead agency coordination, task forces and bargaining, and decentralized networks. We look in depth at the experience of eight cities that employ these different arrangements to identify the specific design considerations within each and assess their consequences. A key takeaway from this research regards the importance of an influential leader or lead unit to maintaining robust local sustainability efforts. Related to this, and because by our definition they do not have a clearly designated lead, decentralized networks appear less effective as an administrative arrangement for overcoming intracity FCA dilemmas. This finding offers a cautionary message about the long-term potential of decentralized collaborative governance in FCA settings and provides detailed descriptions of the challenges to its effectiveness.

Structure of the Book

This is a study of how U.S. cities that have adopted sustainability as a local objective organize to overcome coordination and collective action challenges to achieve its successful implementation. It is the culmination of a three-year research process supported by the National Science Foundation's Science of Organizations program. We use a mixed-methods research approach, and our findings and analysis are based on an extensive original data collection effort. The Smart and Sustainable Cities survey, sent to all cities in the United States with populations over twenty thousand, is the source of our quantitative data. It allows us to map out the general landscape for how local sustainability is being administered, as well as to investigate, in a generalizable manner, the causes and consequences of these local decisions. It also provided the basis for our selection of eight case study cities, which we examined in depth via interviews and network analysis. The case study portion of the research allows us to add context and nuance to the macro-level view provided by the survey.

Chapter 2 presents the big picture of how cities in the United States view sustainability, what actions they are taking to advance it, and how they have organized internally to implement them. We use results from the 2015–2016 Smart and Sustainable Cities survey to develop descriptive statistics characterizing the relative levels of attention that U.S. cities are giving to various sustainability objectives and how frequently different policy actions are being pursued. We compare these findings to results from past studies to provide a sense of how the substance and organization of local sustainability efforts have evolved over time. This chapter also uses correlation analysis to quantify the relationships between priority sustainability issues and the implementation of related policies, and cluster analysis to understand the broader patterns of city sustainability actions and their association with city contextual and organizational characteristics.

In Chapter 3 we develop a general theory of FCA. We build off literature on ICA (Feiock 2013), which was developed to understand how independent cities in a metropolitan region can coordinate to address transboundary problems, and apply its insights to *intra*city coordination challenges. We identify and describe four basic administrative arrangements that institutions can organize to overcome *internal* functional divides and apply these to local sustainability—an objective that requires input from numerous agencies within a government to be comprehensively addressed. The administrative arrangements are developed based on the relative levels of authority and decentralization associated with local sustainability efforts. In Chapter 3 we also reach back to our survey results to characterize cities on these dimensions. The chapter closes with a discussion of the selection of our eight case study cities, which were chosen, in large part, to obtain a maximum variation in the administrative arrangements they use to overcome FCA challenges in their sustainability efforts.

Chapters 4 through 7 are each themed around one of the general arrangements identified to overcome FCA and describe the specific structures and experiences of the case study cities using them. Chapter 4 focuses on lead agency consolidation and describes the experiences of Fort Collins, Colorado. Chapter 5 considers cities' use of lead agency coordination through the experiences of Orlando, Florida, and Kansas City, Missouri. Chapter 6 uses case studies of Ann Arbor, Michigan, Providence, Rhode Island, and Oakland, California to discuss relationships and bargaining as arrangements to overcome FCA. Finally, through the experience of Gainesville, Florida, and El Paso, Texas, Chapter 7 assesses the use of decentralized networks. These four chapters all follow a similar structure and provide basic background on the case cities, describe the organizational arrangement within the city government used to administer sustainability, identify the mechanisms each uses to integrate sustainability functions across units, and assess the implications of these mechanisms and arrangements on the focus, implementation, and output of city efforts.

In Chapter 8 we take a step back and consider themes and patterns that emerged across the case study cities. We visualize and summarize the intracity dynamic that exists around sustainability for a subset of our cases via social network analyses. This chapter highlights the informal network structures that have emerged in these cities in attempt to match administrative processes and boundaries to the sustainability issues.

Applying the lens of FCA, Chapter 9 combines insights from our national survey results with the case study and network analyses to answer the question of how U.S. cities organize to administer their sustainability efforts and the implications of those strategies on their abilities to overcome FCA dilemmas. Using a comparative analysis, we identify the relative strengths and weaknesses of the various organizational arrangements employed and each general mechanism to overcome FCA. We conclude that decentralization of effort is not as effective, because initiatives need some institutionalized center of gravity to be administered effectively and produce durable activities and impacts. We make the case that because modern policy problems are increasingly complex and require the cooperation of multiple semi-independent units within a government to be effectively addressed, it is imperative that governments identify ways to overcome functional divides. Although the focus of this book is local sustainability, we posit that many of the approaches and mechanisms highlighted as effective for it are transferable to other policy issues as well.

2

Setting the Stage

A Quantitative Overview of Cities and Sustainability

This chapter offers a ten-thousand-foot view of local sustainability initiatives in the United States. Using data from a nationwide survey of more than five hundred cities, we present an overview of the relevant efforts being pursued by U.S. municipalities and the administrative arrangements that they are using to do so. Descriptive statistics and cluster analysis are used to identify and help assess broad patterns of activity. This allows us to update and fortify the research on sustainability initiatives summarized in Chapter 1. It also sets the stage for the in-depth city case studies to follow later in the book by situating them in the broader context.

Attempts to define or, using the parlance of economists, definitively "identify" urban sustainability have consumed a large amount of effort over the pasts several decades. One of its early and most widely referenced understandings comes from the 1987 United Nations–sponsored Brundtland Report, which describes sustainable development as development that "meets the needs of the present without compromising the ability of future generations to meet their own needs" (Brundtland et al. 1987, 24). Subsequent conceptualizations emphasize the achievement of long-term balance between environmental, social, and economic well-being and suggest that the initiatives pursued in any given locale should reflect and compensate for place-specific weaknesses in pursuit of that balance (Mori and Yamashita 2015; Portney 2013). Thus, while there is general agreement about the core concepts of urban sustainability, the specifics as well as the actions perceived as necessary to achieve it vary (Zeemering 2009).

Now almost two decades into its treatment as a local objective, most city government leaders have an awareness of what sustainability is, as well as a basic knowledge about the types of actions and policies that contribute to its improvement. Moreover, although they are not always explicitly bundled into a single comprehensive concept and labeled "sustainability," the majority of cities consider these actions as components of locally important economic, environmental, and social programs. Although climate change, and the policies meant to mitigate it, simultaneously looms over and directly affects the long-term viability of actions in each of these three areas, it receives a more mixed reception across U.S. cities. Still, as a group, cities remain more explicitly committed to greenhouse gas mitigation than most other governments in the United States (Portney 2013).

Local initiatives are designed, adopted, and implemented in a dynamic landscape. Particularly when responding to issues like sustainability and climate change, which do not adhere to political boundaries, local initiatives exist as part of a fragmented and multilevel policy setting. City governments' policy actions respond to the political, financial, and issue priority shifts that occur in their own communities, while also being influenced and constrained by those taking place at the state, federal, and international levels (Betsill and Bulkeley 2006; Homsy 2018; Krause 2011a). This policy landscape is likewise shaped by regional dynamics, whereby the actions (or inactions) of neighboring municipalities can create new challenges as well as opportunities for collaborations and innovative solutions. The geographic proximity of communities in a metropolitan area often result in regional spillovers or externalities, which occur when the policy decisions made by one impose costs or benefits on others (Feiock 2009). For example, a city's decision to construct a new roadway may affect the traffic, air quality, and/or economic activity in neighboring jurisdictions.

In these varied settings, policy windows can open and close quickly, necessitating rapid response to take advantage of opportunities. One of the more important policy windows that opened around climate and sustainability issues for U.S. cities resulted from the 2009 American Recovery and Reinvestment Act (ARRA) and the $3.2 billion in Energy Efficiency and Conservation Block Grants (EECBGs) it made available. The pursuit and use of these funds influenced the way many cities structured their approach to energy and climate change, as well as to sustainability more broadly. Approximately 60 percent of EECBG funds were distributed directly from the Department of Energy to local governments according to a formula, with an additional $400 million available to be allocated via competitive, and often project specific, grants (U.S. Department of Energy 2009). To receive either type of grant, however, local governments were required to complete an application and provide a description detailing how their funds would be spent to advance energy conservation and sustainability. Spending resources and, by extension, creating jobs as quickly as possible was an emphasis of ARRA-funded programs (Terman and Feiock 2015). Although some of the cities receiving money had a sustainability agenda in place beforehand, a majority did not. For example, less than 40 percent of cities had climate or energy efficiency goals in their planning documents by 2010, suggesting that they were creating the organizational capacity to manage these funds as they were being received (Terman and Feiock 2015). Reflecting this, many cities used the EECBG monies they received to create and fund a new sustainability coordinator position. However, in the absence of a clear template or set of best practices, significant variation resulted across cities as to the specific title, administrative location, and scope of responsibility and authority location assigned to it.

This observation segues into a key theme underlying the current research—namely, that cities' sustainability efforts are characterized by heterogeneity in their aims and administrative and organizational arrangements. The implications of these decisions, and the extent to which one influences the other, are not clear. Although there are exceptions to be sure, cities' choices about how they administer sustainability have often been ad hoc, influenced by personalities and budgetary convenience more than by strategic considerations or plans (Krause, Feiock, and Hawkins 2016; Portney 2013). There is reason to believe that agency assignment and administrative choices matter substantively. For example, agency location, such as whether a unit is in the executive or legislative branch or buried deep within the bureaucracy, affects the degree to which political pressures shape policy decisions (Krause and Douglas 2004). This, in turn, may affect the accuracy of technical information produced as well as influence expectations about the likelihood of long-term programmatic continuation (Horn 1995). Administrative location within the larger organizational structure also shapes an agency's ability to integrate policy and coordinate functions across other units within a government (Feiock, Krause, and Hawkins 2017). However, both in general and around local sustainability specifically, relatively little is known about the factors that shape these choices or the full nature of their implications.

This chapter provides a snapshot of the priorities, actions, and administrative arrangements that U.S. cities had in place in late 2015 and early 2016 related to sustainability. It begins by providing an overview of the data source and proceeds to offer a quantitatively grounded description of the amount of attention that U.S. cities give different dimensions of sustainability, the frequency with which they pursue different policy actions, and how they organize to administer sustainability. We use correlational analyses to gain an initial idea of how these factors relate to each other and to identify the characteristics of cities associated with different types of actions. The insights gained from this quantitative overview are used to provide context and frame questions regarding effect that organizational form and institutional characteristics have on cities' abilities to overcome collective action dilemmas, which are addressed in depth throughout the rest of the book.

Smart and Sustainable Cities Survey

The analyses presented in the following pages of this chapter are based on data gathered via the Smart and Sustainable Cities Survey, administered from late 2015 through early 2016 to all U.S. cities with populations over twenty thousand. According to the 2015 census, 1,282 cities exceeded this population threshold. The survey questionnaire consisted of thirty-three questions and required about twenty minutes to complete. It is divided into sections asking local officials about their city's sustainability priorities, the allocation of administrative responsibility for the design and implementation of sustainability initiatives, the formal and informal mechanisms used to coordinate relevant efforts between departments, the status of a variety of sustainability-related policy actions, the extent of collaboration with various units inside and outside of the city government, and perceived programmatic impacts (see Appendix A for the full survey instrument).

The survey was sent directly to the staff member in each city government deemed "most responsible" for leading and coordinating its sustainability efforts. To identify the appropriate individual, we went to each of the cities' websites and searched for the terms "sustainability," "green," "climate," and/or "environment." Frequently, the results of this search directed us to the person or department responsible for leading relevant efforts. If, via the website search, we were able to identify the appropriate person, their position title, departmental home, direct email address, and mailing address online, we moved to the next city. When this information or the identity of the appropriate person was not available, we called the city and asked for the information directly. Using this approach, we were able to obtain the contact information of a designated individual for all but 17 of the 1,282 cities in the sample. For the remaining cities, we used generic city or departmental contact information (e.g., mayor@city.gov or publicworks@city.gov) and removed salutations from the invitation (see Appendix B for the survey invitation). When possible, we gathered contact information for two people in the city and used the second as a backup if our primary contact did not respond. While respondents were housed in a wide variety of departments, the majority were located in departments of planning, community development, and public works.

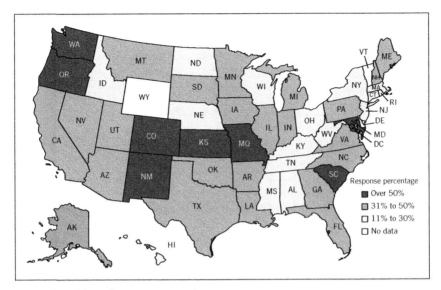

Figure 2.1 Map of survey respondents

The survey was designed and administered using Qualtrics survey software. Following Don Dillman, Jolene D. Smyth, and Leah Melani Christian's (2014) tailored design method, we emailed recipients about the survey in advance. Several days later, we sent a personalized invitation, which included an electronic link to the survey. Over the next several weeks, up to three electronic reminders were sent to nonrespondents. If the primary city contact did not respond after these follow-ups, a secondary contact in the cities for which one was available was invited to participate. The secondary contact received one electronic follow-up. Finally, a paper version of the survey was sent via First-Class Mail to the work address of individuals who did not respond electronically.

Completed responses were received from 504 cities, located in forty-eight states and Washington, D.C., for a response rate of 39.4 percent. Figure 2.1 shows the geographic distribution of responses. Approximately eighty additional cities provided partial responses.

On the basis of demographic indicators, as shown in Table 2.1, cities that responded to the survey appear similar to those that did not respond. The only metric on which they are significantly ($\alpha = 0.05$) different is the mean percentage of their populations with a bachelor's degree or higher: respondent cities have slightly more educated populations. However, the difference is modest, with 2.5 percent more adults in the responding cities having obtained at least a bachelor's degree. As with any survey, the threat of selection bias cannot be eliminated. However, the similarity observed between the responding and nonresponding cities mitigates that concern

TABLE 2.1: COMPARISON OF RESPONDENT AND NONRESPONDENT CITIES

	Respondents (n = 504)	Partial or nonrespondents (n = 778)	Significantly different at α = 0.05
Population (2010)	107,221	102,035	No
Median household income	54,661	55,046	No
Percentage in poverty	10.82	10.71	No
Education (bachelor's+)	31.71	29.21	Yes
Percentage non-Hispanic white	59.21	60.40	No

and allows us to claim basic generalizability across U.S. cities larger than twenty thousand.

Approximately 41 percent of the U.S. public lives in cities that have populations over twenty thousand, making this an important set of jurisdictions to examine. On the flip side, this means that almost 60 percent of Americans live either in unincorporated areas or in municipalities sized under this threshold. Thus, one could argue that this research fails to consider the dynamics of the local government institutions in which a majority of people live. Although this critique is accurate and, to a degree, reflects a valid shortcoming, we posit that our sampling strategy is appropriate given both the focus of our research and the practical trade-offs involved with expanding it.

First, this research explicitly focuses on how incorporated places are administering sustainability efforts. Incorporated places, which are commonly referred to holistically as "cities," technically include all cities, towns, villages, and boroughs that have undertaken a legal procedure to form a municipal government. Unincorporated places are typically managed by county governments but have not formed their own governing institutions and thus are not relevant to our study. In 2013, 62.7 percent of the U.S. population lived in one of the country's 19,508 incorporated places (Cohen 2015). By limiting the scope of our study to cities with over twenty thousand people, we exclude relevant jurisdictions that are home to approximately 22 percent of the population. This decision was shaped by considerations of practical and theoretical trade-offs. The first practical consideration revolves around sheer numbers; there are over eighteen thousand cities in the U.S. with populations under twenty thousand (Cohen 2015). This itself increases the data collection burden considerably. Moreover, in small cities where staff may be spread thin and city websites are more often lacking, it can be difficult to identify the appropriate person to receive a sustainability survey. Finally, and likely related to the previous points, a review of several recent studies using sustainability surveys suggests that those which include small cities in their sample frames tend yield response rates around 25 percent (ICMA 2010, 2016; Hultquist, Wood, and Romsdahl 2017; National League of Cities 2010), whereas those that focus exclusively on larger cities often have response rates of 40 percent or higher (Feiock, Krause, et al. 2014). Lower response rates can exacerbate selection bias issues.

Substantively, small cities are characterized by a different decision-making and administrative dynamic than larger ones. They generally have fewer employees and less professional capacity than larger cities, which can make it more difficult to pursue initiatives that extend beyond core services (Homsy and Warner 2013; Hultquist, Wood, and Romsdahl 2017). Moreover, the range of organizational forms we are considering around sustainability, which often include designated staff or units, are likely not viable for very small cities. In sum, although it does not cover the universe of local governments in the United States, our focus on cities with populations over twenty thousand is practical and logical given the motivation of this research.

Overview of Cities' Priorities, Actions, and Policies

Because it is a relatively new and nontraditional local objective, almost all cities with sustainability initiatives have engaged in some degree of recent policy change. The expansive policy change literature highlights agenda setting as a key initial step in the process. In their now classic piece, Roger William Cobb and Charles Elder (1972) describe systemic and institutional agendas as the two basic agenda types that exist in most political systems. Systemic agendas can be understood as discussion agendas and comprise the broad body of issues that a community perceives as warranting public attention. Institutional agendas are narrower and more concrete, consisting of just those issues that policy makers intend to devote serious attention to and take action on (Anderson 2008).

Our quantitative description of sustainability initiatives in U.S. cities starts with an overview of the issue's status on the local agenda. To make it onto a city government's institutional agenda, sustainability must first be an issue on its systemic agenda. The greater a priority it is there, the better a chance it has of proceeding on and eventually being a subject of policy action. Table 2.2 presents the degree to which different dimensions of sustainability are considered a priority in respondent municipalities. Less than 4 percent of cities describe any one of its primary dimensions—economy, environment, and social equity—as "not at all" a priority. The majority consider each of these as a priority of moderate importance or higher. A different dynamic is observed for climate change mitigation and adaptation,

TABLE 2.2: CITIES' PRIORITIZATION OF THE DIFFERENT DIMENSIONS OF SUSTAINABILITY

Sustainability dimension	Not at all (0)	Low (1)	Moderate (2)	High (3)	Very high (4)	Mean (on 0–4 scale)
Economy	0.3%	0.7%	10.5%	37.6%	50.8%	3.38
Environment	0.7%	7.6%	31.3%	44.8%	15.6%	2.67
Social justice/equity	2.6%	13.5%	38.6%	31.7%	13.7%	2.40
Climate change mitigation	15.0%	29.1%	31.5%	17.0%	7.5%	1.73
Climate change adaptation	15.3%	29.4%	32.8%	15.0%	7.5%	1.70

which are considered low or nonexistent priorities in almost 45 percent of our respondent cities.

There is no threshold level of prioritization that ensures the movement of an issue from the systemic to the institutional agenda, and policy action is not guaranteed even if it does make that jump. However, when sustainability, or a particular dimension of it, is perceived as a high community priority, its chances are improved. Discrete policy actions have received focus in the local sustainability literature because they demonstrate a city's commitment and ambition in ways that are more than just symbolic (Portney 2013; Krause 2011b). Because sustainability outcome metrics are not widely available or comparable across cities, policy actions are often the best metric available (Chavez and Ramaswami 2013; Satterthwaite 2008). Indexes are widely used, by both academics and sustainability practitioners, in attempt to form an accurate picture of the breadth and depth of relevant sustainability actions. In developing an index, one often faces a parsimony-comprehensiveness trade-off; too few indicators can lead to a distorted or incomplete picture, but too many indicators can be unwieldy and present practical data collection and aggregation challenges that limit its widespread use.

A sampling of existing indexes includes Kent Portney's "Index of Taking Sustainable Cities Seriously," in which thirty-eight indicators were applied to the fifty-five largest cities in the United States (2013, 72–73). XiaoHu Wang and colleagues' "National Survey of Sustainability Management in US Cities" (the results of which they analyze in their 2012 "Capacity to Sustain Sustainability") collected information about fifty-one indicators of sustainability from 264 cities, and subsequent research used this data to develop indexes that ranged from between five and seven (Wang, Liu, and Hawkins 2017; Wang, Hawkins, and Berman 2014) to eleven (Hawkins and Wang 2013) sustainability-related policies. STAR Communities and the

Urban Sustainability Directors Network use twenty-one indicators in their Leading STAR Community Indicators, which is based on city self-reports and third-party vetting and has been piloted by forty-five U.S. cities (STAR Communities, n.d.).

Here we consider fifteen different policy actions, five each associated with environmental, economic, and social sustainability. This is far from a comprehensive list of relevant actions and fewer than what has been used by some other indexes. However, given that the primary focus of the survey was on sustainability-related organization and administration, we were constrained in the number of questions about policy actions that could reasonably be asked. As such, we were intentional and systematic in their selection. In arriving at the fifteen policy actions indicated in Table 2.3, we referenced previously administered surveys to identify select questions for replication. We aimed to include policies that are neither low-hanging

TABLE 2.3: PERCENTAGE OF CITIES IMPLEMENTING SELECT SUSTAINABILITY-RELATED ACTIONS AND POLICIES

Action	Percentage
Economic	
Implements "buy local" campaigns	48.2
Works with business on strategies to green operations	38.9
Uses public procurement policies to create green product demand	17.3
Provides incentives for renewable energy sector	11.5
Offers tax credits for LEED-certified commercial buildings	5.2
Average economic implementation rate	24.2
Social	
Requires sidewalks in new developments	85.7
Supports local farmers' markets	74.2
Provides supportive housing options for the elderly	40.7
Provides citywide access to internet/information technology	23.8
Funds public health initiatives for low-income residents	23.2
Average social implementation rate	49.5
Environmental	
Encourages mixed-use development	81.0
Promotes green or open space preservation	76.6
Encourages residential water conservation	64.0
Promotes brownfield site repurposing	47.8
Encourages reduced use of plastic bags	16.0
Average environmental implementation rate	57.1

fruits, which almost all cities have already implemented, nor extremely un-common in U.S. cities. Finally, the selected actions cover a cross section of target populations, beneficiaries, and policy instrument types and reflect a diversity of relevant issues within each dimension.

Table 2.3 shows the percentage of cities that have implemented select policy actions related to economic, social, and environmental sustainability. Environmental actions have the highest implementation rates, with cities having an average of 57 percent of the five identified environmental policies in place. By comparison, cities have implemented an average of 49 percent of social policies and 24 percent of economic policies. There are only moder-ate positive correlations between the implementation rates of cities across dimensions: 0.30 between social and economic, 0.22 between social and environmental, and 0.23 between environmental and economic. This means that, for example, cities that have implemented a larger number of environ-mental sustainability actions also tend to have greater number of social and economic sustainability actions in place, but the strength of this tendency is weak. The correlation between the individual actions making up these categories is also almost universally positive, but none exceeds 0.30.

These results depend on the nature of the particular policy actions con-sidered, which are far from a comprehensive sampling of all relevant poli-cies. It may be that the five economic sustainability actions selected are systematically narrower or more difficult for cities to achieve than the cor-responding actions related to social or environmental sustainability. That said, the considerably lower average implementation rate for the economic activities is notable—and surprising given the high prioritization of eco-nomic health indicated in Table 2.2. Table 2.4 reports the correlation be-tween the stated prioritization of each dimension and the average imple-mentation of its component policies. In each case, the correlations are positive, as expected, but they are also modest and, in the case of economic sustainability, only minimally different from zero. Higher issue prioritiza-tion is only weakly associated with greater policy action.

In addition to sustainability in general, a significant number of cities have embraced climate protection as a local objective. This was the issue that first generated widespread municipal action around a global sustainability concern. Since 2005, over a thousand U.S. cities have signed one or more pledges to reduce their greenhouse gas (GHG) emissions. A smaller number of them have taken substantive steps to achieve their promised reductions. Completing a GHG emissions inventory to map the amount and sources of local emissions is a common initial step in this regard (Krause and Martel 2018). Cities often conduct distinct inventories to separately focus on mu-nicipal government operations and the wider community. Of the 504 cities in our sample, 57 percent have completed a GHG inventory measuring

TABLE 2.4: CORRELATION OF PRIORITY AND POLICY ACTION BY SUSTAINABILITY DIMENSION

Index	Dimension-specific prioritization
Economic policy index	0.04
Environmental policy index	0.28
Social policy index	0.17

emissions from their own government operations—which generally include those sourced from energy used by city buildings, vehicle fleets, street and traffic lights, and wastewater treatment facilities. Emissions produced in municipally operated landfills are less consistently included. Of the cities with government inventories, 77 percent reported that the inventory stimulated policy changes that resulted in at least some reduction of GHG emissions. By comparison, smaller numbers are seen for both the percentage of cities that have completed community-wide inventories (47 percent) and the subportion of those in which at least some emissions reduction occurred as a result (64 percent). Because community-wide emission inventories are much broader in scope and more data intensive to complete, these smaller numbers are not surprising. Local governments also have considerably less control over the GHG-generating behavior and consumption choices of their publics than they do over their own employees. That said, since city government operations usually comprise less than 3 percent of an entire community's emissions (Krause 2012), the net impact of their mitigation is inherently limited.

Patterns in Cities' Organization of Sustainability

Although few existing studies on local sustainability examine the administrative arrangements that have been employed to implement their initiatives, many of the studies that seek to explain observed variation in cities' sustainably commitment or activity levels focus on capacity as a key variable. A meta-analysis of the urban sustainability literature points to organizational capacity, often measured by financial and human resources, as the most consistent statistically significant driver of local sustainability action (Swann and Deslatte 2018). The presence and arrangement of dedicated staff within a city government is a central component of this book's focus on the organizational mechanisms and arrangements cities use to overcome functional collective action (FCA) challenges.

The results of the Smart and Sustainable Cities Survey indicate that 46 percent of the cities in our sample have staff whose jobs are dedicated to sustainability. Table 2.5 shows how that staffing manifests across the

TABLE 2.5: LOCATION OF DEDICATED SUSTAINABILITY STAFF

Office/department	Percentage of cities
In the city/town manager's office or equivalent	7.6
In the mayor's or council's office	3.9
Within a single line department	23.1
Spread across multiple departments	16.1

respondent cities. It is important to note that the categories included in Table 2.5 are not mutually exclusive. For example, a city could reasonably have sustainability staff located in the mayor's office *and* spread across multiple line departments. However, only 3.6 percent of cities have staff placed in more than one of the options indicated. Separate from this dedicated staffing, 18 percent of cities have assembled a task force, committee, or commission that is comprised of employees from across city departments to work on sustainability issues. In slightly over half of these cities (56 percent), the committees or task forces are in addition to, rather than instead of, dedicated staffing.

As noted previously, just under half of the cities in our sample have staff with jobs focused on sustainability. Because it is a broad objective, however, multiple city units and staff members—whether explicitly tasked with sustainability functions or not—often share responsibility for the development and implementation of related programs or actions. The number of units (i.e., independent city offices or departments) involved can affect the design and outcomes of sustainability initiatives. For example, the extant research indicates that sustainability and related issues like climate protection are often technically demanding and require expertise in multiple program areas (Gordon et al. 2019). Thus, the involvement of multiple specialized units may improve effort effectiveness. One study finds that when more units assist in implementation, sustainability initiatives have larger scopes and greater integration, on average (Feiock, Krause, and Hawkins 2017). Conversely, when a larger number of independent city units share responsibility for sustainability, FCA problems can grow. In addition to simple coordination challenges, reduced accountability, fuzzy boundaries of responsibly, and externalities in the allocation of credit or recognition for success all have the potential to increase along with the number of independent agencies involved, complicating efforts to achieve collective action. Figure 2.2 shows the distribution of the number of units that are involved in sustainability efforts across our respondent cities. Approximately seven different units are active on average. A single unit is entirely responsible for efforts in only a few cities, so some degree of internal collaboration appears almost universal.

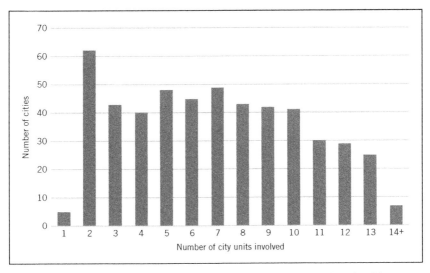

Figure 2.2 Distribution of the number of administrative units involved in sustainability initiatives across cities

In nearly all the city governments in our sample, a number of different offices and departments work together on sustainability-related initiatives. Despite the shared nature of the effort, however, one unit is typically designated as the lead. Depending on the city, this unit may actually design and implement a majority of sustainability actions, direct and coordinate the actions of other units, and/or provide encouragement and assistance to other units on their own relevant efforts. Figure 2.3 shows the headquarters unit for sustainability in the 575 that answered this question in our survey. Thirty-one cities stated that their efforts are completely decentralized, but all the rest were able to pinpoint a specific unit that, either formally or informally, is most in charge.

The identity of this headquarters unit is relevant to overcoming FCA challenges and can influence the specific priorities, issues, and strategies a city opts to pursue. For example, it is reasonable to believe that if, in any particular city, sustainability initiatives were led by a public works department, they would likely look different than if a planning department was charged with the same general function. Each department's professional norms, resources, expertise, and preexisting core responsibilities shape its approach to sustainability. If tasked to lead efforts citywide, those influences will be felt more broadly.

Moreover, a unit's place in a city's organizational hierarchy is anticipated to affect how well cities are able to address FCA challenges. FCA challenges are likely to emerge when collaboration is needed between multiple

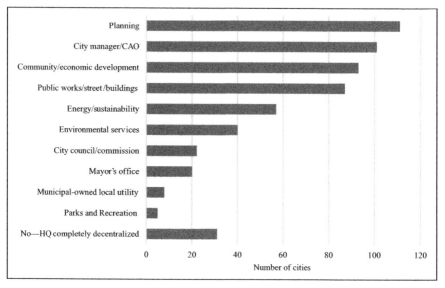

Figure 2.3 Primary unit for coordinating implementation of sustainability initiatives

functionally independent units to achieve a single organization-wide objective around which none has complete ownership. Administrative units, such as those inside line departments that occupy a lower position within the hierarchy are presumed to have less authority compared with the units above them in the hierarchy—for instance, department managers compared to the city administrator. The latter position generally has more direct access to elected officials who sit atop the administrative structure. As well, directives typically flow in a singular direction down a hierarchy. Cities, largely independent of the form of government they use, share this general hierarchical governing arrangement. This leads to the expectation that when sustainability is headquartered in a unit located high within the administrative hierarchy, initiatives should suffer fewer FCA problems.

Only limited empirical work has been done assessing this proposition. However, the research that does exist does not find meaningful support for it, and generally concludes with calls for a deeper look (Feiock, Krause, and Hawkins 2017). One reason for the insignificance of findings may be tied to the nested nature of many units within cities, which render simple "line versus executive" location characterizations overly crude. Under this approach, a city with a large and explicitly focused sustainability unit may be categorized the same as one which headquarters it within a department that has other core functions and priorities, such as public works. Figure 2.4 gives an initial look at how the specific headquarters units identified in

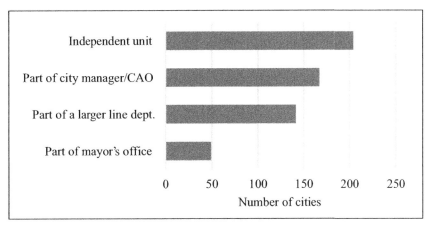

Figure 2.4 Location of primary unit within larger city structure

Figure 2.3 nest within higher units. The role that the identity of the lead unit plays—and how its position within the larger city government affects the nature of sustainability actions, outcomes, and efforts to overcome FCA dilemmas—requires a closer, more nuanced look.

Cities' decisions about what unit to designate as the organizational home for sustainability have been critiqued as being often unsystematic and based on managerial personalities or budgetary conveniences rather than as part of a larger plan or strategy (Krause, Feiock, and Hawkins 2016; Portney 2013). However, because sustainability remains a relatively new function and best practices for its administration have not been established, shaping decisions on budgetary or personnel considerations is, perhaps, not unreasonable. That said, as sustainability matures as a local objective, cities may determine that certain units make more effective headquarters than others, and reorganize accordingly.

Along those lines, we asked survey respondents if, to the best of their knowledge, the unit they identified as primarily responsible for managing the implementation of sustainability (as indicated in Figure 2.3) has had this responsibility since 2010. The results suggest relative stability over the approximately five-year period in question; eighty cities, or almost 16 percent, had changed their administrative headquarters. An assessment of the past and present headquarters units reveals no clear pattern in the movement of these changes across cities. It does, however, indicate that cities are not becoming meaningfully more homogenous in terms of where they headquarter sustainability. Of the eleven city departments listed in Figure 2.3, the largest net increase between 2010 and 2015 was seen in the use of specialized energy/sustainability headquarters units. During this time, thirteen cities created these specialized units, and three disbanded them, for a net gain of ten.

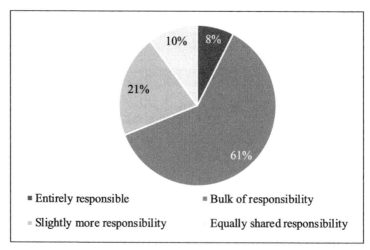

Figure 2.5 Share of overall responsibility for implementation management held by headquarters unit

Relative to other units in a city government, the sustainability lead generally has somewhat more sustainability-related programmatic and coordination responsibilities. However, multiple factors—including official job descriptions, expectations of the chief administrative officer, and levels of buy-in from the managers and staff in other units—result in considerable variation as to how responsibility, and how much of it, is shared across city departments. On one end of the spectrum, the lead unit may be the only entity in a city actively engaged in sustainability and shoulder responsibility for managing related efforts entirely by itself. On the other end of the spectrum, the headquarters unit may share that responsibility and act as one of several equal internal players in pursuit of local sustainability. Figure 2.5 shows that most cities fall between these extremes. Almost 60 percent of cities describe their headquarters unit as shouldering "the bulk of responsibility" for coordinating and managing the sustainability initiatives, relative to other units. Another 20 percent of cities indicate that this department has "slightly more responsibility than others." Significantly fewer cities describe the headquarters unit as being either "entirely responsible" or as "one of several essentially equal players."

A full 99 percent of the 504 respondents that completed the Smart and Sustainable Cities Survey stated that at least two separate units in their city government assist with its sustainability efforts. In over 50 percent of cities, seven or more units have been identified as participants. Any time the efforts of more than one functional unit are needed to advance an overarching objective, the potential of FCA dilemmas arises and thus there is a need to coordinate activities and ensure integration. Having mechanisms in place to facilitate communication and coordination between the involved units is a first basic step to minimizing FCA problems. As will be discussed in more detail in Chapter 3, the mechanisms to do this are often characterized as formal or informal. Informal mechanisms are simultaneously based on and facilitate the development of norms and relationships supportive of bottom-up integration. Formal mechanisms result from institutionalized hierarchy and authority and take a top-down approach toward integration.

Table 2.6 contains a series of informal and formal approaches and indicates their frequency of use by cities. The first column shows the percentage of respondent cities that, based on a five-point Likert scale, frequently or very frequently use each mechanism to coordinate or collaborate between departments on sustainability initiatives. The second column shows those that sometimes use each mechanism, and the third column indicates those that infrequently or never do. The mechanisms are loosely listed according to increasing formality. Although the specifics of this ordering are somewhat subjective, the first three mechanisms are decidedly informal, spontaneous, and/or reflective of a bottom-up approach to coordination. The latter three are based on directives from city leadership.

While there are clear distinctions between formal and informal approaches toward integration, this is not to suggest their use is an either-or proposition. Rather, cities typically use a combination of mechanisms that

TABLE 2.6: FREQUENCY OF CITIES' USE OF COORDINATION MECHANISMS ON SUSTAINABILITY

Mechanisms for interdepartmental coordination/collaboration	Percentage of cities that frequently or very frequently use the mechanism	Percentage of cities that sometimes use the mechanism	Percentage of cities that infrequently or never use the mechanism
Unplanned staff interactions	34.4	26.7	29.2
Ad hoc meetings	34.7	36.4	38.6
Self-organized interdepartmental task force	31.3	22.3	47.3
Appointed/standing sustainability task force	28.8	19.5	51.7
Collaboration requirement from city leaders	22.9	25.3	51.8
Formal agreement between department managers	22.4	21.4	55.3

Note: Cities that frequently or very frequently use the mechanism scored a 4 or 5 on the Likert scale. Those that sometimes use the mechanism scored a 3, and those that infrequently or never used the mechanism scored a 1 or 2.

differ in their formality to encourage interdepartmental coordination and collaboration. Focusing on the first numerical column, an initial observation is that the three informal mechanisms are consistently employed more frequently than formal ones. Moreover, based on this loose ordering of mechanisms within the formal and informal subcategories, the decline of use and increase of formality occur neatly in tandem with each other. Over half of the cities either never or only infrequently rely on formal interdepartmental agreements, mandates from above, or formally appointed task forces to facilitate collaboration around sustainability. There is a strand in the collaboration literature that sees formalization and centralization as potentially detrimental to effective collaboration (Agranoff and McGuire 2004; Kim and Lee 2006; Willem and Buelens 2007), as well as an ongoing debate about the relative roles of supportive formal and informal structures in successful collaboration (Provan and Milward 1995; Thomson and Perry 2006; Yang and Maxwell 2011). Research by Angela Park and colleagues (2018), conducted in the context of interdepartmental collaboration on local sustainability, finds that informal mechanisms have positive and significant effects promoting collaboration. Formal mechanisms, on the other hand, were found not to affect collaboration directly but instead to significantly support the occurrence of informal mechanisms, thus having an indirect effect on interdepartmental collaboration. We explore the various integration mechanisms and the interactions between them in greater detail in the city case studies in Chapters 4–7.

Table 2.7 shows how the use of the various mechanisms correlates with different organizational features of cities' sustainability initiatives. Although none of the correlations are particularly high (none exceed 0.3), there are some associations worthy of note. First, having a dedicated sustainability staff is associated with the more frequent use of every mechanism. The strongest correlation is seen between a staff presence and the use of an interdepartmental sustainability task force. There also are modest positive correlations between the various mechanisms and number of units partnering on sustainability, which are slightly stronger for the formal mechanisms than the informal ones. The location of the headquarters unit, specifically whether it is part of the executive branch, has negligible association with mechanism use.

Separating cities into groups that share similarities in how they approach sustainability can provide additional insight into the organizational and administrative characteristics associated with different policy outputs. Based on patterns in their implementation of the fifteen actions listed in Table 2.3—five each that correspond to the environmental, social, and economic dimensions of sustainability—we can identify general types of cities and then describe the characteristics of each. We do this using cluster

TABLE 2.7: CORRELATION OF STRUCTURAL ADMINISTRATIVE
CHARACTERISTICS WITH COORDINATION MECHANISMS

Mechanisms for interdepartmental coordination	Dedicated sustainability staff	Number of city units active in sustainability	Headquarters unit located in executive branch
Unplanned staff interactions	0.11	0.02	0.02
Ad hoc meetings	0.14	0.17	0.00
Self-organized interdepart-mental task force	0.17	0.17	0.02
Appointed/standing sustain-ability task force	0.26	0.22	0.01
Collaboration requirement from city leaders	0.15	0.21	0.10
Formal agreements between department managers	0.19	0.21	0.03

analysis, an exploratory technique that aims to establish groups or categories within data that are similar on select attributes. It does not generate *p*-values and thus is more appropriate for hypothesis development than hypothesis testing (Everitt 1993). It arranges observations so that resulting clusters have as much internal homogeneity as possible and are as different from other clusters as possible (Aldenderfer and Blashfield 1984). The cluster analysis employed in this study applies hierarchical agglomerative clustering methods, using Ward's linkage and the Jaccard similarity measure, to dichotomous variables indicating whether cities have implemented each of the fifteen previously identified sustainability policies. Ward's linkage minimizes the within-group error sum of squares for each cluster. The Jaccard binary similarity coefficient forms clusters based only on positive matches. In other words, when searching for clusters of like cities, it considers only the sustainability actions that cities do have in place and not those that they do not have in place.

The analysis suggests a three-cluster solution. Table 2.8 shows these three groupings of cities and the descriptive statistics that correspond with each. The first cluster contains 170 cities and has the highest overall sustainability policy activity; cities in this group have implemented an average of between eight and nine (58.1 percent) of the fifteen policies considered. They also tend to exhibit the best-rounded treatment of sustainability; group 1 cities have the highest implementation rates of policies associated with each of its three dimensions. The largest number of cities cluster into the group characterized in Table 2.4 as having mid-level policy activity and a

TABLE 2.8: CITY CLUSTERS AND DESCRIPTIVE STATISTICS

	G1: Highest policy activity, multidimensional sustainability ($n = 170$)	G2: Mid-level policy activity, environmental-focused sustainability ($n = 203$)	G3: Lowest policy activity, socially focused sustainability ($n = 136$)
Policy activity			
Sustainability policies implemented	58.1%*	39.9%†	31.8%
Environmental policies	73.2%*	62.0%†	31.4%
Social policies	65.8%*	40.0%	43.4%
Economic policies	35.4%*	17.6%	20.6%
Community characteristics			
Median population size	80,260*	56,741	58,461
Education (% bachelor's degree+)	34.3%*	29.7%	31.3%
Median income	56,494	52,096†	56,528
Racial composition (% non-Hispanic white)	58.9%	59.7%	59.6%
Political leaning (% Democratic voters)	55.3%	53.5%	52.3%
City government administration characteristics			
Form of government (% mayor-council)	27.6%	36.9%	33.8%
Dedicated sustainability staff	67.6%*	46.3%	45.6%
Energy/sustainability lead unit	12.90%	8.87%	8.09%
Number partner units	6.6*	5.7	5.2
Headquarters unit identity			
Public works/environmental services	27.65	22.17	27.95
Executive management	24.12	24.63	22.8
Planning/development	32.85	39.9	35.3
Energy/sustainability	12.94	8.87	8.09
N/A—completely decentralized	2.94	4.43	5.88

* Values for group 1 cities are different from those of groups 2 and 3 at $\alpha = 0.05$.
† Values for group 2 cities are different from those of group 3 at $\alpha = 0.05$.

sustainability orientation that emphasizes the environment. The 203 cities in this group 2 have implemented an average of approximately 40 percent of the identified policy actions and have 62 percent of the environmental policies in place. Although this is still less than the environmental implementation rate of group 1 cities, it remains quite high and is proportionately much less of a drop than is seen in the other dimensions. The third group of cities has implemented the fewest sustainability actions; about 32 percent or an average of four to five of the possible fifteen. Compared to the other two groupings of cities, group 3 cities see a large drop in the number of environmental actions implemented. However, their implementation of economic and socially focused policy actions remains relatively stable and on average is slightly higher than for cities in the second group. The most meaningful distinction between the cities clustered into groups 2 and 3 is their respective emphasis on environmental versus social and economic policies.

These three clusters of cities illustrate different patterns of municipal policy choices around sustainability. They also enable examination of the general characteristics of cities associated with different approaches. Specifically, a comparison of the descriptive statistics characterizing each group, as shown in Table 2.8, provides initial insight regarding whether there are community or city government organizational features that tend to be shared by the cities within each group.

The high-activity cities clustered in group 1 stand out from the others in that they are, on average, larger and have residents who are more highly educated. These differences are statistically significant at $\alpha = 0.05$. Their organizational arrangements are significantly more likely to have a dedicated sustainability staff. This is consistent with previous literature that frequently finds both that larger cities tend to be better resourced and are more likely to have specialized staff (Hawkins et al. 2015), and that specialized sustainability staff is associated with greater policy activity (Homsy and Warner 2015; Pitt 2010; Wang et al. 2012). The high-activity cities also have a significantly larger number of city units partnering in the implementation of their efforts.

The second and third groups of cities have more modest overall implementation rates and, although they differ in the focus of their activities, they generally appear more similar to each other than they do to the cities in the first group. As described previously, their clustering reflects their differential implementation of environmental as opposed to social and economic sustainability activities. The one community characteristic in which the cities in these groups are significantly different from one another is in residents' median household income, where the cities in the cluster that share an emphasis on environmental policies are less well-off. This is interesting, as it does not align with the oft-expressed notion that environmental quality is a luxury good and that cities that are less economically robust are more inclined to focus on economic and social policies. That said, the economic and social policies identified here are nontraditional and have a definite quality-of-life emphasis. Finally, the departmental home for cities' sustainability headquarters does not meaningfully vary across groups. We aggregate similar departments together for the sake of illustration (for example, planning and zoning, community development, and economic development are all contained under "planning" in Table 2.4), but the level of aggregation does not meaningfully change the observation that there is no particular headquarters location systematically associated with any of the general policy approaches identified by the cluster analysis.

Conclusion

The overarching objective of this book is to understand how cities organize to overcome FCA problems in sustainability. Surveys have been a primary tool used to collect data on local sustainability policy (Feiock, Krause, et al. 2014; Deslatte and Swann 2014), the analysis of which has informed a large and growing body of research. Our contribution to this base of knowledge, both in this chapter and throughout the book as a whole, is to complement existing research on *what* cities are doing in regard to sustainability activities and *why,* with new evidence of how they are using administrative arrangements and integration mechanisms to design and manage implementation of these efforts. We employ descriptive and correlational analysis in this chapter to answer basic questions related to this objective and help address a fundamental gap in the literature on urban sustainability.

As described in Chapter 1, cities are critically important for sustainability, and, therefore, understanding their priorities and actions, along with their administrative arrangements, is important for advancing theoretical inquiry and, in turn, on-the-ground improvements. The sheer number of cities and the variety of approaches they use to address sustainability, while sharing basic similarities in governmental institutions, provide fertile ground for the examination of FCA. Advancing research on these subjects is important in light of the broad FCA challenges that are noted in Chapter 1 and described in greater detail in Chapter 3. The descriptive findings presented in this chapter provide initial quantitative examinations relevant to FCA while setting the path for a more nuanced qualitative assessment in Chapters 4–7.

The results of the Smart and Sustainable Cities Survey demonstrate general variation in the priority U.S. cities give to economic, environmental, and social dimensions of sustainability. Perhaps not surprising to many readers familiar with urban policy, the survey finds that cities in our sample give priority to the economic dimension. The relative prioritization of the other two dimensions is not particularly close; the number of respondents that describe local economic health as a "very high" priority for their city is over 35 percent greater than those that do for environmental or social well-being. However, despite high levels of stated prioritization, its corresponding policies have low implementation rates. Notably, of those identified, environmental policies see considerably higher average rates of implementation.

Some of this may be an artifact of our policy choice; neither the five economic nor the five environmental policies we examined are comprehensive of their entire dimensions. However, their low implementation rates suggest that green approaches to economic development are not being pursued by cities with great frequency. It also points to less than straightforward links between policy actions and a particular sustainability dimension. In this case, several of the policies that comprise the environmental dimension include land use. Managing land use is an important local responsibility, and doing this in a way that enhances environmental well-being may provide economic co-benefits. Improving and maintaining the quality of environmental amenities and redeveloping existing infrastructure are generally representative of "smart growth" policies that also offer a pathway to economic benefits. Although their focus may be primarily environmental, they provide an opportunity to move the needle on economic condition and competitiveness.

While policy action is important for results and signifies a commitment to sustainability, as previous research demonstrates, capacity, and in particular having a professional and dedicated sustainability staff, is important for translating policy into implementation (Krause 2010; Swann and Deslatte 2018). However, the survey results presented in this chapter show that less than half of midsize to large cities in the United States have staff dedicated to their sustainability efforts. Although our analysis does not consider causal relationships, the results of the correlation and cluster analysis suggest that the presence of sustainability staff is associated with cities that have the higher and better-rounded policy activity. Additionally, staff presence is associated with the use of more integration mechanisms, suggesting that having employees explicitly tasked with sustainability responsibilities may be important to coordination.

Another important result from the survey is that sustainability is widely decentralized in terms of the number of units involved in local initiatives. In the average city, seven different units actively contribute to its development and execution. Having a larger number of units engaged can result in more transaction costs and FCA challenges; however, it can also lead to a broader scope and more-comprehensive efforts. The cluster analysis appears to support the more positive of these interpretations: the grouping of cities characterized as having the highest and broadest policy activity, likewise, has the highest average number of functional partners. Also, perhaps out of necessity, the number of partners correlates positively with the use of integration mechanisms.

The identity of sustainability's headquarters location is also thought to produce distinct programmatic priorities as well as their own sets of challenges and advantages associated with FCA. Our survey results show that four units—departments of planning, community and economic development, and public works and the city manager's office—are responsible for coordinating the implementation of sustainability initiatives for a relatively large proportion of the cities in our sample, and often shoulder the bulk of responsibility. However, both our associative analysis and previous explanatory research demonstrates mixed and null findings about the impact of the headquarters' programmatic identity (Feiock, Krause, and Hawkins 2017). This, as well as the qualitative research in subsequent chapters, suggests a more complex and less straightforward relationship between headquarters location and integration.

3

Functional Collective Action Framework

A s the previous chapters make clear, local governments are acting as
leaders in climate and sustainability policy. However, since sustainability is both complex and untraditional as a function of city government, it does not easily fit within existing organizational arrangements
or administrative silos. The environmental, economic, and social dimensions of sustainability necessitate a link between multiple local government
functions, but the traditional separation of responsibility for them across
departments can lead to intracity collective action or coordination problems. Fragmented service responsibilities necessarily affect the design and
implementation of local sustainability efforts and require that organizational and administrative structures and processes play a role in mitigating
the challenges associated with coordinating activities across administrative
units in city governments.

Chapter 2 offers a high-level view of local sustainability efforts in cities
throughout the United States and the various ways they organize in relation
to sustainability. This statistical overview offers insights into the patterns of
organizational structures employed in the design and implementation of
sustainability initiatives. In this chapter we advance a theoretical approach
to account for the observed differences in the ways cities organize sustainability efforts.

Although the administrative structures and organizational arrangements through which cities pursue sustainability vary considerably, relatively little is known about what implication this variation has for the

adoption and implementation of sustainability actions in cities. This chapter addresses questions of coordination and collective action among functional agencies or departments within city governments. We offer a framework that provides insight into both the formal control systems for integration and the ways in which the various units within a government informally influence one another. We then add the degree of centralization characterizing policy design and implementation to this framework to produce a typology of administrative arrangements available to integrate policy across functional departments within a single government.

The long-recognized problem of fragmentation and cross-department coordination (Kaufman 1960; Peters 2002) has direct consequences for city residents. For example, a relatively minor category 1 hurricane in 2015 left thousands of Tallahassee, Florida, residents and businesses without power for over a week, largely as a result of difficulties in coordinating clearing roads, repairing power lines, and removing debris. The respective units responsible for streets, electric utilities, and solid waste management were challenged by working together to implement a timely response. Even in more routine or proactive circumstances, collective action and coordination problems across city departments can lead to undesirable outcomes and inefficiencies. For example, the successful implementation of a "green building" or local energy efficiency policy for rental properties, developed and adopted by a city's planning department, may ultimately hinge on the ability to get the city's building code inspectors to learn about, check for, and enforce the new requirements. Code inspectors may perceive these tasks as additional to their primary mandate of protecting life and safety. However, if inconsistently or incorrectly applied, legitimate stakeholder complaints and dissatisfaction could challenge the overall policy.

The next section of this chapter summarizes insights from several related disciplines to describe the governance and management issues that arise from the fragmentation of responsibilities inherent in governmental structures organized by functionally defined agencies and departments. We then review the institutional collective action (ICA) framework, which has been articulated as a response to this fragmentation and use it as a foundation to advance a functional collective action (FCA) approach. Although they are relevant in different settings, both institutional and functional collective action describe arrangements that can be used to integrate broad complex functions, such as sustainability. They are both generally rooted in considerations of reliance on formal authority versus informal influence for integration and on the relative breadth of partners involved (Feiock 2013). Based on these dimensions, we define four general administrative arrangements for interagency integration of sustainability. In the chapter's final section, we identify cities that use each of these arrangements and pave the way for the in-depth case study examinations to follow in subsequent chapters.

Administrative Silos and Management
of Complex Urban Problems

Considerable theoretical and empirical work over several decades has explored problems of interjurisdictional fragmentation among governments and the various approaches available to promote integration or collaboration across them (Ostrom, Bish, and Ostrom 1988; Feiock 2009; Feiock and Scholz 2010; Jimenez 2014). Much less attention has been directed to problems of fragmented responsibilities *within* governmental organizations. The problems associated with administrative silos and the "fuzzy boundaries" that can arise when objectives, policies, or services cross independent units within a single government have been long recognized (Kettl 2002, 59–60). However, there is little systematic study of these phenomena, the administrative mechanisms for mitigating it, or the consequences that these administrative arrangements have on policy choice, policy implementation, and organizational performance.

Issues related to coordination across administrative agencies have been a long-standing concern in the study of public administration (Kaufman 1960). For example, Donald Kettl (2011) provides an insightful diagnosis of the problem of interagency coordination and offers examples of its dysfunctional consequences. Guy Peters (1992) offers a rich description of administrative coordination issues. These works provide an understanding of the historic roots of relevant coordination challenges and help set the stage for our theoretical approach to establishing the range of alternative integration mechanisms and their consequences. However, and despite a considerable awareness about the problem of administrative silos, a systematic theory of administrative integration is lacking.

Although they do not address this issue directly, several additional lines of work also contribute relevant partial insights, which we assemble to build the theoretical foundation for the FCA approach proposed here. These research lines include management science-based research on interdepartmental integration as an approach to performance improvement, public administration literature investigating administrative reorganizations and city-county consolidations, political science work on administrative delegation and agency assignment, and policy studies research on complexity and network multiplexity. We review the most pertinent studies in each of these literatures in turn.

Management of Interdepartmental Integration

To produce desired benefits and expected outcomes, coordination and cooperation across administrative silos may need to occur within a supportive managerial context. For example, in an early work, Kenneth Kahn (1996) examined whether improved interdepartmental integration yields improved product development performance. He defined increased interdepartmental integration procedurally, that is, more meetings and the presence of formal information flows between functional subunits of an organization. He contrasted these procedural integration mechanisms with collaboration, defined as various departments working collectively toward common goals. Both collaboration and integration between departments were hypothesized to positively influence product development and management performance. The results indicated, however, that collaboration but not integration improved performance.

Building from this work, Alexander Ellinger, Scott Keller, and Andrea Ellinger (2000) contrasted two methods of interdepartmental integration in organizations: interdepartmental interaction and collaboration. They specify that, according to the interaction perspective, the "interdepartmental integration process is largely mandatory and tangible, while the collaborative process is predominately voluntary and intangible" (Ellinger, Keller, and Ellinger 2000, 44). The classification of interaction versus collaboration-based integration roughly corresponds with the formal/informal authority distinction within the FCA framework we advance here.

Administrative Reorganization

A second relevant line of research deals with administrative reorganization. Reorganization within a city government is generally considered the restructuring of distinct administrative units, and may include a merger or consolidation of departments, divisions, or offices. Administrative reorganization is a common activity of city government, but it remains relatively understudied.

Early work by Peters (1992) advanced three approaches to studying administrative reorganization that are relevant to the organization of sustainability in cities. The first, purposive reform, is undertaken to achieve a particular end goal or outcome and may be seen as a political act. The second approach, environmental dependency, views administrative reorganization as a response to changes in the larger-environment context. It is considered passive adaptation rather than as a result of a willful decision. The third approach, institutionalism, views organizational change as a collective decision to shift administrative structure in order to better reflect the organization's values or culture. The latter approach, Peters posits, "makes change at once more understandable and less predictable" (1992, 213).

Building on the work of program performance by Edward Jennings (1994), Edward Jennings and Ann Ewalt (1998) focus on reorganization and coordination together to explain outcomes related to job training. They find that both coordination, measured as an index of administrative techniques, and administrative consolidation, indicated by whether the two primary agencies responsible for program implementation were represented as one administrative unit, make a difference for outcomes. While overall coordination is positively related to outcomes in three of the ten measures of program outcome, administrative consolidation shows strong, positive effects on six of the outcome measures.

Research on city-county consolidation is also relevant—particularly work that examines collaborative mechanisms as an alternative to consolidation. Unification of existing governments occurs primarily through a merger or consolidation. A merger refers to the joining of two or more incorporated government units of the same level, whereas a consolidation involves the unification of two or more governments of different levels, such as in combining city and county governments. The former approach to government unification is much more common than the latter, but at a general level, both are pursued for potential cost savings in service delivery and efficiency gains. However, associated transaction costs and questions of efficacy have driven criticism of these approaches and spawned studies on alternative mechanisms—including municipal annexation, interlocal agreements, and the use of special district governments—for achieving purported goals of consolidation (Carr and Feiock 2004). Recent work points to interlocal agreements as a promising means to achieve the potential benefits of consolidation without its associated costs. A key benefit of interlocal agreements, and collaborative approaches generally, is that they allow individual governments to preserve their autonomy. Similarly, within a city government, a collaborative agreement between two administrative units can minimize conflicts involved in revoking authority or identity from units. Compared to administrative reorganization, the process of creating and amending their own rules as part of a collaborative effort may generate greater legitimacy among participants (Feiock and Scholz 2010).

Administrative Delegation

The structural design thesis in political science predicts that agencies that are highly buffered from political influence produce more accurate and less biased policy information than agencies that have weaker institutional autonomy (Krause and Douglas 2004). The underlying logic of this thesis is that better-insulated agencies have a greater capacity to resist political pressures placed on them to produce policy information that is compatible with elected officials' goals. If policy information produced by technical experts within government is politicized, and generated in response to political demands, it may be contrary to information produced through expert and independent analyses (Moe 1991). It is also argued that, when administrative responsibility is insulated from political interference, there is a stronger credible commitment or institutional guarantee that revenue for a particular program or policy will not be rescinded in the future (Horn 1995).

The issue of legislative assignment of responsibilities to specific bureaucratic agencies or departments is central to agency authority in the political science literature. Agency design at the national level has been linked to political incentives that shape future agency decisions as well as to factors that influence their exposure to future political interventions (Moe 1991). Most of the political science literature considers the federal rather than local government level and focuses almost exclusively on congressional design of administrative agency responsibilities in the legislative appropriation process. The principal agent approach applied in much of this work yields important insight, but its focus on delegation and agency structure addresses assignment only indirectly.

At the local level, Arnold Fleischmann and Gary Green (1991) investigated whether primary responsibilities for economic development are housed within the chief executive office, as a separate specialized agency, as part of a larger agency, or in a decentralized line department. Jongsun Park and Richard Feiock (2012) similarly examine changes in the location of development responsibility over time. These studies report that larger cities and those with a greater number of development programs are more likely to have a specialized separate department for promoting economic development (Fleischmann and Green 1991) and that demographically homogenous communities were more likely to locate functions in the chief executive office (Park and Feiock 2012).

Policy Complexity

The fourth line of relevant literature is centered on a growing policy studies literature that explores how self-organizing networks can coordinate complex multi-actor problems. Complex and crosscutting issues such as water resource management, emergency management, or sustainability require the cooperation of multiple semi-independent units to effectively address collective-actions problems and overcome functional divides. The network governance literature focuses on integration across multiple public and/or private organizations by framing their interactions as an ecology of games

(Lubell 2013). The relationships are facilitated by venues, meetings, and associations in which various actors jointly participate.

These same network mechanisms can operate within a single organization to coordinate across functions. Multiplexity refers to the tendency of network members to develop interorganizational ties across different sets of activities, deepening or fortifying the relationship between actors (Andrew and Kendra 2009). Extensive research has focused on how autonomous but interdependent organizations or governments can coordinate to address transboundary problems. Building from this literature, we describe intracity coordination challenges in governing city sustainability efforts. By advancing a framework around the administrative arrangements used to integrate sustainability, we draw on studies examining mechanisms for mitigating vertical and horizontal ICA dilemmas, which argues that the appropriate mechanisms to mitigate the fragmentation of public authority are shaped by the nature of the problem, the interests of the actors involved, and the existing set of institutions in place (Feiock and Scholz 2010; Feiock 2013). We also draw from literature on administrative agency design in the legislative appropriation process, presidents, and the politics of agency design (Lewis 2003; Krause 1999), as well as from our recent work of sustainability agency assignment (Krause, Feiock, and Hawkins 2016; Feiock, Krause, and Hawkins 2017).

Administrative Organization for Sustainability

Municipal sustainability offers an ideal lens through which to study FCA dilemmas generally, since sustainability involves and depends on actions that many of the departments or agencies existing within cities can potentially address (Feiock, Portney, et al. 2014; Feiock, Krause, and Hawkins 2017). However, because of its complexity, and because sustainability is new to the local agenda, an administrative apparatus has not been systematically developed to coordinate its implementation and facilitate policy success.

The organizational structures and administrative mechanisms available to resolve FCA problems and support effective sustainability implementation remained largely unexamined until recently. General knowledge of the way sustainability functions are, or should be, organized in cities is limited (Portney 2013). It is thus difficult to assess, a priori, whether local governments have established the administrative and institutional arrangements necessary to facilitate the success of their sustainability efforts. The implications of this extend to issues of policy design, implementation, and eventual outcomes that lie at the center of local policy and public administration research.

Sara Burch's (2010) study of barriers to carbon reduction in three Canadian cities was one of the first efforts to link the administrative structure for pursuing sustainability to outcomes. Applying a new institutional theory approach, municipal institutions were presumed to deeply influence the context within which responses to climate change are designed and implemented, because they are part of the historically evolved and path-dependent structures that have been shown to limit the options of actors.

> Structural/Operational barriers arise from the location of climate change and/or sustainability in the organizational hierarchy, the job descriptions that set priorities and performance criteria for individuals, the organizational mechanisms for facilitating interdepartmental collaboration, the presence or absence of a political party system, and the structure of the budgetary system. (Burch 2010, 7578)

In the case study of Vancouver, some officials argued that the sustainability unit should be directly affiliated with the city manager's office to demonstrate the strength of the city's political will with regard to climate change and sustainability issues (Burch 2010).

Recent work extending the ICA framework to interdepartmental collaboration and integration represents the first attempt to advance a broader theory of administrative organization and integration for local sustainability (Krause, Feiock, and Hawkins 2016; Feiock, Krause, and Hawkins 2017). This lays a foundation for the FCA approach developed in this book by directing attention to the importance of which unit in local government serves as the headquarters for sustainability efforts.

The following sections describe the ICA framework and then apply it specifically to the problem of functional fragmentation of local sustainability initiatives to develop a systematic FCA approach that can be applied to the eight city case studies that follow.

Institutional Collective Action

ICA dilemmas are fundamentally a result of divided or partitioned authority that arises when decisions made by one governmental actor in a specific jurisdiction or functional area affect other jurisdictions, actors, or functions (Feiock 2013). If significant externalities are present, then individual actors' pursuit of their own short-term goals may result in collectively inefficient policies. The ICA framework compares alternative mechanisms to mitigate horizontal, vertical, and FCA problems. Horizontal dilemmas occur when the jurisdictional boundaries of the governmental units with authority to address a problem are not large enough to effectively solve the problem individually and/or the consequences of their actions spill over to affect their neighbors. Vertical ICA dilemmas arise when different levels of government pursue similar or overlapping policy objectives. FCA problems are defined by the connectedness of services, policies, and resource systems. Unlike vertical and horizontal dilemmas focused on intergovernmental relationships, FCA dilemmas are a product of functional fragmentation of authority among departments and agencies within a single government (Feiock 2013; Shrestha, Berardo, and Feiock 2014; Feiock, Krause, and Hawkins 2017).

An expansive body of literature investigates the fragmentation of authority among governments in metropolitan areas and the mechanisms available to integrate or coordinate decision making in polycentric systems (Feiock 2009; Feiock and Scholz 2010; Ostrom, Bish, and Ostrom 1988). The study of ICA dilemmas has produced a taxonomy of mechanisms for mitigating collective dilemmas that vary along two dimensions (Feiock and Scholz 2010; Feiock 2013). The first dimension is the degree of encompassment. Mechanisms range from bilateral relationships between two units to multilateral or multifunctional processes that include all relevant actors. Although broader in scope, participating in more-encompassing mechanisms may create additional transaction costs or divert a unit from its primary mission. As a result, individual actors may prefer ICA mitigation mechanisms that are less complex. The second dimension along which mechanisms vary is the extent to which they rely on informal commitments versus formal mandates imposed by higher authorities (Feiock 2009). As before, the costs of participating increase when formal arrangements force actors away from their preferred policy path. Because of this potential loss of autonomy, actors are often thought to favor less-formal engagements with their peers.

Both transaction costs and collaboration risks can shape individual actors' support for an integration mechanism and its likely effectiveness (Terman, Feiock, and Youm 2020). The ICA framework presumes that local governments, or functional agencies within a local government, will seek to collaborate when the utility of doing so outweighs the benefits of inaction or going it alone (Feiock and Scholz 2010). When the benefits of joint action are sufficient, local managers can choose from among a variety of available collaboration mechanisms (Feiock 2013). The potential integration mechanisms for all three types of ICA dilemmas involve elements of both self-organization and authoritative design in addition to network management. Figure 3.1 presents the mechanism that results from combining the two dimensions defined in the framework when applied to the dilemmas of integration across governments within a region. A rich body of literature has developed around efforts to mitigate vertical and horizontal ICA dilemmas, but with the exception of the authors' 2017 study, functional ICA mechanisms have remained unexplored (Feiock, Krause, and Hawkins 2017).

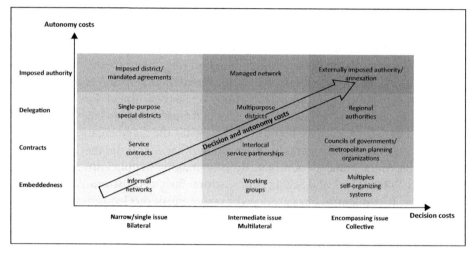

Figure 3.1 Transaction costs and ICA mechanisms

Functional Collective Action

Functional coordination and collective action problems within a single government are similar to the ICA problems that arise from fragmented governmental authority more generally (Feiock and Scholz 2010; Feiock 2013). In each instance, the connectedness of services, objectives, and resource systems produces positive and negative externalities (Feiock 2013). However, in FCA situations those externalities exist between distinct units within a single government. For example, a development decision made by a city's planning department may have consequences for the city's infrastructure maintenance (that is the responsibility of the public works department), its natural resources (environmental management), and its transportation system (managed by an internal transport authority), as well as numerous other agencies and divisions within the city government that did not have direct input on the policy decision. In situations such as this, absent an integrative coordination mechanism, the policy decisions made by a single unit can generate interagency spillovers that lead to inefficient outcomes and stymie citywide goals. Although functional coordination has long been a concern within public administration, these issues are not emphasized in contemporary policy theories (Kim et al. 2020).

Drawing from and extending theories of ICA, we identify four general types of administrative arrangements available to integrate sustainability across a city government and the specific design considerations within each. Figure 3.2 arrays these four arrangements along two dimensions. The first dimension involves the assignment of primary responsibility for sustain-

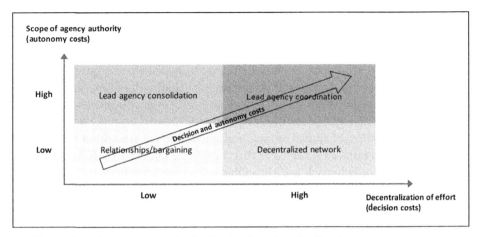

Figure 3.2 Arrangements for facilitating functional collective action

ability and indicates the scope and degree of authority held by this lead agency. The second dimension captures the number of independent entities within a government that share some responsibility for sustainability.

One option to minimize intraorganizational collective action on sustainability is to consolidate all or most of the services and functions of government that deal with this issue, as depicted in the upper-left quadrant. This is the approach that many states took to environmental protection in the 1970s by consolidating soil and lands, air pollution, water resource management, and public health functions into a super agency with strong regulatory power. The advantage of this arrangement is that the integration of sustainability internalizes functional spillovers. Such an approach, however, might be politically difficult and diminish the ability of agencies to carry out traditional functions. This makes the agency assignment decision critical (Krause, Feiock, and Hawkins 2016).

The upper-right quadrant represents a lead agency coordination arrangement, in which several administrative units share responsibility for sustainability activities, but an authoritative lead agency is empowered to direct their actions. The lead agency is endowed with a formal, often hierarchically based, authority or influence over other relevant units, which facilitates the implementation of its policy preferences. This is similar to the model of an interorganizational managed network with a strong lead agency that has become popular in intergovernmental or intersectoral service delivery collaboration.

The lower-left cell of Figure 3.2 represents a situation where an agency with primary responsibility does not have strong authority, but it is clearly identified as the relevant lead. Moreover, the number of other administrative units involved in implementation is limited in scope. In this case, integration might be pursued through approaches led by the primary unit that include bargaining, the use of task forces, and the cultivation of personal relationships and mission buy-in with relevant staff. Full coordination under this structure may be elusive because units within city government will likely still be protective of their resources, including staff time, and want to maintain their relative autonomy and authority over policy decisions.

In the lower-right "decentralized network" quadrant, responsibilities for sustainability are spread among multiple agencies throughout the government with none empowered to direct citywide efforts. In this situation, if integration is achieved, it is through a self-organizing network or communication and coordination among individual units. Studies of crosscutting development issues indicate that self-organizing networks can operate as a complement to, or a substitute for, more formal mechanisms to achieve collaboration among governments (Kwon, Feiock, and Bae 2014).

City Case Study Selection

Over the next four chapters of this book, we present in-depth case studies of eight cities whose sustainability-related actions and arrangements are characterized by each of the quadrants depicted in Figure 3.2. In selecting case study cities, we sought to capture examples of city governments that have strong sustainability programs and together use a cross section of the four previously described arrangements to overcome FCA challenges: (1) lead agency consolidation, (2) lead agency coordination, (3) relationships and bargaining, and (4) decentralized networks.

We used the results of the Smart and Sustainable Cities Survey, described in Chapter 2, to identify a list of candidate cities. First, we operationalized "high achieving" cities as those which had implemented seven or more of the fifteen sustainability policy actions asked about in the survey (see Table 2.3 for the list of policy actions). Among the 504 cities that completed the survey, the mean implementation rate was 6.5 policies. Thus, the 339 cities that had implemented at least seven are considered "above average" and remained in consideration as candidate cities.

Next, we divided these high-achieving cities into groups according to the two dimensions in Figure 3.2—that is, the extent of authority and decentralization that characterize their sustainability effort. This enabled us to identify cities that, on the basis of our working hypotheses, were expected to represent each of the four possible administrative arrangements available to overcome FCA. We used the location of the sustainability headquarters unit in the city government hierarchy as a proxy for authority, reflecting the hypothesis that units in the executive branch are, all else being equal, endowed with greater authority than those in line departments. Data on the number of city units that partner on sustainability were used to represent the decentralization of effort. The average number of partner units working on sustainability for the cities in our sample is 6.8. We use this as the point at which to divide cities into two categories representing more and less administrative centralization.

All 339 above-average cities in the sample were placed into one of the four quadrants based on these rules. Two cities from each quadrant were selected as case studies. The selection of specific cities was also influenced by a consideration of size. We chose to examine medium to large (but not extremely large) cities, and settled on a population range of between one hundred thousand and seven hundred thousand. Obtaining a relatively even geographic spread of cities across the country as well as sufficient variation in their forms of government were also objectives considered in city selection.

The left side of Figure 3.3 shows the case study cities' placement in the quadrants as originally conceived. Although we used a systematic approach in attempt to identify two cities in each quadrant, the completion of the case study research provided additional and more nuanced information that led us to somewhat recharacterize their placement. The right side of Figure 3.3 shows the post–case study characterization of cities according to their administrative arrangements. Notably, the changes reflect a more comprehensive understanding of the role of authority. The case study research makes clear that the simple notion of hierarchical authority, as represented by the executive or line placement of headquarters units, does not consistently shape the type of administrative arrangement used. Rather, lead unit *influence*, a more complicated and harder to measure dynamic, emerges as key in shaping how cities can and do overcome FCA dilemmas. This complexity is explored throughout the remainder of the book and particularly in the case study chapters, which are organized around the groups in the right side of Figure 3.3.

Tables 3.1 and 3.2 provide a basic comparison of the eight case study cities on key city government and community characteristics, respectively. Figure 3.4 maps the geographic location of the case study cities.

Cities organized based on selection criteria

Headquarters in executive branch	*Lead agency consolidation*	*Lead agency coordination*
	Providence, RI El Paso, TX	Orlando, FL Kansas City, MO
Headquarters in line department	*Relationships/ bargaining*	*Decentralized network*
	Fort Collins, CO Gainesville, FL	Ann Arbor, MI Oakland, CA
	Fewer units involved	**More units involved**

Cities organized based on case study outcome

Headquarters has more authority/ influence	*Lead agency consolidation*	*Lead agency coordination*
	Fort Collins, CO	Orlando, FL Kansas City, MO
Headquarters has less authority/influence	*Relationships/ bargaining* Ann Arbor, MI Oakland, CA Providence, RI	*Decentralized network* El Paso, TX Gainesville, FL
	More centralization	**Less centralization**

Figure 3.3 Initial and final distribution of case study cities by quadrant

TABLE 3.1: COMPARISON OF CASE STUDY CITIES ON CITY GOVERNMENT CHARACTERISTICS

City	Form of government	FY17 total budget (millions)	FY17 general funds (millions)	Number of city employees (FTE)	Number of council members + mayor	City operates electric utility	City operates drinking water utility
Ann Arbor	Council-manager	$370.8	$54.4	729	11	No	Yes
El Paso	Council-manager	$900.0	$381.0	6,000	9	No	No
Fort Collins	Council-manager	$451.6	$152.0	1,200	7	Yes	Yes
Gainesville	Council-manager	$330.3	$116.6	1,390	7	Yes	Yes
Kansas City	Council-manager	$1,594.0	$478.4	4,369	13	No	Yes
Oakland	Mayor-council	$1,331.6	$570.5	4,299	9	No	No
Orlando	Mayor-council	$1,172.4	$423.1	3,284	7	Yes	Yes
Providence	Mayor-council	$716.8	$454.6	5,045*	16	No	No

* 3,316 of the city employees work in the Providence school system.

TABLE 3.2: COMPARISON OF CASE STUDY CITIES ON COMMUNITY CHARACTERISTICS

City	2010 population	Median household income	Education (bachelor's or higher)	Race: non-Hispanic white	Democrat votes (2016 general election)*
Ann Arbor, MI	115,204	$52,625	71.1%	70.4%	68.4%
El Paso, TX	628,923	$37,428	21.4%	14.2%	69.1%
Fort Collins, CO	140,082	$49,589	50.1%	83.1%	58.5%
Gainesville, FL	124,271	$30,036	43.8%	57.8%	47.5%
Kansas City, MO	454,876	$44,113	29.6%	54.9%	55.7%
Oakland, CA	390,724	$49,721	36.3%	25.9%	79.3%
Orlando, FL	233,707	$42,355	32.7%	41.3%	60.4%
Providence, RI	178,286	$36,925	28.9%	37.6%	59.0%

* County-level aggregation.

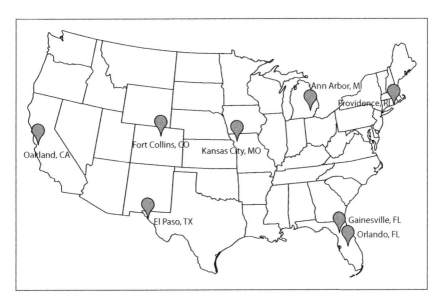

Figure 3.4 Map of case study cities (Map data © 2019 Google)

Chapter 4, which examines the city of Fort Collins, Colorado, as an exemplar of lead agency consolidation, is the first of four chapters organized around administrative arrangements. The experience of Fort Collins and its unique Sustainability Services Area offers an illustration of how lead agency consolidation can serve as an arrangement to overcome FCA challenges around sustainability. This chapter provides a profile of the Fort Collins community and city government; it describes the Sustainability Services Area, its development and functioning; and it identifies the formal and informal mechanisms the city government uses to integrate sustainability functions across departments. The chapter ends with an assessment of how the organization strategy used in Fort Collins has shaped its subsequent sustainability outputs and outcomes.

Lead agency coordination is next explored in the contexts of Kansas City, Missouri, and Orlando, Florida. Kansas City's and Orlando's experiences illustrate how cities can use lead agency coordination to implement their sustainability initiatives. The lead agencies in both cities, Kansas City's Office of Environmental Quality and Green Works Orlando, are part of their city's executive branch, and this chapter describes their evolution and functioning. Each case study begins with a profile of the community and city government context, highlighting their primary pressures and sustainability-related priorities. It identifies the formal and informal mechanisms each city uses to determine and integrate sustainability objectives across departments citywide. We comparatively assess the two cities' lead agency coordination experiences and assess the impact that the use of this arrangement has had on their subsequent sustainability outputs and outcomes.

Three cities are drawn on to illustrate relationships and bargaining: Providence, Rhode Island; Ann Arbor, Michigan; and Oakland, California. These three cities each have lead sustainability units that are clearly identifiable but have relatively little authority over other units in the government. As such, they use relationships and bargaining as primary mechanisms to overcome FCA challenges. We profile the city government and community context surrounding each of their sustainability arrangements and identify the approaches they use to integrate sustainability functions. The chapter ends with a comparison of the three cities' experiences with the arrangement and an assessment of the impact it has had on the outputs and outcomes in each city.

Finally, Gainesville, Florida, and El Paso, Texas, offer examples of two cities that use a decentralized network approach to sustainability. As with the other case study chapters, we describe the local government and community context of each city, describe the evolution of their organizational arrangements, identify the sustainability integration mechanisms used, and comparatively assess the two cities' experiences.

4

Lead Agency Consolidation

Fort Collins, Colorado

When an issue is so complex that it touches everyone or so
ambiguous that there is no leader—we take it on.
—Jackie Kozak Thiel
(chief sustainability officer, Fort Collins, Colorado),
interview by the authors, June 1, 2017

One way to minimize intraorganizational collective action challenges
around sustainability goals is to consolidate all or most of the services and government functions that pertain to sustainability. The
advantage of this arrangement is that the integration of sustainability
within a single unit mitigates accountability problems resulting from fuzzy
boundaries. Consolidation also internalizes functional spillovers to reduce
the likelihood that the presence of positive externalities (e.g., shared credit,
recognition, or financial savings) will reduce departments' incentive to invest their own time and energy in the pursuit of a shared objective.

The headquarters unit into which relevant functions are grouped may
have either considerable or quite limited authority to manage the daily affairs of other units and shape how sustainability is addressed citywide. As
described in Chapter 3 and depicted in Figure 3.2, when a city consolidates
its sustainability functions into a single unit and endows it with considerable formal authority to shape the issue's overall treatment, we characterize
the administrative apparatus used as lead agency consolidation. This is the
least common arrangement used to administer sustainability in U.S. cities
because it requires the largest departure from the organizational status quo
and is likely to be resisted by at least some existing units (Brierly 2004). The
city of Fort Collins, Colorado, and its unique Sustainability Services Area
(SSA), exemplifies the characteristics of a consolidated agency arrangement.

The city of Fort Collins is organized into seven service areas, which are
umbrella units that each consist of several functionally related departments

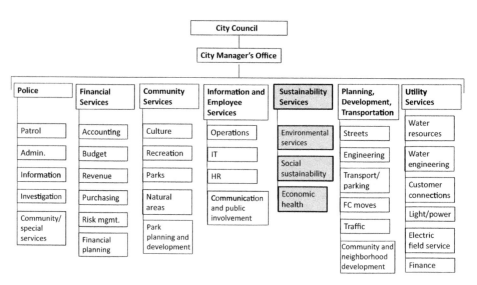

Figure 4.1 City of Fort Collins organizational chart

(see Figure 4.1). The SSA comprises three departments—Environmental Services, Economic Health, and Social Sustainability—and is headed by a chief sustainability officer (CSO) who is a member of the city's Executive Leadership Team. As the city manager told us, the expressed purpose of this structure is to institutionalize a triple-bottom-line approach to sustainability and ensure that it is pursued "enterprise-wide." Along those lines, it is important not to overstate the centralization of sustainability in the SSA. Although responsibility for coordination and the delivery of many services directly related to sustainability are consolidated within it, sustainability as an objective remains explicitly co-owned by many different departments outside the SSA.

The Fort Collins community context enabled the development of the SSA. Fort Collins is perceived by city staff as a demanding community that expects a lot from its local government. It is Democratic leaning but politically mixed, with politics described by interviewees as "rational" and kept in check by a "healthy tension." Although not without pockets of pushback, including from a conservative chamber of commerce, the community has shown a longtime commitment to conservation and environmental stewardship. In recent years strong advocacy groups have organized around climate protection and homelessness. The community and its overall support of sustainability "gives the city permission to be aspirational," according to interviewees. The SSA—and its attempt at aligning vision, resources, and structure—is one operationalization of this aspiration.

The data informing this chapter were primarily gathered from eleven hour-long in-person semistructured interviews conducted with Fort Collins executive leadership and city staff in June 2017, including people holding the following positions:

- City manager
- Chief sustainability officer
- Environmental services director
- Social sustainability director
- Economic health director
- Deputy city manager
- Climate program manager
- Sustainability impact manager
- Social sustainability officer
- Sustainability financial analyst
- Communications manager

Appendix C contains the general template of the questions we asked interviewees across all eight case study cities. The city website, reports, and planning documents, as well as local newspaper stories, supplement the interview data. The next section of this chapter describes the rationale and dynamic that led to the SSA's creation and provides greater insight into its structure and priorities.[1] We then identify specific formal and informal mechanisms used to integrate sustainability across the city government and assess how they are used in the context of Fort Collins's particular consolidated lead agency arrangement. Finally, we assess the SSA's success in overcoming functional collective action (FCA) dilemmas and other operational challenges. A general overview of Fort Collins, which provides its governmental and community context, is available in Appendix D.

How the Sustainability Services Area Came to Be

Fort Collins, both as a community and a city government, has a demonstrated commitment to environmental stewardship, which initially focused on land preservation and water quality, reaching back to the 1950s. For much of this time, Fort Collins was an economic magnet for the region and did well economically, as one interviewee put it, "without even really trying." Longtime city staff described a skepticism in Fort Collins around ideas

---

1. This is a point-in-time description of the city's goals and structure as they were in 2017, when data were collected.

of growth, to the point where "economic development" was an intentionally avoided term. Social issues were also not a major local concern. This began to change in the early 2000s, when there was a notable shift in perception about the city's regional economic competitiveness, and social concerns, particularly high rates of local homelessness, became more visible. This started a transition to a more holistic approach to sustainability. Darin Atteberry, the Fort Collins city manager, who has more than twenty years' tenure with the city, used the metaphor of a sustainability stool to explain that in response to the city's changing situation, "a new structure was needed to lengthen the other two legs of the stool. It was not about reducing the environmental but increasing the social and economic ones."

For some years before the creation of the SSA, Fort Collins used a model akin to the lead agency coordination approach described in Chapter 3, by which there was a sustainability coordinator in the City Manager's Office tasked with facilitating efforts in other departments. This strategy, however, proved unsatisfactory in achieving desired outcomes. Atteberry told us, "It just didn't work. We needed structure around it." The services area structure had already been used in the city, starting with planning, development, and transportation services, which was perceived as successfully overcoming a "classic professional divide" by getting planners and engineers to regularly talk to each other, he said. Atteberry described his approach to management as being "very clear about vision, giving it resources, and structuring your organization around it. . . . Then collecting data, monitoring, and benchmarking." With the help of a supportive city council and Bruce Hendee, a former landscape architect who joined the city specifically to formulate its sustainability plan and who eventually became its first CSO (Ferrier 2015), Atteberry developed the SSA to give cohesive structure to sustainability's triple bottom line.

The SSA came into fruition in 2012, bringing Environmental Services, Economic Health, and Social Sustainability under a single administrative umbrella as sibling departments. Each department has its own distinct history: Environmental Services had previously been embedded in the city's Natural Resources Department. In its move to the SSA, it brought with it responsibility over efforts related to indoor and outdoor air quality, climate action planning, waste reduction, and recycling. It is not responsible for environmental sustainability relating to natural areas, transportation, or utilities, all of which are housed in other service areas. Economic Health was a small unit, previously housed in the City Manager's Office and most recently in Financial Services, that pursued a traditional local economic development agenda with a focus on business retention. The Social Sustainability Department was newly created along with the SSA. It initially pulled together staff from the existing Planning and Community Development

Departments, including the city employees who managed grants from the U.S. Department of Housing and Urban Development.

By 2017, five years after its start, the SSA had a dedicated budget of $7.1 million and 25 full-time-equivalent employees: 11.5 worked for Environmental Services, 7.5 for Social Sustainability, 3 for Economic Health, and another 3, including the city's CSO, at the SSA level. One interviewee described the SSA's financial and staff capacity, which is enhanced somewhat by interns and hourly staff, as creating an organizational context in which they "are stretched but not constrained."

The expressed purpose of the SSA is to integrate, and not just cohouse, the three departments representing the triple bottom line. Moreover, sustainability in Fort Collins is a citywide goal, and the consolidation of many sustainability functions into the SSA does not imply that the cooperation of other units is not still necessary. Jackie Kozak Thiel, the city's second CSO, who entered the position in 2015, observed, "We [the SSA] have the responsibility for *coordinating* efforts, but the achievement of outcome needs to be a shared goal." Although the consolidation of relevant functions in the SSA decreases the collective action challenges associated with administering sustainability, the integration of sustainability, both within the SSA and across other service areas, remains an intentional objective in Fort Collins.

Sustainability Priorities

There are two clear sustainability priorities in Fort Collins that consume a considerable portion of the SSA's workload and effort from the city government as a whole: the implementation of the Climate Action Plan (CAP) and improving equity, particularly as it involves addressing the local homelessness problem. Both issues benefit from having strong, vocal community advocacy groups that push the city to adopt ambitious initiatives and monitor the progress in carrying them out.

Climate Action

In 2015, the seven members of the Fort Collins city council unanimously boosted the city's greenhouse gas (GHG) reductions goals and adopted a CAP framework, which sets out specific steps and incremental quantitative benchmarks to guide the effort. The city is committed to mitigating community-wide GHG emissions so that they are 20 percent below 2005 levels in 2020, 80 percent below by 2030, and carbon neutral by 2050 (City of Fort Collins 2015a).

The Environmental Services Department's Climate Action Team is leading a citywide effort to achieve what have been described as some of the most aggressive mitigation goals in the world (Kozak Thiel 2015). Planning and implementing change for their achievement is a major undertaking, both substantively and organizationally. Substantively, it has been estimated that implementing the CAP could cost $600 million by 2020, not accounting for efficiency-based cost savings (Duggan 2015). Organizationally, one staff member observed, "the way we have set up the CAP is fundamentally changing the way we do governance" in the city.

Approximately seventy staff members from a range of city departments are participating in one of eleven different CAP Strategic Initiative (SI) teams, formed around actions necessary to reach GHG reduction goals. Some of the SI teams directly implement climate action programs (e.g., Energy Efficiency and the Road to Zero Waste), and others play support roles, such as performance measurement and messaging and engagement (City of Fort Collins 2016). The SI teams have specific impact targets and responsibilities, which the interviewees credit as important to the CAP's continued prioritization. In addition to the SI teams, there is a CAP Core Team, composed of the two leads of each of the eleven SI teams, and a CAP Executive Team consisting of seven top-level city officials, including the deputy city manager, chief financial officer, chief sustainability officer, and utilities executive director. The CAP Executive Team provides strategic vision particularly in regard to how the city will transition to achieve the 2030 CAP goals. Each of these teams has standing monthly or bimonthly meetings. A fourteen-member CAP Community Advisory Committee provides regular community feedback on the effort.

The city set up an online climate dashboard to provide the public with regular updates on progress. As of 2016, annual emissions in Fort Collins were 12 percent, 2.1 million tons of carbon dioxide equivalent, below 2005 levels.

Equity and Homelessness

In Fort Collin's 2017 point-in-time homeless count, 331 people were identified as homeless (Kyle 2017). This is slightly higher than the national average of 17.7 homeless per 10,000 people (National Alliance to End Homelessness 2016). However, several recent visible incidents in the city's downtown involving members of the homeless and transient population brought the situation to the forefront. Homelessness, in the broader context of equity, community wellness, and affordability, has become a significant focus for the city council, and a strong group of local homelessness advocates keeps the issue on the agenda. The Social Sustainability Department is the key player in the city's homelessness response. Social Sustainability is not a direct service provider, in that it does not run homeless shelters, but it plays a large outreach and coordination role with relevant city departments, such as police services, community nonprofits, and regional partners. As noted by one SSA employee, "It convenes and collaborates and sometimes funds, but it's others who implement."

The SSA structure is credited for equity issues becoming a local priority. The social sustainability director noted, "By having a department and being explicit about it [equity], we can bring all the necessary people together." The city manager elaborated: "The structure allowed us to get up to speak about these issues and make the change happen—a delightful unexpected, unanticipated consequence for city."

Authority, Leadership, and Influence

Formally, the CSO heads the SSA and has authority over the operations of the three departments that compose it. As a line unit, however, the SSA does not have hierarchical authority over other service areas or their composite departments, many of which play a role in sustainability. Although consolidating many of the responsibilities for coordination and service delivery into a single unit reduces the potential for FCA challenges, it does not eliminate it; the cooperation of other units is still necessary. Despite not having formal authority over them or the ability to require their participation, the SSA and its leadership wield significant influence. This influence comes from four main sources: the CSO's position as a member in the city's Executive Leadership Team, the person of the CSO, the clear and consistent support from the city manager, and the vocal support and pressure from the public, which acts as a check to the larger system.

The Fort Collins Executive Leadership Team is made up of the deputy city manager and service area division heads: the chief finance officer; police chief; utilities executive officer; director of planning, development, and transportation; employee services director; community services director; and CSO. The Executive Leadership Team meets regularly and is tasked with shaping the implementation of the city's strategic plan. The CSO's participation in the Executive Leadership Team increases the influence of the SSA and sustainability as an objective in two major ways. First, it enables the CSO to be in regular contact with all the city division heads and to be an early participant in their conversations about new projects and directions. This allows sustainability considerations to be a part of projects' entire formation rather than being tacked on at the end. Second, having a seat on the Executive Leadership Team also sends a clear message internally to city staff and externally to the community about the importance of sustainability. As noted by one interviewee, "The position of CSO as part of the executive team leverages huge gravitas and resources. It shows that sustainability is a core government service here—just as much as fire and police."

Another source of the influence that the SSA has over other units is tied to the specific individuals who have held the position of its director. As of 2020, two people have served as CSO since its creation in 2011. The first, Bruce Hendee, joined the city as an assistant to the city manager specifically to help facilitate the organizational transition and bring Environmental Services, Economic Health, and Social Sustainability under the umbrella of a single service area. He assumed the role of the city's first CSO upon the SSA's approval by the city council. He is described by SSA staff as being "visionary" with a "big-picture perspective" and is credited with getting the city leadership and community to think in hundred-year time horizons. The city's second CSO, Jackie Kozak Thiel, took over in 2015 and brings implementation expertise. She is described by staff as particularly skilled at "turning ideas into action" and as a "relationship-based leader" able to foster collaboration across different departments. The personal characteristics and professional skills of both CSOs facilitate buy-in from colleagues across the city and contribute to the ability of the SSA to minimize FCA dilemmas.

The SSA, and sustainability as an objective, has benefited from the consistent and explicit support of the city manager. The city manager in place in 2020 has been in that position since 2004, and his long tenure has helped make sustainability a part of the organization's values. The creation of the SSA was largely his brainchild. In this context, even though the CSO might not have authority over units outside the SSA, the city manager does, and his implicit support of the SSA's mission makes getting buy-in easier than it otherwise would be. Finally, the city manager serves at the pleasure of the city council, which serves at the pleasure of the people of Fort Collins. In addition to benefiting from general support from the public at large, well-organized community advocacy groups keep sustainability issues, particularly climate action and homelessness, on the agenda of city leaders. This influence trickles down and shapes daily operational decisions.

Integration Mechanisms

The SSA was constructed to serve as a comprehensive headquarters for sustainability in the Fort Collins city government. It is tasked with the responsibility of coordinating efforts citywide and for providing a significant portion, but far from all, of the city's sustainability-related services. In so doing, it reduces the FCA challenges and blurred lines of accountability that could otherwise hinder implementation. That said, simply lumping together several related functions into a single unit does not necessarily ensure their integration. Moreover, creating an integrative sustainability headquarters runs the risk that other units in the government will become overly reliant on it and/or view sustainability as "their" responsibility rather than "our" responsivity. The Fort Collins leadership is aware of these potential pitfalls and has engaged in explicit efforts to minimize them. As noted by one SSA employee, "There is a real intentionality about integration here."

Given the structure, integration is needed at two levels: internally within the SSA and across the entire city government. The SSA was created through a process of reorganization, in which staff were identified from across the government to be part of the new service area. Existing personnel and programmatic responsibilities were reshaped to be consistent with a holistic sustainability objective. This resulted in some initial challenges in both determining an appropriate approach to integration and finding the necessary capacity to implement it. As one SSA department director explained, "When it was originally formed, each employee came from an existing department already having a full workload—climate action planning, urban renewal authority, housing affordability. How do we find the capacity to integrate?" This perspective was shared by another department director: "When it started out, we all already had day jobs, and then we had to also figure out what this sustainability thing was. But five years in, we coordinate every day, and this feeling of extra-ness has decreased." The consensus among SSA staff is that it is the right organizational home for all the functions within it and that significant progress has been made in integrating the departments; however, there is still more work to be done.

Integration Mechanisms within the Sustainability Services Area

The structure of the SSA itself forms the basis for cohesion around the triple bottom line, but in addition to the three departments simply being a part of the same overarching unit, a number of formal and informal mechanisms have been used to help integrate the functions of the departments. According to an interviewee, a stated goal of the integration efforts "is to get rid of the mind-set of policy trade-offs among the three legs of sustainability and shift our mind-set to think about: What are the places where economic and social and environmental overlap and mutually reinforce each other to really optimize the outcomes?"

On the formal side, the SSA holds weekly team lead meetings—which are attended by the CSO, the three department directors, and SSA-level communications and finance staff—to discuss near-term priorities and any immediate actions needed to respond to requests from city leadership. These standing meetings are a key to ensuring that departments are kept abreast of one another's activities. The handful of staff employed at the SSA level—that is, those in finance and communications—also attend each department's staff meetings and serve an important bridging role.

Using a common format and a common language, departments within the SSA have developed a strategic plan to clarify their individual and joint missions. Interestingly, the seemingly minor decision to use a shared style and format for the three plans was pointed to as important in building connections between the departments. The upcoming development of an SSA synthesis plan is expected to further strengthen this commitment.

Finally, the SSA has an explicit Integration Team, which illustrates the intentionality with which integration is approached. One team member explains that it was born out of "the realization that we don't even have a good definition of integration and so don't know how to achieve it." In response, the team, which consists of two representatives from each department, engages in active dialogues about what integration really means and how the SSA will know when it is achieved. The team helps organize the full SSA staff meetings that occur quarterly. Some of the exercises during these meetings have included brainstorms to gather multidisciplinary views about what integration means and activities to identify what integration feels like and what it looks like. The team also tracks opportunities and projects that would benefit from having more cross-departmental participation.

In addition to these formal efforts, several informal mechanisms have helped integrate the three departments in the SSA. Staff point to the simple passage of time and shared experiences that have resulted in a natural accumulation of trust and understanding between the departments. This natural integration was enhanced dramatically with the service area's move to a shared space. Although it took four years after the SSA's formation to occur, all of its employees now share one floor of a building. Being in the same space facilitates informal staff connections made through casual conversations. It also makes certain beneficial but ad hoc practices, such as doing dry runs of important presentations in front of one another to get experience with different audiences, easier and more frequent.

Citywide Integration Mechanisms

Although headquartered within the SSA, sustainability is intended to be co-owned by all service areas and departments. Three mechanisms emerged as important to facilitating a shared agenda and coordinated action around sustainability throughout the city as a whole. First, the CAP requires cooperation from across the city government to achieve the city's ambitious GHG mitigation goals. For Fort Collins to be carbon neutral by 2050, fundamental changes are needed from both the government and the larger community. As previously described, several interdepartmental teams—the CAP Executive Team, the CAP Core Team, and eleven SI teams—were established to help plan and execute the actions needed to achieve GHG goals. Together the teams are staffed by over seventy individuals from across various service areas. The teams have substantive responsibilities, and their progress is monitored as part of the CAP. As a result, they are active, meet regularly, and effectively spread responsibility for carbon mitigation beyond the SSA.

A second important mechanism for integrating sustainability across the entire city government is a recently modified sustainability assessment tool called the Triple Bottom Line Scan (TBL-S). Although it has not yet reached its full potential, SSA staff and the city's executive leadership have high expectations for its potential to integrate sustainability thinking into all departments' business-as-usual operations. The TBL-S includes a series of standardized questions that generate a visualization that summarizes the overall impact of a project on the three sustainability dimensions. Its use is expected to help evaluate triple-bottom-line impacts, articulate trade-offs, and foster transparency. A completed assessment is a required part of the materials shared with the city council any time a project goes to it for approval. The city has employed a version of the TBL-S for several years and is revising it to be more simple, efficient, and comprehensive. Pending a successful reboot, the TBL-S is envisioned to serve as a useful decision tool for the council and a useful project management tool for service areas and departments. The latter function is where its integrative potential is most relevant: employees from across all departments will use the tool, at an early stage in their projects, to systematically think about how their work will affect the three dimensions of sustainability.

Third, the city's strategic plan and the Budgeting for Outcomes process it employs together link units across the city to the larger sustainability agenda. Although the strategic plan and its seven strategic objectives do not use the language of sustainability, staff members note that the plan and objectives are all closely tied to the triple bottom line. The feature that makes the strategic plan important for integration is its role in the budget process. Fort Collins uses a Budgeting for Outcomes approach, which takes the perspective of "buying results" rather than paying for costs. As an initial step in each budget cycle, the city council determines community outcomes and priorities. Service areas and departments make "offers" to the city leadership of the services they seek to provide. These offers are ranked and "bought" by the city in the order of that ranking until funds are spent (City of Fort Collins, n.d.a). When making budget offers, units must explicitly

TABLE 4.1: MECHANISMS USED TO INTEGRATE SUSTAINABILITY IN FORT COLLINS CITY GOVERNMENT

Sustainability Services Area	Citywide
Formal	
• SSA structure itself • Weekly team lead meetings • SSA Integration Team • Quarterly all-staff meetings • Common development of departmental strategic plans	• Climate Action Plan and its associated teams • Triple Bottom Line Scan sustainability assessment tool • City strategic plan and the Budgeting for Outcomes process
Informal	
• Shared space • SSA-level staff ability "float" between departments • Rehearsing big presentations in front of an interdisciplinary audience • Overall intentionality from leadership	• Shared culture

link their proposed services back to the strategic plan objectives. This ends up acting as a de facto requirement that all city services proposed for funding are tied back to the city's broad sustainability vision.

The procedural connection between the strategic plan and budgeting process is what enables the former to have influence on integration. This dynamic comes into sharper relief when contrasting the influence of the strategic plan with the city plan. Although still relevant, the city plan plays a clear secondary role in the sustainability integration process because it lacks the budgetary lever. Table 4.1 summarizes the mechanisms used to integrate responsibility for sustainability within the SSA and across the city government.

Assessment of Functional Collective Action in Fort Collins

An explicit administrative philosophy underlies governance in Fort Collins and shapes the way sustainability is structured in the city. Originating from the city's executive leadership, the philosophy emphasizes having a clear vision of desired outcomes, providing resources to support that vision, and logically structuring the organization around it. The development of the SSA is the operationalization of this philosophy around the issue of sustainability. The overall administrative approach in Fort Collins gives as much attention to process as outcome. Rather than operating in the background, the various processes of governance and implementation are subject to explicit attention, examination, and critique. As expressed by an interviewee,

"We are so about process in this organization!" By institutionalizing and consolidating the key functions associated with the triple bottom line, the SSA is seen by all interviewees as an improvement over the more distributed models the city previously used.

Across service areas and departments, most staff members are perceived as willing to engage on sustainability. Although there some instances of perceived overreliance on the SSA, FCA challenges are not a serious impediment to getting sustainability done in Fort Collins. This is in part because, although it is a line department with little formal authority over other units in the government, the SSA exerts a fairly strong influence over their relevant operations. Sustainability is clearly a priority of the city manager, which is structurally reinforced by the CSO's position in the Executive Leadership Team. In addition, sustainability is a shared value of the Fort Collins public and most of the city staff. Unlike in some cities, there is little debate about its worthiness as an objective. Finally, staff membership on different sustainability-related teams (e.g., equity, climate action, business engagement) is intentionally aligned with their core jobs, to minimize the extent to which it is extra. Some staff even consider participation on these teams to be a reward or professional development opportunity.

The majority of the challenges expressed by interviewees regarding the SSA and Fort Collins's approach to sustainability share a single root—namely, that the mission of the SSA is not sufficiently defined, and its scope is too broad. Some expressed a desire for specific quantitative goals, such as are included in the CAP, for the SSA. Others sought a more explicit qualitative prioritization of actions and a defined boundary around the SSA's responsibilities. The lack of clear parameters is seen as contributing to an insufficient understanding of the SSA by some units in the city government, as well as by some stakeholders in the community. This manifests in two almost contradictory ways. On the one hand, it allows for an overreliance on the SSA, by which other city units feel that they do not have to be as involved in sustainability objectives. On the other hand, it is perceived as feeding an almost dismissive attitude toward the SSA and the idea that what it does is "advocacy" or "fluff." A combination of increased mission clarity and better communication is seen as a potential remedy for both of these reactions.

5

Lead Agency Coordination

Kansas City, Missouri, and Orlando, Florida

It is key that we have someone who pushes and keeps cohesion
in the vision. I'm in fleets. I don't really know what is going on
in planning. It is important to have someone who does.

—SAM SWEARNGIN
(fleet administrator, Kansas City, Missouri),
interview by the authors, November 28, 2016

The functional fragmentation of sustainability and its consequences are a central theme of this book. There is virtually no city or government structure in which sustainability fits neatly or completely under a single administrative unit. Some degree of intraorganizational collaboration is therefore needed to pursue it successfully—which is part of what makes it substantively interesting to study. However, the extent of decentralization varies, and in some city governments, the scope of administrative units that share responsibility for the design and implementation of sustainability activities is broad. In these situations, (1) individual administrative units may act independently or as part of a loosely organized network in pursuit of their own sustainability goals, or (2) an authoritative lead unit or individual may be empowered to direct their actions in a more cohesive manner. The latter arrangement, what we call *lead agency coordination*, is the focus of this chapter.

Under lead agency coordination, an identifiable unit and/or person is tasked with leading a city's sustainability effort. That unit or staff person is endowed with a meaningful degree of authority or influence over other units in the city government and is thus able to direct their actions on this issue. Given their importance to the realization of lead agency coordination, it is worth clarifying our distinction between authority and influence: whereby authority is derived from formal position within a hierarchy, influence is broader and is shaped by both formal and informal characteristics of the lead unit and its staff. A key feature of this arrangement is that rather than relying on favors, bargaining, or goodwill from other units asked to contribute to overall sustainability efforts, the lead unit is able to issue directives and (largely) expect that they get done. Although this arrangement uses a top-down approach, it in no way precludes two-way conversations or relationship-based efforts to facilitate buy-in.

Kansas City, Missouri, and Orlando, Florida, have employed different variations of lead agency coordination to successfully overcome many of the functional divides that could otherwise stymie municipal sustainability efforts. In Kansas City, the Office of Environmental Quality (OEQ), which is located within the City Manager's Office, champions and coordinates the city's efforts. Orlando's sustainability efforts are orchestrated by its Green Works team, which was created as a mayoral initiative and reports directly to the city's chief administrative officer (CAO). Both cities locate their sustainability headquarters units in the office of the chief executive rather than as or within a line department. Although not a requisite part of this arrangement, the executive branch is a common home for the headquarters unit in many cities that use lead agency coordination for sustainability. The position in the hierarchy and, perhaps more important, the influence that comes from its proximity to the mayor or city manager is key to the mitigation of functional collective action (FCA) challenges and the successful functioning of this arrangement.

This chapter explores the administrative structures used in Kansas City and Orlando to illustrate how a lead agency can facilitate citywide sustainability efforts. The data informing this chapter were collected via semistructured interviews and are supplemented by information from city plans, websites, and stories published in the local newspapers. In-person interviews were conducted in October and November 2016 with ten members of Kansas City government staff and one active member of the public:

- City manager
- Chief environmental officer
- Performance officer
- Sustainability coordinator
- Sustainability analyst
- Fleet manager
- Environmental compliance manager
- Management fellow
- Senior planner
- Water quality educator
- Environmental Management Commission cochair (citizen)

Eight interviews were held during the same time period with current and former staff of the city of Orlando:

- Director of sustainability
- Assistant city attorney
- City planning manager
- Director of public works
- Fleet and facilities manager
- Former director of sustainability
- Deputy chief administrative officer
- Economic development director

The chapter focuses first on Kansas City and presents the general context for sustainability in the city. It describes the structure, background, and operations of the OEQ and identifies the key mechanisms used to facilitate city-wide integration. This approach is repeated for Orlando.[1] The final sections of the chapter provide a comparative assessment of the use of lead agency coordination in the two cities. A general overview providing the larger community and government context for each city is available in Appendixes E and F.

Sustainability in Kansas City, Missouri

Since 2000, Kansas City, Missouri, has bolted from among the ranks of environmental underperformers to become a regional and national leader in the local sustainability movement (Krause and Martel 2018). Aided by consistent support from elected officials, as well as from the current and previous city managers, Kansas City has made notable strides on issues related to energy efficiency, stormwater management, and, more recently, community equity. An interviewee described sustainability as a "surprisingly non-political issue" in the city and noted that "going green, or pursing the more sustainable alternative in a given situation," has, in recent years, become expected by many city staff members, particularly when they present new policies or programmatic initiatives to the city council. Although sustainability efforts in the city face what might be characterized as low-level challenges, perhaps most notably the general reluctance of staff to do the "extra work" required to implement new initiatives, it has, to a large degree, become ingrained in the city government's culture. The establishment of a "sustainability norm" simultaneously aids and has been aided by the leadership efforts of the OEQ and its director, the city's chief environmental officer (CEO).

---

1. The chapter presents point-in-time descriptions of the cities' structures and operations as they were in 2016, when data were collected.

Office of Environmental Quality: Structure and History

The OEQ is a nine-person unit located within the City Manager's Office. Its responsibilities include sustainability, environmental compliance, clean air, and acting as an environmental liaison with organizations in the community (City of Kansas City, City Manager's Office 2019). Although the majority of the OEQ staff are tasked with environmental compliance—that is, making sure that city facilities are following relevant environmental regulations—two of its positions are explicitly focused on sustainability. The sustainability coordinator is a manager-level position that has existed in the city since 2006; a sustainability analyst position was added in 2015. The main responsibilities of these positions include (1) developing and implementing sustainability programs, such as the 2015 Energy Empowerment Ordinance, which is a reporting and benchmarking requirement for large buildings in the city, (2) gathering and assembling relevant performance data, such as for the city's greenhouse gas (GHG) inventory updates, and (3) working with staff to break down administrative silos and facilitate citywide sustainability efforts.

Although they do considerable work in coordinating and carrying out sustainability initiatives in the city government, the two staff positions do not, themselves, have the authority or influence to be characterized as engaging in lead agency coordination. That is attached to the position of the OEQ director, the city's CEO. At the time of the interviews, the CEO was Dennis Murphey, who had held that position since it was established in 2006. He described his role as an "internal champion for sustainability" and as "akin to an orchestra conductor." His broad perspective and focus on encouragement and facilitation have been widely appreciated by city staff and his requests have carried considerable weight. As one city employee described, "His position is taken seriously. . . . The departments recognize that his encouragement reflects the priority of the city manager, the mayor, the leadership." This influence is in part due to the OEQ's location in the City Manager's Office. As is discussed in more detail below, the proximity to leadership and the "freedom to roam" that this placement affords is seen as providing a tremendous advantage and being instrumental to success of the city's sustainability efforts.

The OEQ was established in the City Manager's Office in 2006, but its history is longer and rooted in environmental compliance. In the early 1990s, the Kansas City government was found to have been operating a hazardous waste storage facility, nicknamed "Fort Hazard," for years without a permit (*St. Louis Post-Dispatch* 1993). As part of its negotiated consent decree with the federal government, the city was required to create an environmental compliance manager position to audit all city facilities and ensure regulatory adherence. Environmental compliance was originally housed in the City Manager's Office and grew to include other environmental functions such as recycling and Leadership in Energy and Environmental Design (LEED) projects. It eventually transitioned into the Department of Environmental Management, a line department with additional operational responsibilities such as solid waste collection. This move, which changed its position in the city's organizational hierarchy, was perceived by some as limiting the compliance officer's effectiveness and creating more friction because, as one interviewee put it, "each department is its own little fiefdom. It is hard to tell departments what to do when you are just another department."

In 2005–2006, three related decisions resulted in the emergence of the current incarnation of the OEQ and the expansion of its focus from compliance to sustainability. First, then mayor Kay Barnes signed on to the U.S. Mayors' Climate Protection Agreement committing the city to meaningfully reduce its GHG emissions. Second, the then city manager Wayne Cauthen advanced a vision of Kansas City as an environmental leader and committed to reorganizing city government units to help accomplish it. Third, the CEO position was created, placed in the City Manager's Office, and offered to Dennis Murphey (Dillon 2006; Krause and Martel 2018). The subsequent city manager, Troy Shulte, expressed that because sustainability is a citywide goal, "it just makes sense" to have sustainability as a component of the City Manager's Office. Other citywide, policy-driven units are housed there as well, including the arts office, emergency management, and performance management.

The OEQ has served as the central unit for overseeing environmental and sustainability activities across the city and as a single contact point for the mayor and the council. However, despite it still playing a central role, its sustainability efforts have become increasingly decentralized in the yearssince its explicit emergence on the local agenda. Along these lines, the interviewed CEO noted, "Ten years ago I could have told you every sustainability-related action being undertaken in the city well before it happened. I can't do that anymore. Actions are occurring at all levels, often organically."

Sustainability Priorities

Several city staff members described Kansas City's sustainability efforts as "strategically opportunistic." Many of the specific programs and actions that it has implemented were shaped by the availability of external funding that matched with the city's larger priorities. Three of the most significant and overarching sustainability priorities for the Kansas City government are energy and climate protection, social equity, and stormwater management.

Climate and Energy

In 2008, the Kansas City city council unanimously adopted its Climate Protection Plan (CPP) aimed at achieving a GHG reduction goal of 30 percent below 2000 levels by 2020 and 80 percent by 2050. These targets apply both to municipal operations and the community as whole. The CPP was "citizen-driven," and over eighty citizen volunteers served on work groups to inform its content and recommendations (City of Kansas City Office of Environmental Quality 2013). Implementing the CPP remains an explicit priority for city leadership, but it operates more in the background for most staff members. One mid-level manager observed that the CPP "at the operational level underlies lot of what we do—although it is not obvious to everyone."

One key policy outcome of the CPP, and the GHG emissions inventories that have been conducted in support of it, is the identification of large buildings as a critically important target for reductions. The GHG inventory found that largest 3 percent of buildings in the city were responsible for almost 33 percent of the city's total energy consumption (City of Kansas City 2015). This paved the way for the city's passage of a 2015 Energy Empowerment Ordinance, which requires that municipal buildings over ten thousand square feet and commercial and multifamily buildings over fifty thousand square feet report and benchmark their energy use with an aim of reduction. The development of this ordinance was facilitated by Kansas City's participation in the City Energy Project, coordinated by the Institute for Market Transformation and the Natural Resources Defense Council, as well as its acceptance into the U.S. Department of Energy's Better Buildings Energy Data Accelerator program, during which it partnered with the regional investor-owned electrical utility, Kansas City Power and Light, to develop a data access solution.

Energy conservation and efficiency are priority issues for Kansas City's sustainability program, in part because of their GHG implications, but also because they enable the OEQ staff to show a definite financial return on the city's investments. For example, since 2010, the city government has tracked its own energy use in city buildings through the Enterprise Sustainability Platform, an automated monitoring system, which is able to help quickly diagnosis problems and eliminate spikes in usage. It is credited with reducing utility costs by 24 percent to 30 percent across nine city buildings (City of Kansas City Office of Environmental Quality 2013). The ability to save money through reduced energy costs resonates well across city departments—many of which are billed separately for at least some of their energy expenses. Moreover, many of Kansas City's investments in efficiency and renewables have been supported, at least in part, through external funds. Notably, the city received $4.8 million in formula grants and $20 million in competitive grants from the Energy Efficiency and Conservation Block Grants distributed in 2009.

Social Equity

For all the progress made over recent decades, Kansas City remains a racially segregated and economically disparate big city. Bridging that divide has become an important objective. Advancing equity and shared opportunity was a top priority for the mayor, the city manager, and the city council at the time of our interviews. It is also a primary focus for some departments in the city. For example, one of the Health Department's top concerns is health disparities. Data released by the city show that residents of the city's wealthier zip codes live an average of ten to fifteen years longer than residents of the poorer zip codes near the city core (Marso 2017; KCStat 2017). These data have proven galvanizing, and they provide a metric to shape and assess the Health Department's efforts.

Kansas City uses a comprehensive definition of sustainability to guide its policies, and reducing social inequities—including those highlighted in the public health data—falls squarely within its scope. However, it was noted by interviewees that in practice, social equity tends to be treated as distinct by city leaders and in program implementation. Compared to the other two dimensions of Kansas City's triple bottom line, social equity efforts have proven more challenging to integrate. The perception that it is the weakest sustainability dimension in the city has helped propel it to the top of the priority list. One of the ways social equity is being explicitly tied into sustainability efforts is through climate resilience and the recognition that climate impacts will place a disproportionate burden on the city's poorest and most vulnerable residents (Rodgers 2016).

Stormwater Management

The third sustainability issue that is receiving considerable time and attention, stormwater management and overflow control, differs from the others in that it is, to a large degree, legally driven. As described in Chapter 1, Kansas City's antiquated combined sewer overflow system resulted in untreated sewage being released into area surface waters after heavy rains, causing Clean Water Act violations. As part of the nearly $4.5 billion consent decree issued by the Environmental Protection Agency in 2010 to address the issue, the city embarked on an innovative effort to use green infrastructure (e.g., rain gardens and retention ponds) rather than just gray infrastructure (e.g., building new sewer lines). The city's Water Services

Department is the lead actor on this and has embraced the "green infra-structure bandwagon" as a way to enhance overall city sustainability. It also ties into the city's other, previously highlighted, sustainability priorities. The implementation of the consent decree has been driving water rates up each year to the point that they are a serious social equity concern. The aver-age monthly residential water bill in Kansas City was $102 in 2017, more than twice what it was in 2009 (Horsley 2017). A city employee further ob-served that approximately one-third of the city's energy bill is from Water Services, "which makes the water-energy nexus clear." Finally, several inter-viewees noted the expectation that climate change will bring more-intense storms and more-frequent flooding to the region. They tied successful stormwater management to part of the city's larger, and nascent, climate-resiliency strategy.

Interdepartmental Influence

The CEO supervises the eight employees in the OEQ, only two of which are dedicated to sustainability. Although the OEQ serves as a central node and coordination point, most of the actions, policies, and programs that contrib-ute to sustainability originate outside of the OEQ. Neither the CEO nor his or her office has formal authority to determine the actions of any other unit in the city. Nonetheless, since 2006, they have been influential in developing a government-wide culture of sustainability and in getting other departments to engage in supportive policy and programming. FCA challenges have not posed a serious obstacle to sustainability in the Kansas City government, and the initial challenges that did exist appear to have diminished considerably. Three dynamics and sources of influence are credited for this: the organiza-tional placement of the OEQ in the City Manager's Office, having consistent support from top city leadership, and the leadership of the longtime CEO.

Being part of the City Manager's Office gives OEQ staff, and particularly the CEO, regular access to decision makers throughout the city govern-ment. It also provides the CEO with, as one interviewee suggested, a "gravi-tas" and the unit with a flexibility not common to other departments. The CEO meets with the city manager regularly and attends all meetings the city manager has with department directors. The CEO interviewed described the fact that he was "at the table and invited to be a part of the conversation" with department directors as conferring a huge advantage. Being involved in these conversations enabled him to have input on high-level mission-defining decisions as well as the development of citywide policy resolutions and ordinances. Involvement also allows the CEO to be informed of projects during their early stages, which allows him or her to help nudge them in a sustainable direction before their details solidify and are more difficult to change. The CEO explained that being at a higher point in the organizational hierarchy compared to line departments gives him both an ability and "more permission than most to meddle in other departments' affairs." Moreover, the position's close connection with the city manager means that staff across departments take the position seriously and interpret the CEO's encouragement as reflecting the priority of the city leadership. (See Figure 1.1 for Kansas City's organizational chart.)

This ties to the second dynamic that facilitates overcoming FCA dilemmas: strong, consistent support from city leadership has made it clear that sustainability is not a passing fad in the city. Since it has become a city objective, the Kansas City city council has unanimously passed most of the sustainability legislation put in front of it (Rodgers 2016), which sends a clear message to city employees across all departments. One interviewee stated, "The city council has been green for decades . . . to the point where staff has to justify any decisions about not going green to them." Several interviewees described a resistance on the part of some departments and department heads during the first years that sustainability was being explicitly pursued in the city. This resistance was characterized as a general reluctance to do new things and as pushback against the extra work that is often associated with new procedures and responsibilities. Although it has not disappeared completely, the long-term support it has received from leadership, which has extended over the last three mayors and two city managers, has helped to get buy-in. Moreover, city leadership considers sustainability as a factor when allocating money and making investments. Departments' recognition of this has helped motivate their incorporation of sustainability principles as a way to receive more resources from the city. One interviewee observed, "It's all about collaboration, but leadership from the top is a critical element."

One important element of leadership is exemplified by longtime CEO Dennis Murphey, who took the position when it was created in 2006. He has a background in biochemistry and previously headed Cincinnati's Office of Environment and Sustainability and was a chief regulator for the Oregon Department of Environmental Quality. He entered the position with considerable relevant policy knowledge and professional experience, which he described as enabling him to be an "internal champion" for sustainability. Staff across departments have described him as a "facilitator and an enabler," and these personality characteristics emerged as important factors in minimizing potential FCA challenges. A member of the city's performance management team described the importance of "having somebody at the helm who has a collaborative nature rather than using a typical carrot-and-stick approach and who truly believes in sustainability principles. It comes from a place of authenticity." Another described Dennis as "adept at identifying how different groups and departments can benefit from engaging in sustainability and . . . persistent, too." The combination of having a collaboration-oriented champion, in a position with significant access and flexibility, for an issue that is clearly supported by city leadership facilitates intradepartmental collective action.

Integration Mechanisms

The cross-functional and transboundary nature of sustainability makes it susceptible to free-riding and responsibility shirking. Where a specified lead unit has been designated, but its small dedicated staff makes success dependent on the actions of multiple other departments, as is the case in Kansas City, there is a potential for noncooperation to stymie organization-wide goals. A staff member in the OEQ tasked with coordinating the city's sustainability efforts observed that primary resistance to new initiatives in the city tends to occur with mid-level management: "It is much easier to get directors to say yes to things because they can delegate." The burden then falls on mid-level managers, who are tasked with figuring out the specifics of implementing a new project or procedure. "That is where the bottlenecks can occur," the staff member noted. Relatedly, there is a general feeling among staff that sustainability efforts in the city rely too much on goodwill and volunteerism. For many, sustainability initiatives have an "extra credit" feel—they are valued and encouraged but are not a part of most employees' core responsibilities. They thus can get pushed to the back burner. However, the leadership and organizational characteristics described in the previous section have largely prevented these challenges from becoming overly detrimental to the city's efforts. This has also been aided by a series of mechanisms that the city uses, although not always with this conscious intention, to integrate sustainability across departments. Table 5.1 organizes them into formal and informal categories.

Formal Mechanisms

Formal integration mechanisms are those that have been codified or are a part of the city's standard operating procedure. Many of them are explicitly intended to institutionalize sustainability and extend responsibility for its achievement across city departments. Other mechanisms, most notably the citywide business plan and KCStat, are not substantively focused on sustainability, yet their use has an integrative effect. Importantly, several of these formal mechanisms reinforce one another. For example, in isolation something like KCStat would likely only make minor contributions to sustainability integration, but in the presence of an administrative structure that makes use of it for this purpose, its impact as an integration mechanism is amplified.

TABLE 5.1: MECHANISMS USED TO INTEGRATE SUSTAINABILITY IN KANSAS CITY GOVERNMENT

Formal
- Office of Environmental Quality and its sustainability staff
- Climate Protection Plan (CPP)
- Interdepartmental Green Solutions Steering Committee and Green Teams
- Administrative regulations
- Citizen advisory groups
- Five-year citywide business plan
- Citywide data and performance measurement initiatives: KCStats and STAR Communities
- New employee orientation—sustainability training

Informal
- Consistent support from city leadership
- Recognition events
- City government culture

Office of Environmental Quality and Its Sustainability Staff

The OEQ, its director, and staff are arguably the most significant forces behind the government-wide integration of sustainability. Approximately 4.0 full-time-equivalent staff positions are dedicated to sustainability work in Kansas City, 2.5 of which have sustainability as their explicit primary function and the rest is patched together from other OEQ staff who have sustainability-related responsibilities, such as managing the city's four interdepartmental Green Teams. Although they are a relatively small staff, a majority of their time is spent working with partners across the city government and larger community. The OEQ's placement in the City Manager's Office affords staff with a greater "freedom to roam," access, and—particularly for the CEO—influence than they otherwise might have. Still, interpersonal relationships and informal quid pro quo arrangements provide a critical base for getting interdepartmental buy-in for new policies. Along these lines, the sustainability coordinator, who frequently taps staff across departments for reporting data and implementation assistance, described one of his approaches to fostering cooperation: "It is best to be able to give something to get something. I try to help out staff in other departments when I can—usually by providing information—and that makes them more willing to help me."

Climate Protection Plan

The city's CPP is a second important driver and integrator of sustainability across the city. The continued support it has received from the mayor and city council since its 2008 adoption has enabled it to provide a solid foundation for city action. Its influence is most prominent at the director level and it is often used to shape or justify departmental budget requests. For most staff members, the CPP operates as a background document. However, when staff members approach the council with proposals for specific policies or projects, they are expected to describe how their proposal aligns with the CPP and assess its broad intergenerational effects. As one interviewee noted, "It forces us all to ask and answer how a particular action or ordinance is good for the kids."

Interdepartmental Steering Committee and Green Teams

The interdepartmental Green Solutions Steering Committee is tasked with directing the city's green solutions efforts and "promoting sustainability in all city operations" (City of Kansas City 2011). It is cochaired by the city manager and CEO and is composed of director-level members, appointed by the city manager. The staff-level counterparts to the steering committee are four Green Teams structured around the issues of green infrastructure, resource management, regulation and policy, and education and outreach. These teams function as working groups tasked with developing strategies, which are then submitted to the steering committee, for incorporation into city policies. Their actions are guided by a sustainability blueprint consisting of eighty-one initiatives, divided between the four teams.

Staff participation in the Green Teams is voluntary, and the four teams have about forty members citywide. Although they are credited with some significant accomplishments (e.g., designing a KCGreen brand for project labeling in the community and advancing a new citywide green procurement policy), their overall performance has been mixed, and obtaining consistent and appropriate participation has been hard. One OEQ staff member, who was also a Green Team member, observed, "Green Teams are great, but participation is inconsistent. Sometimes it is just the two people from our office at the meetings. People are busy. They don't want to come to city hall and look for parking. It's just the normal dumb stuff that gets in the way." Another interviewee described the key challenge as finding the right chairperson and staff to serve on each team, which "requires matching people's interests and passion with where their expertise is needed. But because participation is voluntary, we can't force this match." After several years of stagnation on the part of three of the four Green Teams, they were intentionally reinvigorated so that a single Green Team coordinator helps create accountability among the teams and transitions activities from one to another as necessary.

Administrative Regulations

Administrative regulations (ARs) are approved by the city manager and require certain actions and behaviors on the part of staff. Several ARs been passed related to sustainability, including those which established a LEED

Gold requirement for the construction of all city-owned facilities, a sustainable procurement policy, and the Green Solutions Steering Committee and Green Teams described above. Of the integrative mechanisms identified, ARs appear to have the most impact on the day-to-day operations of staff who otherwise are not directly working on sustainability. An interviewee stated, "If an AR happens, we do it." Additionally, the fact sheet accompanying any proposed resolution or ordinance, regardless of its content, must answer the question "How does this contribute to a sustainable Kansas City?"

Citizen Commissions and Advisory Groups
CEO Dennis Murphey stated, "When I came [into the position], the city was primed for a conversation about sustainability. A few key citizens had built a coalition and put a value on environmental quality in the community." Many of these engaged citizens serve or have served on one of two citizen advisory groups that provide input and guidance to the city government on sustainability. The Environmental Management Commission is a long-standing citizen group consisting of seventeen members who are appointed by the mayor. It was established by ordinance and assigns members the task of "(1) Reviewing the plans, budgets, programs and actions of the City which substantially impact the City's environment; (2) Providing for the preparation of a comprehensive plan for addressing the long-term environmental needs of the City; and (3) Monitoring the City's actions for compliance with state and federal environmental laws and regulations" (City of Kansas City, City Manager's Office 2019). The Environmental Management Commission, according to a staff member interviewee, is credited as being the "original advocates for developing a local climate protection plan." The second group, the Climate Protection Steering Committee (CPSC), was put together during the development of the CPP and continues to function in an oversight role. It consists of eleven members, including a former longtime city council member who, as one interviewee explained, "carries a lot of weight and knows how to get things done."

Together these groups keep pressure on city leadership to ensure that sustainability remains a citywide priority. One example of their success involves jump-starting GHG inventory updates. There had been no update to the GHG inventory for many years after it was first completed in 2006—financial problems prevented a scheduled 2010 update. The Environmental Management Commission and CPSC recommended to the mayor and city council that they include a line in the 2014 budget to hire a consultant to do an update and to develop customized software to enable the city to do its own updates in the future. This was done, and now the OEQ conducts inventory updates in-house.

Five-Year Citywide Business Plan

In 2014, Kansas City adopted its first five-year citywide business plan, intended to provide an overall road map for funding the city's priorities. The business plan is an integrative effort aimed at linking "vital but as yet disconnected efforts (performance measurement, trends analyses, structured change management, citizen surveys) into one comprehensive platform. The plan is an important first step in breaking a pattern of successive single-year fixes, often implemented without a long-term view" (City of Kansas City Finance Department 2014, 4). From this perspective, the business plan simultaneously serves as a vision document, a budgeting tool, and a data management guide. Its priority goals, updated by the city council in 2017, target the areas of (1) customer service and communication, (2) finance and governance, (3) neighborhoods and healthy communities, (4) planning, zoning, and economic development, (5) public safety, (6) transportation and infrastructure, and (7) housing.

Sustainability is not included as an overarching goal in the business plan, but several of the specified objectives and strategies under each goal relate directly to sustainability. It is through the latter that it serves as a mechanism for integrating sustainability efforts across city departments. In accordance with the plan, departments are required to develop and modify their own strategic plans based on the relevant goals and objectives. This influences what departments include in their budget requests. Moreover, departments are required to report data on the progress of their plans every six months. One interviewee described the business plan's impact on sustainability as "more of an accountability mechanism and less of a change-pushing one. There was enough leadership in place before, and there are plenty of one-off sustainability projects. This becomes important for ongoing projects." The data collection requirements ensure that departments discuss relevant sustainability-related objectives and strategies at least twice a year.

Citywide Data and Performance Measurement Initiatives

"KCMO is a data-centric city," one interviewee told us. Particularly since 2013, the city has embarked on performance measurement and big data initiatives and has an Office of Performance Management that reports directly to the city manager. Much of this effort is funneled toward KCStat, which is billed as Kansas City's "data driven approach to improve city services" (KCStat 2017). KCStat is the mechanism used to monitor progress toward the priorities in the citywide business plan, and its "dashboard" serves as outward-facing platform to communicate city progress and efforts to the public. In relation to sustainability, it is credited with helping to identify barriers to achievement, although not necessarily solutions. A staff member in the city's Performance Management Office offered an illustrative anecdote: "Data show our achievements with waste management and recycling have plateaued. It is clear that this is in part a resource issue—we don't own our facilities for sorting recycling, so we are at the mercy of our contractor. Another limit to progress is we don't offer recycling for multifamily units. Changing this will be hard, but at least we know where the problems are. The data collection and KCStat keep it on the table." Moreover, because of the biannual reporting requirements imposed by the citywide business plan, conversations like this are regular and reoccurring.

A second citywide data collection initiative involves Kansas City's participation in STAR Communities, which is a rating system designed to help communities become "more transparent, accountable, and sustainable" (STAR Communities, n.d.). Participating municipalities collect information about progress on over five hundred indicators (actions and outcomes) corresponding to seven different sustainability goals and get certified on a one-to five-star scale. In 2016, Kansas City was certified a four-star city. The data collection effort was led by a full-time intern who spent a quarter of his time on STAR. (The intern told us, "It is a good rating system, well respected. The city had an eye on it for several years but didn't have the manpower to pursue it. That is where I came in.") Prior to the start of data collection, the city manager and CEO informed all department directors of the effort and asked for their support and cooperation. Responsiveness to the intern's data collection requests varied across departments. As he explained, "Some people got why this was important right away. Some required more pestering and bothering. A few said, 'No, this will require too much staff time.'" As indicated previously, the bottlenecks most often occurred with mid-level managers who already felt overburdened. Even among those more resistant to the additional work, the intern expressed hope that the effort "subtly cracked into their consciousness. Knowing what's there to pursue and improve can make people to think about what they should do." Several interviewees also discussed STAR's continued potential in providing structure, guidance, and benchmarking and expressed hope that it will be more formally incorporated into KCStat and the citywide business plan.

New Employee Orientation

Although it had not yet been implemented at the time of our interviews in 2017, the city had just made a change to its new employee orientation to explicitly include sustainability. The sustainability coordinator is tasked with providing an overview of sustainability priorities and ongoing efforts as part of every new employee's orientation and training, which he or she predicts will have significant impact in facilitating further cross-departmental collaboration.

Informal Mechanisms

The informal mechanisms that integrate sustainability across city departments—particularly the consistent support sustainability has received from elected and administrative city leadership, which has permeated the city government's organizational culture—directly enable and enhance the formal mechanisms identified above. Recognition events straddle the formal/informal line and are used to boost morale and enthusiasm around the actions that various people and departments are taking that go above and beyond to incorporate sustainability into their jobs. The Environmental Management Commission, for example, sponsors an Environmental Achievement Award to recognize and reinforce staff sustainability efforts.

Sustainability in Orlando, Florida

Orlando, Florida, is the second city government profiled in this book that uses lead agency coordination as its approach to overcome the FCA challenges associated with the administration of sustainability. The city of Orlando organizes its sustainability efforts through the Green Works Orlando initiative. Green Works, as it is simply referred to by city staff and community stakeholders, is a mayoral initiative located in the city administrator's office and has emerged as the face of the city's energy efficiency programs, smart cities projects, and fleet and facilities investments, among other initiatives focused community-wide and on municipal operations.

City government leaders are known to vary in their interpretations of sustainability and have different ideas about what issues fall under its broad umbrella (Zeemering 2009). Orlando takes a decidedly environmental approach to sustainability, with a secondary focus on cost savings and job creation. At its core, Green Works is the administrative unit responsible for designing and monitoring Orlando's environmental sustainability initiatives and for promoting the integration of these efforts throughout the city's line departments, which are responsible for their implementation. Since 2007, the Green Works initiative transformed what had been a largely a siloed approach, consisting of ad hoc department-level efforts, into a comprehensive effort organized around explicit citywide environmental sustainability goals.

Green Works Orlando: History and Structure

Since its formation, Green Works has formalized and provided structure to the city's department-driven environmental management and sustainability innovations. As a formal administrative unit, it serves as a connecter between divisions to promote a crosscutting culture of sustainability. The

Green Works team is responsible for designing new programs and working with departments and divisions on their implementation to achieve the goals outlined in the city's two sustainability plans. Green Works was described by a city staff member as playing an important "consultant role to divisions."

The sustainability efforts in Orlando, including the formation of Green Works, were largely driven by the city's mayor at the time, Buddy Dyer. Orlando has a strong mayor-commissioner form of government. Green Works was established in 2007 to advance the mayor's vision for the city to become a national leader on energy and climate change issues. Prior to the mayor launching the Green Works initiative and establishing its administrative arm within the executive branch, sustainability efforts were largely driven by a small self-organized group of staff in the Public Works, Fleet and Facilities, and Planning Departments. These efforts were relatively narrow in scope, and the lens of sustainability was primarily applied to guiding how public works activities could save money and minimize environmental impacts. Although these uncoordinated efforts put the issue of environmental sustainability on the radar, they were hampered by the absence of city-wide sustainability-focused policies and the lack of links to larger organizational priorities. In the early 2000s, the city also was without financial resources earmarked for sustainability, and lacked a formal organizational structure, or planning documents to provide support or institutionalize efforts.

These relatively small and fragmented efforts eventually evolved into an informal citywide committee in which the assistant CAO and the directors of Public Works and Fleet and Facilities led regular multidepartmental conversations around environment and energy issues. These self-organized efforts, combined with leadership from the mayor, laid the foundation for the establishment of Green Works. The first director of sustainability, who served from 2008 to 2015, was hired from within the city and had previously worked in the Planning Department. Like many other cities at the time, Orlando was focused on developing practical, cost-effective ways to improve sustainability and deal with climate change by identifying the most critical city needs and building support for proposed solutions.

At the time of our interviews, the Green Works office had three core staff members: a director of sustainability (DoS) and two sustainability project managers. Each manager works with departments to facilitate project implementation in three specified issue areas. The first manager focuses on livability, local food, and solid waste, and the second on energy, water, and transportation. The DoS's role primarily revolves around gathering research, designing new policies, promoting and encouraging buy-in to sustainability efforts, serving as a liaison between departments and with city leadership, and resolving conflicts when necessary.

During the interview, the DoS at the time, Chris Castro, who had held the position since 2016, shared that he was working to increase the size of the sustainability staff, and this happened shortly thereafter. One additional sustainability project manager has since been hired, and several additional city staff now associated with Green Works are housed in other departments. Namely, the city's energy project manager is located in Fleet and Facilities Management, and a sustainability associate, public outreach coordinator, and the Keep Orlando Beautiful coordinator are housed in Public Works but have a formal affiliation with Green Works. Funding for Green Works is generated through city enterprise funds and grant monies; the office does not have a dedicated budget. The city's Solid Waste Division pays for the salaries of two of the project managers and several of the affiliated staff.

Functionally, although Green Works is a part of the mayor's office, the DoS reports directly to the city's CAO (see Figure 5.1). The CAO approves ideas for new sustainability initiatives before bringing them to the mayor and relevant department heads as part of what was described to us by Chris Castro as a "mini-cabinet meeting," through which they undergo a second round of vetting. As a result, the initiatives that the mayor ultimately moves forward on have been scrutinized from both operational and policy perspectives. One interviewee suggested that although this process of "double vetting" can be frustrating and often means that policy development takes more time; "it has the effect of allowing only the best ideas to rise to the top." Moreover, because multiple departments often have a role to play in implementing sustainability initiatives, this vetting process provides an opportunity for each to weigh in to offer their perspective and help ensure that the

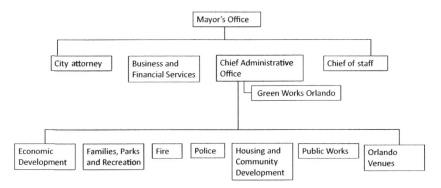

Figure 5.1 City of Orlando organizational chart

city has not overlooked anything. This process is particularly significant for achieving broad buy-in across the city government.

Sustainability Priorities

Reflecting its form of government, policy priorities in the city of Orlando are largely shaped by the mayor. During Mayor Dyer's long tenure, sustainability has benefited from being one of the issues he championed, with the stated vision to "transform Orlando into one of the most environmentally-friendly, economically- and socially-vibrant communities in the nation" (City of Orlando 2012, 4). In practice, Orlando uses a traditional, environmentally focused view of sustainability. Although social issues, including ending homelessness and creating a just and equitable city, are key objectives, they are largely treated as distinct from sustainability and do not fall under the responsibilities of Green Works. Economic development, the third pillar of sustainability, has received considerably more attention, particularly through policies that seek to use improvements in environmental quality and energy conservation to produce positive economic returns. Many of the city's recent priorities integrate environmental and economic objectives.

Green Works began in 2007 as a top-down initiative from the mayor's office that established city goals and set an aspirational tone for what Orlando can become. The original aspirations to promote environmental sustainability were based on five pillars: (1) conserve natural resource and protect the environment, (2) invest in green buildings, vehicles, and materials, (3) foster alternative transportation options, (4) increase the amount of green spaces and tree coverage in the city, and (5) work together as a community to combat the urgent threat of global climate change. Administratively, the initiative was organized to give the city staff leading it the flexibility to innovate and to make programs that would advance the mayor's vision. To update these focus areas, the city implemented a planning process in 2012–2013, led by Green Works staff and a task force of twenty representatives from Orlando's business, institutional, and nonprofit organizations. Via this process, the five original pillars evolved into a new set of policy areas that were subsequently outlined in the Green Works Community Action Plan: (1) energy/green buildings, (2) food systems, (3) green economy, (4) livability, (5) solid waste, (6) transportation, and (7) water. While collectively these priority areas are intended to guide decisions to achieve the goal of "making Orlando the most sustainable City in America by the year 2040" (City of Orlando 2013), there are two specific sustainability priorities that have shaped many of the policy and programmatic initiatives undertaken by Green Works: reducing energy consumption by encouraging green building practices and promoting energy efficiency, and the application of smart cities technologies.

Energy Consumption and Efficiency

Approximately 76 percent of Orlando's GHG emissions come from buildings; thus, the city has set aggressive sustainability goals, including ensuring that 100 percent of new and existing buildings meet green building standards by 2040, reducing GHG emissions by 90 percent by 2040, and reducing total electricity consumption by 20 percent by 2040 (City of Orlando 2013). Although commercial, institutional, and multifamily buildings larger than fifty thousand square feet cover less than 5 percent of Orlando's buildings, they account for nearly 50 percent of total energy and water used by all buildings citywide. As a result, the Green Works team has been involved in an extended effort to develop policies that address the energy inefficiencies of the city's largest buildings. This included partnering with the City Energy Project, an initiative from the Natural Resources Defense Council and the Institute for Market Transformation, to develop the Building Energy and Water Efficiency Strategy (BEWES). This policy, formalized via ordinance, requires the owners or managers of targeted buildings to report their annual energy consumption, and for those buildings that underperform on efficiency metrics, to conduct an energy audit.

Orlando's efforts to curb energy use have definite environmental underpinnings, but many of its initiatives are also pursued to generate positive economic spillovers. Several interviewees mentioned that the initiatives that they have helped design or implement often had more to do with being innovative and increasing efficiencies than being sustainable. Orlando's deputy CAO spoke at length about the importance of identifying ways that departments could save money that might provide environmental co-benefits. The BEWES ordinance, for example, was advocated by Green Works as a mechanism that would, by 2030, save the community approximately $208 million in energy costs and $57 million in public health benefits, spur job creation in high-paying fields, and contribute to the city's economic competitiveness by positioning Orlando as a leading sustainable city that is attractive to new businesses and investors (City of Orlando, n.d.a). Another illustration involved the Solid Waste Division's journey to find a way to insulate itself from large fluctuations in the price of diesel. Transitioning to vehicles with hybrid and alternative fuel systems made economic sense and provided environmental benefits by reducing the dependence on fossil fuels. Department-level sustainability champions were described as savvy business analysts for their departments, and were praised for finding ways to improve quality, save money, and be more sustainable.

Smart City Technologies

The application of smart technologies is a second priority that overlaps many of the city's energy-related sustainability priorities. To explore innovative and smarter solutions to address environmental challenges, Green Works has spearheaded the Smart ORL initiative, which is described by the mayor as combining "our work across all departments and explor[ing] ways to use digital technologies to improve our city operations, save money, and make the city more livable for years to come" (Dyer 2017). Through Smart ORL, the mayor envisions Orlando becoming the "experimental prototype city of the 21st century" and a "living lab and test-bed for smart and sustainable technologies" (Dyer 2017). Green Works received financial support from a Smart Cities Council Readiness Challenge Grant to develop a roadmap for the Smart ORL effort. Through this grant the Smart Cities Council and Green Works staff are developing a comprehensive smart city plan that integrates multiple city departments and regional stakeholders with a focus on smart transportation solutions, in particular the application of sensors and advanced communication systems.

Reflecting the largely environmental focus of the city's sustainability efforts, Smart ORL aims to tackle climate change by reducing congestion and vehicle emissions and promoting energy conservation through the city's transportation and mobility projects. The application of smart city technologies will require data collection and management practices that translate information into on-the-ground changes in city operations and service delivery. This, in turn, requires greater policy integration and the active participation of multiple departments across the city, particularly Public Works and Fleet and Facilities Management. As the mayor noted in an announcement of Smart ORL, the broad focus areas of Green Works "demonstrate how seriously we take the concept of environmental sustainability: clean energy, green buildings, multi-modal transportation, water quality, local food systems, waste innovations, and more" (Dyer 2017).

Authority and Influence

The Green Works office is largely responsible for designing and driving the city of Orlando's sustainability initiatives. It relies on other units in the city government to help implement the projects it designs, but neither Green Works nor its director have true authority over them, in that they are unable to mandate that those other units take specified actions. Rather, Green Works' ability to overcome would-be FCA problems around sustainability has three main sources: (1) its location in the executive branch and organizational proximity to the mayor and CAO, (2) environmental sustainability being a personal and political priority of the mayor, and (3) the recognition of what Green Works staff have achieved as the city's experts on sustainable solutions.

One interviewee described a general dynamic in the city in which "departments are more responsive to those above them then those next to them." Green Works' position, in which it represents an initiative begun by the mayor but reporting to the CAO, puts it near the top of Orlando's administrative hierarchy while also enabling its director to share the same reporting structure as other department directors. This is important because, even though Green Works is not a department per the city hierarchical structure, it is treated as on the same administrative level when meetings are called between department directors and the CAO.

Green Works' positioning enables its director to have regular interaction with both the mayor and the CAO. The DoS and CAO work together when determining how to respond to sustainability-related requests made by elected officials, as well as on budget issues that may affect the success of Green Works–led projects. The DoS and CAO also consult with each other prior to providing the mayor with policy updates or soliciting the mayor's support on new initiatives or policy proposals. As a result of their regular interactions, the Green Works staff are able to have an open dialogue with the CAO about proposed and ongoing initiatives. They also are afforded a clear view of the city's financial realities and often have the opportunity to make financial adjustments before proposing new projects. This degree of administrative vetting has helped achieve a 100 percent track record with the mayor. As Chris Castro described the process, after consulting with the CAO, "we pitch it to the mayor, who gives us a green light or red light at that point. We haven't received a red light so far."

This ties in to the second source of the unit's influence. Sustainability is a known priority and expectation of the mayor, who ultimately is the boss of every city employee. The Green Works office has considerable clout and is effective in shaping the relevant actions of departments across the city. Moreover, the DoS has been able to leverage the mayor's personal and political interests in advancing an ambitious environmental agenda to shape the decisions of individual departments and overcome FCA problems as they emerge. According to Castro, the mayor is ultimately the face of the program and serves as a strong and visible champion for Green Works. The director, in turn, champions the mayor's initiative to become greener and more sustainable. Having Green Works positioned as a mayor's initiative enables the director to be aggressive in how he approaches opportunities to integrate sustainability across departments. Being in the shadow of the mayor enables Green Works to play the role of lead agency coordinator effectively. It provides the office with significant influence over other departments, which are generally responsive to its requests for assisting in implementing initiatives.

The third factor that helps Green Works achieve cooperation from other city departments on the sustainability initiatives it leads is linked to the role its staff plays as experts and providers of information. The Green Works director and staff are widely recognized as the city's experts on sustainable solutions. The director's participation in several professional sustainability associations and national-level networks creates the expectation that he is best able to identify the innovations and best practices that can be applied in Orlando. Moreover, because Green Works represents the mayor, there is a particular onus on Green Works staff to emphasize due diligence in the preparation of their research findings and be knowledgeable about any new initiatives that may emerge from them. This expert perspective does not preclude other departments from suggesting pathways, programs, and their own initiatives to advance sustainability. However, they often need assistance in translating their ideas, often learned through their own professional networks, into citywide action. In this regard, the Green Works staff play an important consultant role. Finally, it was noted by staff in the public works department that the office "is populated with people who have very good communication skills. They can share the value of what they are doing and know how to create win-win situations."

The Role of the Mayor

Mayor Buddy Dyer looms large in discussions of Orlando's sustainability efforts. As of 2020, it has been his explicit political priority, he has been its most visible champion, and Green Works is a mayoral initiative. This raises the obvious question of what will happen to this initiative once Mr. Dyer is no longer in office. He has served in this capacity since 2003, and the city of Orlando does not have term limits. However, at some point—either as a result of his choice, the public's choice, or because of an external change— he will no longer be mayor. All cities experience transitions in leadership that can reshuffle priorities. However, it is generally only in cities with strong mayors that public objectives are explicitly linked to the identity of an individual, which may make the objectives more vulnerable to disruption when that individual departs. Although this is a significant hypothetical concern, the city staff we interviewed did not seem concerned about its potential, suggesting that a sufficiently robust "norm" or "culture" has been created.

To the extent that Mayor Dyer and the Green Works initiative have built the momentum toward greater sustainability, it is the department-level managers who are the leaders in implementation. Department-level managers actively participate in the design of the city's sustainability policies and, in some cases, are the lead policy entrepreneurs on projects that align with their expertise or department focus. Since 2007, the city has devoted substantial financial resources toward upgrading facilities and public property with the goal of improving energy efficiencies, reducing operating costs, and producing positive environmental impacts. While some investments have an immediate financial payoff and have enabled Mayor Dyer and city council members to showcase the economic and environmental benefits of their policy decisions, other investments are noteworthy because of the relatively long time horizon needed for the city to realize monetary benefits. The mayor's popularity among staff and the public enables him to pursue bold initiatives and take more political risks, which sometimes include financial investments and policy decisions that have a delay in monetary returns. Although in his absence, some of these more ambitious policy decisions may no longer be politically feasible, there appears to be general confidence that, after his years of strong leadership on the issue, the city's trajectory will not meaningfully change.

Integration Mechanisms

Green Works was credited by one interviewee as enabling Orlando to achieve a "more comprehensive rather than piecemeal approach to embedding sustainability into all divisions." For many of the reasons already specified, FCA challenges have not meaningfully hampered Orlando's overall progress on sustainability; however, obstacles to interdepartmental collaboration do exist. Of the challenges identified by city staff, several are not specific to sustainability and include the general personality conflicts, general misunderstandings, and miscommunications that can hamper any multiperson effort. Other challenges, noted by one interviewee, result from differences in how departments' professional ideologies lead them to "look at sustainability in ways that don't align." For example, in the Orlando city government, the Planning Department is a subunit of Economic Development, which causes it to be particularly sensitive to concerns that sustainability initiatives might have a negative impact on economic viability. The Planning Department is thus often reluctant to take on policies they think might upset the development community. Other units, like Capital Projects, whose work revolves around front-end investments rather than long-term operations and maintenance, can also have difficulty seeing the benefits of Green Works initiatives, which accumulate over time. Several interviewees noted that budgetary constraints have exacerbated these challenges.

The combination of Florida's broad open records law and the scattered physical locations of offices belonging to Green Works staff, department directors, and city leadership creates another interesting challenge for collaboration. Florida state law makes city employees' electronic communications subject to broad public disclosure. As a result, it was observed that some staff members may be less willing to discuss sustainability—or anything else that could be perceived as remotely controversial—in writing. Therefore, email is often not a sufficiently effective form of communication. However, given that relevant staff are not physically near each other, smaller conversations or check-ins do not always happen. A final challenge relates to the fact that several members of the Green Works staff are relative newcomers to the Orlando city government and may not have a full grasp of its inner workings or of the greater Orlando community. This was pointed to as something that has made collaboration more difficult and was a factor in the longer-than-expected rollout of the BEWES program.

As in most organizations, both formal and informal administrative mechanisms are employed to prevent the relevant challenges to collaboration from escalating into problems. In Orlando, as discussed extensively above, the existence of the Green Works office and its position in the executive branch give it authority and allow it to serve as an important formal force for integrating sustainability across city departments. In addition, two city plans function as important mechanisms for sustainability's integration. The Green Works Orlando Community Action Plan and the Municipal Operations Sustainability Plan lay out shared objectives and provide policy guidelines and linked action items for departments across the city to implement. This, plus the regular practice of mini-cabinet meetings and the practice of other departments helping to support the salaries of Green Works staff, rounds out the key formal mechanisms used in the city of Orlando to facilitate interdepartmental collaboration on sustainability. Support from elected officials and the ability of Green Works staff to leverage their endorsements provide an additional informal means of integration.

Policy Action Plans

For the first several years of the Green Works initiative, the lack of an overall policy framework limited the ability of city government officials to link and align independent, and sometimes competing, departmental initiatives to overarching city goals. As the initiative matured, two significant integration mechanisms were established: the Green Works Community Action Plan and the Municipal Operations Sustainability Plan. These documents establish goals and action items that require both greater integration of sustainability into departmental activities and FCA on citywide initiatives.

Together they reflect the city's attempt to translate the city's vision identified by the mayor into workable policy solutions and action items.

Green Works Community Action Plan

The Green Works Orlando Community Action Plan was adopted in 2013 and aims to guide the community's efforts toward "making Orlando the most sustainable City in America by the year 2040" (City of Orlando 2013, 3). To do this, it identifies goals and actionable strategies in seven focus areas: energy/green buildings, food systems, green economy, livability, solid waste, transportation, and water. As a community-wide plan, it requires broad collective action. In the document's introduction, Mayor Dyer makes this need explicit: "To succeed, the Green Works Orlando Community Action Plan needs the support, cooperation and commitment of our entire City. Government, businesses and residents each have a critical role in the effort to make Orlando an environmentally sustainable, socially inclusive and economically vibrant community" (City of Orlando 2013, 3). To engage these stakeholders early on, the mayor appointed a task force comprising city staff and twenty community members. The Green Works office gave the task force two primary questions to consider when discussing each of the plan's potential goals and policies: What are the environmental impacts of their proposed actions? And what is the potential of each action for creating jobs that positively affect Orlando's economy? These questions reflect the city's attempt to reconcile two priority areas that are often perceived to pull in opposite directions—economic growth and environmental protection. The impact of Orlando's strong development community makes these concerns particularly salient, and the task force met five times to discuss them.

In addition to the task force meetings, two community-wide roundtable meetings were held around each of the seven focus areas. More than two hundred residents attended at least one of the fourteen roundtables, which were used to develop a prioritized list of ten strategies per focus area back to the task force (City of Orlando 2013, 5). This was complemented with public input from an interactive online forum. In general, city staff do not consider the Orlando public as particularly engaged with the local government, but assessed the degree of participation experienced with the Community Action Plan positively.

Although the Green Works Community Action Plan and the public engagement efforts that were a part of its formation have a decidedly outward focus, it also helps city departments to think more holistically about sustainability and consider how their individual decisions affect the ability of other units within the city to achieve sustainability goals. As one example, although the recent construction of a new headquarters building for the

Orlando Police Department was approved without any efficiency requirements, the Green Works Community Action Plan gave standing to the argument that its construction should consider not only public safety requirements but also environmental sustainability objectives. Particularly, Public
Works—which is responsible for the planning, design, construction, and
maintenance of the city's infrastructure—advocated that LEED certification
be pursued for the headquarters by citing the positive long-term environmental and economic impacts achieved by its construction standards. Similarly, Fleet and Facilities Management, which provides preventative maintenance and repair services to city buildings and equipment, advocated for
the electrification of the city's police cars and bikes and the construction of
electric vehicle charging stations. This led to the mayor-endorsed funds to
build an LEED Gold headquarters.

The Green Works Community Action Plan also acts as an umbrella that
spans and links other city plans. This is yet another way it serves as an integrating mechanism. The most significant of the linked plans is the Orlando
Comprehensive Community Plan, which establishes goals and objectives for
future land use, transportation systems, and parks and recreation areas.
Staff members describe the Green Works Community Action Plan and the
Orlando Comprehensive Community Plan as having become self-rein-
forcing. For example, the Comprehensive Community Plan's future land
use element includes policy statements related to the use and management
of land, zoning, and enforcement mechanisms that have long-term implications for city energy systems, including where solar panels can be in-
stalled, how they are designed, and what impact the installation may have
on abutting properties and municipal infrastructure. The Green Works
Community Action Plan, in turn, provides policy reference for city staff
who are developing new long-range growth management policies and updating municipal land use codes.

Municipal Operations Sustainability Plan

The Municipal Operations Sustainability Plan is a second major planning effort to originate under the banner of Green Works Orlando. It was adopted
in 2012, shortly before the community-wide plan, and shares its overarching goal of achieving ambitious sustainability improvements. The municipal operations plan is organized around twelve goals in nine substantive
areas: GHG emissions, green building, electricity, water, city vehicle fleet,
employee commuting, materials management and purchasing, urban forestry, and education. The target year for achieving Municipal Operations
Sustainability Plan goals is ten years earlier than that in the Community
Action Plan, 2030 instead of 2040.

In its role as an integrative mechanism, one of the plan's most important features is its listing of the different city units involved in implementing the action items associated with each goal. For example, under Goal 7, "100% of municipal materials meet environmentally-preferential purchasing and disposal standards by 2030," the first action item is to develop the actual purchasing policy for the city. The city's Procurement and Contracts, Green Works, and Facilities Management offices are identified as jointly responsible for drafting that policy. A second action item under Goal 7 is to explore online options to enable the city to switch to paperless permitting. This responsibility is tasked to the Planning Department and Technology Management Office (City of Orlando 2016). Headway on the municipal operations plan is monitored by Green Works Orlando staff, who develop progress reports. The progress reports are used to update elected officials on the action items that have been implemented by various departments and the extent to which goals have been achieved over the course of a year.

Chief Administrative Officer as an Administrative Focal Point
The CAO's office functions as the hub in the spoke-and-wheel communication structure of Orlando's line departments. Because the CAO's office receives requests and updates from Green Works as well as other departments, it serves as a common administrative point from which information is distributed. Its positioning makes it the third formal integrative mechanism highlighted. The CAO provides a focal point administratively within the city hierarchy where department managers, including the DoS, meet regularly to discuss city issues. This common focal point enables Green Works staff to discuss with the CAO issues that need the participation of other units. It also enables the CAO to discuss with Green Works staff issues that have been raised by other departments across the city. This administrative structure sets up a useful channel of communication between Green Works and other departments.

Mini-Cabinet Meetings
A fourth, and related, formal mechanism that helps nip in the bud potential FCA challenges around sustainability is the city's use of mini-cabinet meetings, in which the DoS has the opportunity to pitch ideas for new initiatives to the mayor and other directors. Ideas are shared at mini-cabinet meetings only after they have already received the CAO's approval, and this forum allows Green Works staff to answer questions and address concerns on the part of city leadership. The mayor ultimately gives each project a green or red light at that point, but having allotted to discuss them with the leaders of departments during these mini-cabinet meetings helps facilitate buy-in.

Support from Elected Leaders

Although not based on formal policy, structure, or procedure, the fact that the mayor and majority of the council are strong advocates of sustainability is an important factor that helps to integrate Green Works' initiatives in units across the city. In particular, operating in the shadow of the mayor makes it easier for Green Works staff to convince other departments that, for example, they should pursue a new project or participate in the implementation of an existing one. One interviewee described the mayor's shadow as a strength in overcoming FCA problems this way: "Green Works is in the mayor's office and is strongly supported by the mayor. . . . Everybody knows that. When Green Works calls, people take notice. It lends credence to the sustainability office's status." Another noted that the mayor has been in office for over a decade, and divisions increasingly understand that to "serve at the pleasure of the mayor," they must be receptive to initiatives from the Green Works office.

The Green Works initiative has developed a reputation for generating new and innovative policy and program solutions for a wide range of sustainability-related issues that require the active involvement of departments to implement. Green Works has been aggressive in identifying potential funding for new initiatives and strives to develop them in a way that also addresses the department-level goals of involved units. As a result of sustained commitment from leadership and the mechanisms highlighted in Table 5.2, sustainability has become ingrained into much of what the departments do on a daily basis, and Green Works staff no longer has to convince their colleagues across the city about the value of sustainability as an objective worth working toward.

Comparative Assessment of Lead Agency Coordination

Sustainability efforts in both Kansas City, Missouri, and Orlando, Florida, are led by relatively small administrative units in the cities' executive branch

TABLE 5.2: MECHANISMS USED TO INTEGRATE SUSTAINABILITY IN ORLANDO CITY GOVERNMENT

Formal
- Green Works Orlando office's positioning in the city's executive branch
- Green Works Orlando 2013 Community Action Plan
- Green Works 2012 Municipal Operations Sustainability Plan
- Use of CAO as an administrative focal point
- Mini-cabinet meetings

Informal
- Support from elected leadership

that are largely responsible for the design and coordination of initiatives, but they rely on line departments for much of their implementation. Thus, these line departments must be persuaded to take on tasks that are typically above and beyond their core responsibilities. This is being accomplished in both cities through a lead agency coordination approach. Lead agency coordination is an organizational strategy to overcome FCA challenges characterized as when a relatively authoritative single unit heads a decentralized larger effort. Authority in this context is traditionally conceived of as the product of top-down hierarchical positioning in the city government that enables one unit to require cooperation from other units (Feiock, Krause, and Hawkins 2017). However, the Kansas City and Orlando case studies suggest a more complicated dynamic at play. Rather than authority, a more holistic picture of lead unit influence emerged as key. It encompasses not only the influence of hierarchy but also proximity to supportive leadership and well-respected and knowledgeable issue champions.

Although these two case studies do not provide the data to make generalizable conclusions, our findings suggest that having the headquarters unit located in the executive branch may be essential for effective lead agency coordination. Almost every interviewee in both cities described this placement as one of the strongest features of how their city administers sustainability. This is in part because executive placement provides that unit with some, albeit usually limited, direct authority over other units. Additionally, and perhaps more important, it provides proximity to the mayor and/or chief administrator—the individuals in the city government with the greatest true authority. Also, by being part of an executive office, sustainability staff can "float" and move into and out of the affairs of other departments as necessary with relative ease. Being located under the mayor versus the city manager appears to matter less to overall effectiveness than does simply being a part of the executive office. Moreover, in both cities, having over a decade of consistent support from city leadership has helped create a norm, or culture, of sustainability that has diminished pushback and eased efforts overtime.

It is interesting to note that both cities shifted from less authoritative models to their current lead agency coordination arrangements at about the same time (2006–2007). Referring to the four general approaches for overcoming FCA dilemmas that were fleshed out in Chapter 3, prior to locating the Office of Environmental Quality in the City Manager's Office, Kansas City used a bargaining-based approach. The lead sustainability unit was in the Department of Environmental Management, where it had much less influence over other city units. The effort was also more centralized than it has become, both because there was more difficulty generating interdepartmental cooperation and because the scope of its relevant mission was smaller than what falls under sustainability in Kansas City today. Orlando previously used a relatively small decentralized network structure. Prior to the creation of Green Works, there was no designated lead, and environmental sustainability was something that Planning, Public Works, and Fleet and Facilities pursued on their own, with modestly coordinated activities. To a person, interviewees perceived the later structure as superior.

Although they share some important similarities, the Kansas City and Orlando approaches to sustainability administration are not mirror images. A first difference rests in their form of government, which provides the institutional context for sustainability administration: Kansas City has a council-manager government, whereas Orlando uses a mayor-council form. A large body of literature has assessed the implications of form of government on policy outcomes and organizational effectiveness (see Carr 2015 for a comprehensive review). The overall empirical evidence on the differential impact resulting from form of government is not as strong as is often hypothesized, perhaps because many modern cities use adapted forms that pull beneficial features from the playbooks of both political and administrative cities (Frederickson 2016).[2] Kansas City's council-manager government is squarely adapted in practice, whereas Orlando's strong mayor and mayor-council form follows a more purely political model. One of the more consistent findings in the literature about form of government is that council-manager governments are more likely to adopt comprehensive policies than their counterparts in mayor-council governments (Carr 2015). This appears to hold true in this two-city comparison in which Kansas City uses a broader definition of sustainability than does Orlando, and pursues policies reflective of that comprehensive conceptualization. Also reflecting the general literature on form of government, Orlando's strong mayor—whose actions as champion and entrepreneur for sustainability—has enabled rapid and visible change.

A second difference in administrative approach is, compared to the OEQ in Kansas City, Green Works Orlando appears considerably more top-down and the efforts it leads are more centralized. This may be a reason that the number of mechanisms for integration used in Orlando are fewer than in Kansas City (seven versus eleven); given its greater authority and narrower scope, additional ones are not necessary. Green Works is responsible for designing Orlando's sustainability initiatives, getting approval from city leadership, and working with departments to implement them. In Kansas City, more of the actual policy design takes place in the departments, with

---

2. H. George Frederickson presents cities' form of government as on a spectrum from purely administrative to purely political (2016). Although every city's charter states its form of government, that label can obscure the many adaptations that can it can take.

the climate action plan serving as their overarching frame and the CEO, with the backing of the city manager, nudging department directors in a more sustainable direction.

Finally, although both cities are pursing sustainability and climate protection in conservative states with legislatures that are often hostile to those objectives, this seems to manifest differently. In general, the potential of upsetting the state government seems to be a more salient concern among staff in Kansas City. In 2013 the Missouri legislature passed a bill banning the use of state money toward sustainability. It was vetoed by the governor but has resulted in what interviewees described as a noticeable "keep your head down" approach and desire to "operate under the radar." An implication of this is the avoidance of policies, such as plastic bag bans, that could attract the ire of the state. The consistent support of the Kansas City public means that local opposition is minimal. In Florida, state and public scrutiny has tended to focus on planning departments and the regulations and ordinances that they may pass. Situating environmental sustainability as a mayoral initiative makes it very visible, but strategically distances it from some of the opposition targeted at planning departments in Florida.

Kansas City and Orlando provide examples of two variations of lead agency coordination. Both have proven remarkably effective and have propelled cities that were unimpressive in terms of sustainability to a place where they are regularly profiled as leaders in best practices.

6

Relationships and Bargaining

Providence, Rhode Island; Ann Arbor, Michigan;
and Oakland, California

> We are very linear but we liaison out. We are the connective
> tissue. We make sure that the sustainability connections
> between departments are at least made.
>
> —JENNIFER LAWSON
> (water resources manager, Ann Arbor, Michigan),
> interview by the authors, June 20, 2017

As we have established in previous chapters, many cities identify a clear headquarters unit charged with promoting and coordinating government-wide sustainability efforts. When these units are large and comprehensive, they can overcome functional collective action (FCA) by consolidating much of the relevant responsibility and providing many of the relevant services themselves (e.g., Fort Collins, Colorado). When efforts are more decentralized, but the lead unit has a significant degree of authority over other units, it can coordinate and direct their actions (e.g., Orlando, Florida, and Kansas City, Missouri). A third organizational arrangement—the one examined in this chapter—involves a headquarters unit that, while clearly identified, is unable to provide the bulk of relevant services and lacks authority over other offices or departments in the government. In this case, it needs extensive assistance from other units but cannot require or even necessarily expect their cooperation. Rather than directing other units to participate, it must ask and persuade—often relying on negotiations, bargaining, or personal relationships to obtain cooperation. Under this organizational arrangement, the headquarters unit functions more as an entrepreneurial partner or colleague rather than manager or boss. Because it lacks authority, but must develop policy responses that span administrative silos, it is required to forge an informal path that complements whatever formal mechanisms may exist in order to establish credibility and responsiveness to implement strategic actions.

Three of the case study cities that we examine exemplify this approach: Providence, Rhode Island; Ann Arbor, Michigan; and Oakland, California. Although they use different arrangements—Providence has a three-person Office of Sustainability in the Mayor's Office, whereas sustainability in Ann Arbor and Oakland is headquartered in multiperson units that are subsets of larger departments—all rely extensively on bargaining and relationships to get things done. A bargaining approach necessitates that the unit responsible for sustainability within the city engages other departments in ways that reduce the transaction costs of coordinating actions among units. As with every approach, there are general strengths and weaknesses associated with its ability to overcome FCA challenges. Compared to others, particularly a consolidated lead agency, arrangements based on relationships and bargaining are less disruptive to the organizational status quo. Its bottom-up orientation has the potential to facilitate widespread buy-in and innovation across city departments. However, collaboration is needed to achieve collective goals and, given its lack of formal authority over other units, there may be little recourse when dealing with resistant units.

This chapter examines the experiences of Providence, Ann Arbor, and Oakland to understand how relationships and bargaining-based approaches can be used by nonauthoritative headquarters units to overcome FCA dilemmas. The information for this chapter comes from twenty-three, primarily in-person, semistructured interviews held with staff from the three cities between February and August 2017. Providence staff interviewed include people holding the following positions:

- Director of sustainability
- Principal planner
- Director of Art, Culture, and Tourism
- Environmental Sustainability Task Force chairperson
- Director of Healthy Communities
- Former sustainability director/former policy director
- Parks and recreation director

Ann Arbor staff interviewed include the following people:

- Systems planning manager
- Planning manager
- Solid waste and recycling coordinator
- Energy programs analyst
- Environmental coordinator
- Stormwater and floodplain program coordinator

- Water resource manager
- Transportation program manager
- Urban forest and natural resources coordinator

Oakland staff interviewed include the following people:

- Sustainability manager
- Department of Transportation Smart City manager
- Energy policy analyst
- Recycling specialist
- Deputy resiliency officer
- Environmental services manager
- Green industry specialist

Appendix C provides the interview template. City plans, website and archival information, and newspaper stories supplement the information obtained from the interviews. The following sections of the chapter provide descriptions of the specific organizational arrangements used by each city to implement sustainability, including the background of how these arrangements evolved and the priority issues that they are addressing.[1] The chapter concludes with a comparison of the integrative mechanisms the cities use to overcome FCA dilemmas and assessments of their relative successes. Appendixes G, H, and I provide a descriptive profile of the three cities.

Overview of Sustainability Efforts
in Providence, Rhode Island

Providence shares characteristics with many typical Northeast and Rust Belt cities in the United States; it faces a declining manufacturing base, financial resource constraints, and eroding physical infrastructure. Despite these challenges, Providence began a renaissance in the early 1980s with major public-private developments that have reshaped much of the downtown landscape and began to rejuvenate the city's economy. Several of these revitalization projects are ongoing, perhaps most notably the redevelopment of land once occupied by a former interstate highway; however, they have been unable to erase the environmental and equity problems of its past. Providence continues to be plagued by the remnants of a long history of heavy manufacturing. Most of the city's surface water bodies remain impaired, urban runoff into

---

1. These are point-in-time descriptions of the cities' structures and operations as they were in spring 2017, when data were collected.

Narragansett Bay continues unabated in some areas, and abandoned buildings and brownfields across the city remain undeveloped because of the environmental risks and the subsequent financial costs of remediation.

The history of sustainability efforts in Providence has been a combination of reactionary responses to state and federal environmental mandates and, to a lesser and more recent degree, proactive locally driven policy initiatives. The city's antiquated stormwater collection system—which led to water pollution violations and a costly consent decree with the U.S. Environmental Protection Agency specifying how the city would address the problem—garnered significant attention and drove much of its first-generation environmental initiatives. Although considerable investments in pollution control and abatement have been made, mandated responses to environmental hazards continue to necessitate significant resources from the city and state governments.

Proactive efforts on the part city government have intensified over the past decade, notably including the establishment of a sustainability office, attempts to improve recycling rates, actions to increase the energy efficiency of municipal infrastructure as well as of residential and commercial properties, and efforts to promote equity in decision making. Even as the city continues to struggle financially, sustainability has been a priority of the last three mayoral administrations. Since Mayor Jorge Elorza took office in 2015, his administration has broadly emphasized equity issues and minority rights, and the operationalization of sustainability in city government has transitioned to be much more socially focused. Nonetheless, the city's long history of budget shortfalls and financial instability amplify the sensitivities surrounding the need for more economic development. Economic development, as one interviewee noted, "is always in the background."

Sustainability Administration: Description, History, and Rationale

Providence's sustainability efforts are headquartered in its Office of Sustainability, which is located in the Mayor's Office and has three employees: the director of sustainability, a municipal energy manager, and a building energy advisor. The Office of Sustainability leads several initiatives focused on energy, resource conservation, and equity, and serves an advisory role to other departments. In that respect, the Office of Sustainability was described by its director as an "in-house consultant" that "helps other departments achieve their respective sustainability goals set out in the ['Sustainable Providence'] plan." This includes tracking metrics and conducting data analysis to document how well the city is meeting its sustainability goals.

Prior to the establishment of the Office of Sustainability, relevant efforts were fragmented across departments. Federal and state environmental requirements provided some of the earliest impetus for interdepartmental collaborations on sustainability-related issues. For example, a federal mandate to address water quality violations required coordinated action among departments that otherwise would not have engaged in joint efforts. While infrastructure retrofits and permitting approvals primarily fell under the purview of Public Works, the city was also expected to improve the quality of the city's surface water bodies and account for future land development. Pressure from Save the Bay—a high-profile statewide environmental advocacy organization—further compelled the city to act. To meet these externally driven pressures, multiple city units began to regularly engage in a more integrated process of decision making. These interactions served as a precursor to the formal establishment of the Sustainability Office.

Providence's broader conceptualization of sustainability began in 2005 when the city signed the U.S. Conference of Mayors' Climate Protection Agreement and committed to reduce greenhouse gas (GHG) emissions. In 2008, the city council adopted GreenPrint Providence, which served as the launchpad for a more comprehensive approach to sustainability. It reported on the city's climate protection efforts, provided a plan to position the city as a leader in the green economy, and offered goals in the areas of energy, the built environment, public space, transportation, waste management, purchasing, and water (City of Providence 2008). Importantly, GreenPrint Providence was where the position of a sustainability officer, who would oversee the development and coordination of energy efficiency and conservation projects, policies, and procedures for city-owned equipment and facilities, was initially proposed.

Shortly thereafter, the director of sustainability position was established by city ordinance, but it remained unfunded and unfilled for several years. In 2011, the city received a one-time federal Energy Efficiency Conservation Block Grant and a portion of these funds were dedicated to supporting this position and establishing the Office of Sustainability. Because it is formally institutionalized by a city ordinance, the director of sustainability position has relative permanence and it is resistant to political shifts. However, the individual holding this position and the issue priorities pursued are determined based on "the pleasure of the mayor" and thus can change with administrations (Code of Ordinances, sec. 2-45). Further, the establishing ordinance says nothing about a larger sustainability office or the sustainability director's placement within the city's organizational hierarchy. Thus, both could change with mayoral discretion. However, the structure—whereby the sustainability director leads a unit within the Mayor's Office and reports to

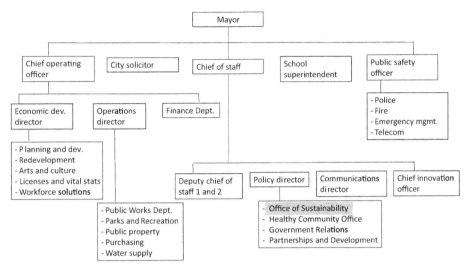

Figure 6.1 City of Providence organizational chart

the city's policy director, who reports to the mayor (see Figure 6.1)—has remained stable across three administrations.

According to ordinance, the sustainability director has the official status of a department head. In practice, however, the position does not operate with the same administrative standing as directors of relatively large departments within the city, such as Planning or Public Works. The sustainability director has relatively little formal access to department directors and does not wield authority over other administrative units. The position was originally conceived of as a technical one, but, in the words of Providence's first sustainability director, the "role became less about being an expert and more about being a connector between community, city employees, and across departments." Despite having relatively little formal authority to fall back on, reliable collaborations have been established with some city departments, including Parks, Recreation, and Planning. Using these interactions as a springboard, the Office of Sustainability, in coordination with the city's longtime Environmental Sustainability Task Force, developed "Sustainable Providence" in 2014. This remains the formal sustainability policy guide for the city.

As the Office of Sustainability has matured as an administrative unit, its initiatives have retained strong roots in environmental and municipal energy issues. It also has increasingly assumed a more outward focus. This shift was accelerated under Mayor Jorge Elorza's SustainPVD initiative, which is focused on making Providence a "greener, healthier, more livable city" (City of Providence, n.d.c). It also intensified and expanded the scope of engagement with low-income and minority communities on social equity and environmental justice issues.

Sustainability Priorities

Cost and financial implications are in the background of every decision made by Providence's cash-strapped city government. The overriding motivation to save money has shaped its sustainability priorities and elevated energy and resource conservation to the top of the list. Energy is one of the city's original sustainability focuses—the sustainability director position was first paid for using federal Energy Efficiency and Conservation Block Grant funds and the ordinance that established it specifies that the director's key responsibilities include documenting the city's energy use and its associated costs, and developing conservation policies. Two of the three staff members in the sustainability office have the word "energy" in their titles and one focuses exclusively on reducing energy consumption and costs in municipal operations.

Although most directly influencing the city's energy efficiency initiatives, cost reduction is also part of what has compelled significant efforts to increase recycling rates. Providence provides residential curbside recycling service and a city ordinance requires its use by residents. However, high levels of contamination caused by people putting dirty or nonrecyclable materials in their recycling bins has been expensive for the city. As a result of its cost, multiple units across the city want to see the issue improved, which has facilitated collaboration around efforts to identify barriers to proper recycling and in the development of education campaigns and recycling pilot projects. Stormwater management is a final "traditional" sustainability priority in the city. As previously described, the strongest push to address this issue comes from external mandates, but its legal and financial implications make it a major internal concern.

More recently, equity in sustainability has become a priority in Providence. Social equity's emergence as a focal point of the city's sustainability initiatives was, in part, a political reaction to residents' demands for a more inclusive approach to the update of the city's comprehensive plan. The emphasis on social equity has also been advanced by several external grants the city received to partner with community organizations to develop and apply a racial equity lens to its sustainability work. Providence's sustainability director, Leah Bamberger, described the effort as "expanding the boundaries of what environmental sustainability means" and intentionally making it take a "more human-centric rather than an environmental-centric approach." Issues of race receive explicit focus. Staff observed that sustainability in Providence is often perceived as "a white upper-middle-class

issue." In attempt to make it more inclusive, the Office of Sustainability assembled a Racial and Environmental Justice Committee and tasked it to "1)
identify key concerns, issues, and needs for communities of color related to
environmental sustainability in Providence; and 2) recommend a long-term
process and structure for collaboration between communities of color and
the Office of Sustainability" (City of Providence, n.d.b). The committee's
recommendations were adopted in 2017.

Influence, Relationships, and Small Victories

Providence's Office of Sustainability has little authority to shape the actions
of other departments. This, coupled with the pressure on departments to
maintain core services with limited financial resources, provides a challenging backdrop for efforts to coordinate sustainability initiatives across the
city government. As explained by a department director, "Working with a
heavily unionized workforce in a very financially strapped environment . . .
the day-to-day stuff like funding to allow for snow removal post-blizzard is
more important than thinking about sustainability efforts. The disconnect
between sustainability and the daily department responsibilities is not necessarily malicious, but rather it is a lack of resources for implementation."
The same department director added, "To make a case for sustainability,
you will have to figure out the financial benefits. Sustainability for sustainability's sake is not enough." Thus, to pursue its citywide initiatives, the
Office of Sustainability is often faced with persuading already-constrained
officials, who are not inherently sold on the mission, to alter their standard
operating procedures in order to assist.

To operate in this context, the Office of Sustainability uses an approach
that it characterizes as "small victories" and attempts to promote sustainably in a way that emphasizes win-wins. Personal relationships and trust
building are key to its success. One example of a small victory relates to the
landscaping used in city parks. Although the Parks Department may, on the
surface, appear to be a natural ally of environmental sustainably objectives,
it has historically focused on maintenance and programming. Office of Sustainability staff engaged directly with the Parks Department director to re-
vise guidelines to encourage natural landscaping, such as rain gardens and
bioretention ponds, and to use repurposed sustainable materials in construction. This effort also required the involvement of the city's Public
Works Department. Although critical to the success of many of the city's
sustainability initiatives, Public Works has been fairly resistant to changes
that could potentially disrupt its daily tasks. However, after multiple informal conversations and interactions to communicate how green infrastructure would minimize infrastructure maintenance needs in city parks, its

leaders eventually warmed to the idea and are implementing the new guidelines. As a result, the Public Works Department is able to redirect staff and financial resources from parks maintenance toward other priority areas and sustainability considerations are more embedded in decisions on infrastructure: win-win.

Integration Mechanisms

Because the Office of Sustainability's capacity to direct the activities of other units in Providence's city government is limited, its ability to overcome FCA challenges around sustainability are successful to the extent that relationships can be negotiated and built horizontally among relevant departments. In the absence of having authority over them, the Office of Sustainability relies on access, trust, and influence to coordinate and shape departmental efforts. This can be challenging to effectively build and sustain, particularly when new initiatives require additional work from departments or expand the scope of their core responsibilities.

Overall, the office's success in overcoming FCA challenges to generate a comprehensive, cohesive approach to sustainability appears mixed. Certain units with functions related to sustainability, including the Healthy Communities Office, the Parks and Recreation Department, and the Planning Department, have emerged as reliable partners. Others have proven less willing to engage. As is the case in many of the other cities profiled in this book, a primary dimension of pushback is resistance to change, exemplified by a "this is how we've always done it" mentality. In the case of Providence, this is exacerbated by the relative newness of explicit sustainability efforts: the city's Office of Sustainability has been functioning since 2011, and its director has held the position since 2015. Sustainability, as a value, has not yet permeated the city organization; nor have the director and staff had enough time to develop the necessary relationships to secure buy-in on new initiatives. A secondary challenge is that, in certain departments, a large percentage of employees are unionized. Although only one part of the larger context of labor relations in the city, unionization is perceived by some interviewees as increasing the challenges associated with getting staff to take on sustainability responsibilities, which often extend beyond standard job descriptions.

Given that many of the formal mechanisms used to integrate sustainability across Providence's city government lack teeth, informal mechanisms ultimately are key to overcoming FCA challenges. That said, the available formal mechanisms—largely the presence of certain administrative bodies and planning documents—help establish the foundation for engaging other city units and create conditions for integration by reducing the

TABLE 6.1: MECHANISMS USED TO INTEGRATE SUSTAINABILITY IN PROVIDENCE CITY GOVERNMENT

Formal
- Sustainability office and the director of sustainability
- "Sustainable Providence" plan
- SustainPVD Dashboard
- Environmental Sustainability Task Force

Informal
- Relationships and negotiations
- Joint grant-seeking efforts

transaction costs of collaborative activities. Table 6.1 lists the primary mechanisms, both formal and informal, which are described in more detail in the following sections.

Formal Mechanisms

Four formal mechanisms—the arrangements, practices, or procedures that have been established by ordinance or formally adopted emerged from the interviews as important to facilitating FCA across Providence's city government on issues of sustainability.

Sustainability Office and Director Position

Facilitating the integration of sustainability policy across city departments in Providence is one of the Office of Sustainability's key responsibilities. The city ordinance that established the director of sustainability position spells out the basic expectations of this position, several of which are integrative in nature. For example, it tasks the director with developing, monitoring, and annually reporting on the implementation of the city's sustainability plan by other city units and with promulgating regulations and ordinances in support of the plan's achievement (Code of Ordinances 2-45). Moreover, the fact that the position and its major responsibilities are established by ordinance helps safeguard their existence in the face of changing political contexts and conveys a message about their permanence to staff across the city government.

The sustainability director reports directly to the policy director, both of whom are located in the Mayor's Office. For several of the other cities profiled in this book, having sustainability headquartered in the executive branch was itself identified as an integrative mechanism. However, in the case of Providence, the executive branch location does not translate into either greater authority or access. One interviewee noted that because the mayor and the city council often have political disagreements, being located in the Mayor's Office can make it difficult for the director to work with some members of the city council. Thus, although the sustainability office and director are clearly integrative, their positioning in the city hierarchy is not.

"Sustainable Providence" Plan

The city's sustainability plan, "Sustainable Providence," released in September 2014, establishes twenty-five strategies to achieve six goals in the areas of zero waste, local and healthy food, transportation, water, sustainable energy, and sustainable land use and development. It also includes thirty high-priority actions and specific metrics to track annual progress. The 2017 update includes a new citywide GHG reduction goal. The plan depends on widespread buy-in across the city government and from the larger community. It is explicitly integrative and includes this observation: "Hundreds of representatives from agencies, City departments, nonprofit organizations, academia, and the community at large will be crucial to the execution of the plan" (City of Providence 2014, 11).

An informal Sustainability Evaluation Tool is included in this plan and gives city departments a mechanism to consider how proposed projects will achieve all six of the city's sustainability goals. The evaluation tool aims to embed the sustainability values of environment, economy, and equity into the city's land use and economic development decision making and is intended to be used by all departments to evaluate development projects based on how well they help the city achieve its sustainability goals. Although departments are not required to apply the evaluation tool, the hope is that it will be integrated into the development review process over time.

SustainPVD Dashboard

To ensure the transparency of its sustainability efforts, the city has implemented the SustainPVD Dashboard. This publicly available data portal is maintained by the Office of Sustainability and displays the progress made toward promoting the six topic areas outlined in the city's sustainability plan. It features the latest progress on implementation of the plan, as well as data for up-to-date reports on performance metrics for "Sustainable Providence." The consistent monitoring and evaluation require data that span multiple administrative units. Thus, the process of collecting and harmonizing the data necessitates some degree of interdepartmental communication and collaboration.

Environmental Sustainability Task Force

The city of Providence relies extensively on its Environmental Sustainability Task Force for policy development and to shape the city's sustainability agenda. The task force was established by ordinance in 2006 primarily to assist the city with its stormwater management issues. Since that time, its involvement has expanded to broader sustainability issues, including recycling and most recently social justice and equity. It has nine community members including four appointed by the mayor, four by the city council, and one by the Environment Council of Rhode Island.

Although it does not use the words "integration mechanism," the ordinance establishing the task force essentially defines its role as such. To help integrate responsibility for sustainability across the city government, the task force is assigned to "work with the Office of Sustainability, the Mayor, the City Council and other city departments to coordinate the City's environmental agenda and provide a level of accountability for the environmental initiatives the City is currently implementing or planning to implement." It also has a public outreach and communication role and is tasked with working with "experts from the City and from the community to discuss and propose innovative, yet achievable, environmental initiatives" (City of Providence, n.d.a). Thus, the task force serves both as a conduit for interests groups wanting action on specific projects and as a liaison between city departments. Finally, the task force provides political backing for sustainability initiatives and petitions the mayor and city council members to support projects that the Office of Sustainability wants to see advance.

Informal Mechanisms

Although the formal mechanisms described above play an important role in Providence's pursuit of sustainability, some have also been problematic. For example, soon after it was established, the Office of Sustainability created a citywide Green Team. The Green Team, which is now defunct, was intended to provide a formal means for the office to solicit input from department directors or their representatives on sustainability policy. This approach, however, resulted in pushback, which interviewees characterized as an attitude of "I'm here only because the mayor said I had to be." This type of resistance resulted in the Green Team being disbanded. Office of Sustainability staff transitioned to holding informal department-by-department conversations to solicit input in attempt to align department-level activities with the objectives and strategies described in formal policy documents. This has proven more successful and reflects an overall theme in the city about the relative success of informal approaches to integration, particularly when those efforts are spearheaded by the Office of Sustainability itself.

Relationships
The success of interdepartmental collaboration on sustainability in Providence depends heavily on the cultivation and maintenance of trusting personal relationships. The quality of the sustainability director's relationships

with the directors of relevant city departments is perceived as particularly important. Although the rest of the sustainability staff often work directly with mid-level managers across the city, getting buy-in at the director level is crucial. There remains a perception among some city employees that the city's sustainability objectives pose an added burden to their core job responsibilities. Department directors are in a key position to minimize or exacerbate that reaction. As noted by the chair of the Environmental Sustainability Task Force, the sustainability staff make explicit efforts to act as partners with other departments by "being available and giving resources where possible so it is a two-way street," which has allowed considerable inroads to be made over time. Critical to this has been the ability of sustainability staff to demonstrate to departments across the city that using a "sustainability lens" does not detract from their primary functions or their ability to achieve their own goals. Finding and cultivating issue champions within each department has been important in this relationship-based strategy.

Grant Seeking and Grant Getting

Providence's sustainability staff are highly engaged in applying for external grant funding. Developing joint projects in the pursuit of grants helps bring everyone to the table. The city's parks and recreation director cited a recent example where the department worked with Planning, Public Works, and the Office of Sustainability on an application for a coastal resiliency grant from the National Oceanic and Atmospheric Administration. The grant would fund the development of a comprehensive coastal resiliency plan, which is important to each department for slightly different reasons. Assembling an application necessitates conversations across departments; and when grants are received, interdepartmental ties are strengthened further.

In sum, sustainability is relatively new as an explicit objective in Providence's city government and not yet fully incorporated into its organizational culture. Although it has the support of city leaders and has a permanent director and staff located within the Mayor's Office, these positions are not endowed with much authority. FCA around sustainability remains a challenge but is being meaningfully minimized through an intentional but informal strategy of cultivating relationships and the achievement of small wins.

Overview of Sustainability Efforts in Ann Arbor, Michigan

Sustainability in Ann Arbor primarily means *environmental* sustainability. Most social sustainability efforts fall to the county and, besides a few basic land use issues, so does economic vitality. Sustainability was described by the interviewees as an important shared value throughout the city government, and it is actively pursued by many individual offices and departments. However, as described in greater detail later, the city's initiatives are generally designed on a project-by-project basis, and as with the other cities profiled in this chapter, the primary thread that connects these initiatives is informal and relationship based. Ann Arbor has designated its interdisciplinary Systems Planning Division as its sustainability lead and has designed a variety of administrative mechanisms to integrate sustainability initiatives across departments. Key among these is an overarching formal Sustainability Framework that integrates multiple fragmented and overlapping plans that have been adopted by the city over the years.

Ann Arbor has a long history of forward-looking environmental sustainability programs. As one illustration, the city has had an Energy Office and an Energy Commission since 1985, which is two decades before movements like the Mayors' Climate Protection Agreement began to mainstream the localization of energy and climate issues in the United States. Although there is some internal identification of priorities, the city's sustainability agenda has largely been shaped in response to community pressure and organized local environmental advocacy organizations. City staff describe Ann Arbor as a very engaged and demanding community. Home to the University of Michigan, it has residents who tend to be highly educated and politically liberal. Both the public at large and the council members they elect prioritize environmental objectives and actively check up on their implementation. One interviewee noted, "It all starts with people—the people who work here, the people who live here. Different places have different public conversations. Here it is important to be green. It is the 'Ann Arbor ethos.'" Traditionally this ethos has centered around the protection of the Huron River, which flows through the city. The value placed on environmental sustainability has enabled associated efforts to persist over the long term despite their relatively limited institutionalization.

Ann Arbor has a council-manager form of government and a relatively stable administrative structure. However, after an economic shock in 2007—the pharmaceutical company Pfizer closed two major research facilities in the city, eliminating almost two thousand jobs and $6 million in annual tax revenue—the local government underwent significant downsizing, which it used as an opportunity to make meaningful organizational changes. Specifically, staff was reduced by almost 30 percent and the city government hierarchy was considerably flattened and reorganized around four main service areas (see the city organizational chart in Figure 6.2). The organization of the city government affects how sustainability is managed and is consistent with the relationship-and-bargaining-based approach highlighted in this chapter.

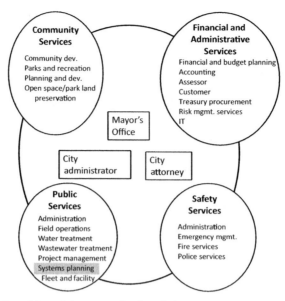

Figure 6.2 City of Ann Arbor organizational chart

Sustainability Administration: Description, History, and Rationale

There is no formal office of sustainability in the Ann Arbor city government, and the word "sustainability" is not explicit in any city employee's job title. In practice, sustainability is headquartered and largely embedded in the city's Systems Planning Division, which is one of seven divisions in the city's more encompassing Public Services Area. Systems Planning consists of a manager and fourteen interdisciplinary staff members who specialize in distinct substantive areas: environment, energy, transportation, forestry, floodplains, water quality, and waste. There are also several systems planning analysts and engineers in the unit. The city's environmental affairs coordinator at the time of interview, Matthew Naud, is considered the point person for most of the environmental sustainability projects and is the city's representative to organizations like the Urban Sustainability Directors Network (USDN).

Together, the Systems Planning staff are responsible for "asset management," which is described by one interviewee as an "infrastructure term for sustainability," and collectively operate as a long-range planning department with a focus on the city's infrastructure. Over time, Systems Planning has evolved into the de facto sustainability unit for the city. Notably, unlike in some cities that strategically avoid the use of the term "sustainability" to minimize political opposition, in Ann Arbor this is largely an artifact of timing. These functions and positions were in place before the development of modern language around local sustainability and they simply have not been changed. As explained by one interviewee, "Systems Planning came about here before 'sustainability' was a buzzword."

Systems Planning emerged in the early 2000s during the time of Ann Arbor's financially motivated organizational change. Its creation was spearheaded by Sue McCormick, the then newly hired director of the city's new Public Services Area. She had previously worked at a regional utility that had a systems planning unit, and she took initiative to re-create it in Ann Arbor. Originally, all the staff who composed the city's Systems Planning division were relocated to it from other departments across the city. Notably, both the energy and environment coordinator positions were part of the City Administrator's Office before joining Systems Planning. Moving these positions to a place deeper in the administrative hierarchy had the effect of reducing their authority, but it also opened up new opportunities for collaborative work. The colocation of the environmental affairs coordinator with other like-minded units smoothed the process of integration, even though the service areas concept created additional layers of administrative reporting. The move was also evaluated as improving funding and security for these positions; as part of Systems Planning, they benefit from stormwater utility fees, which is a reliable source of revenue. To date, this arrangement has persisted through three city administrators.

Systems Planning was described by interviewees as "a very flat unit," with each suboffice reporting to the systems planning unit manager. It is also very broad in terms of its scope of coverage—which has both positive and negative implications. The unit is intentionally comprised of employees with specialized focuses on a range of loosely related issues, which makes it a stimulating place to work (as one interviewee noted, "It is fantastic to have that depth of expertise around so many different issues"). However, this same feature contributes to it becoming, in the words of one interviewee, an "island of misfit projects." Moreover, the degree of staff specialization appears to have something of a siloing effect within Systems Planning itself. One interviewee observed that although it has "the good fortune of having specialists, they can end up trying to achieve results in a more narrow way than our Sustainability Framework does." Still, over time sustainably has emerged as the theme that connects Systems Planning staff as a multidisciplinary team that plans for and develops policy to guide public infrastructure investments.

Sustainability Priorities

As previously described, the city's conceptualization of sustainability has a strong environmental orientation. Although the responsibilities of the

Systems Planning staff all link to this overarching goal, one consequence of the staff's specialized professional orientations is that each person focuses primarily on the issues in her or his area of expertise—be that waste management, energy, transportation, water quality, or floodplain management. Although many issues receive attention, none clearly stand out as the *overriding* sustainability priorities in Ann Arbor, unlike in some of the cities we profile in this book. Instead, efforts appear to be more project driven. They are often determined in response to the needs and demands of community members and are led by the relevant in-house expert in Systems Planning.

Climate change and the implementation of the city's Climate Action Plan (CAP) emerged from interviews as Ann Arbor's most consistent big-picture priority. The CAP was completed in 2012 and, building off of GHG emissions inventories completed in 2000 and 2010, establishes a primary mitigation goal of 25 percent below the year 2000 baseline by 2025 (City of Ann Arbor 2012). To achieve this, it identifies eighty-four specific actions in the areas of energy and buildings, land use and access, resource management, and community and health. The CAP identifies the implementation leaders for each action; often the lead is a particular city government unit, but sometimes includes groups within the community (e.g., residents, nongovernmental organizations) or institutions like the University of Michigan and Ann Arbor Public Schools. The city's energy manager described the CAP as "an outward-facing community GHG mitigation plan," which reflects the fact that only 1.1 percent of community-wide emissions come from city government operations.

Notably, the CAP has not been adopted into Ann Arbor's master plan. One interviewee explained, "There is interest and willingness to incorporate elements of the CAP in the master plan, but there is plan fatigue" in the city. Implementation of the CAP is being funded through nonprogrammatic means and has had a soft-money budget of about $160,000 a year. Although the CAP has not been institutionalized, it is perceived as a living and influential plan. More informally, the city's environmental affairs coordinator and the energy manager work to make sure climate considerations are injected into the planning of all city projects.

Cohesive Efforts in the Absence of Authority

Being tucked away "four-deep in the hierarchy," as one interviewee put it, neither Systems Planning as unit nor the sustainability lead have much formal authority to shape the policy or programmatic actions of city staff. Sustainability integration in the city government is informal and relationship based. For example, Systems Planning staff are not necessarily invited to all relevant meetings, and a staff member having access often depends on having a friend in the department who keeps him or her in the loop informally. Except for a handful of relatively weak mechanisms—such as the Sustainability Framework and portions of the Capital Improvements Plan (CIP), which are described in more detail in the next section—sustainability is not meaningfully institutionalized across the city. The lack of ability to require departments to adjust their traditional operations and incorporate sustainability was mentioned by the interviewees as an occasional problem with a few specific departments. For example, there have been challenges getting the city engineers to protect street trees, consider stormwater runoff, or consider pedestrians or cyclists in their work. One interviewee observed, "I don't get a sense of explicit resistance, but they just don't see it. It is their training and 'this is the way it has always been done' ideas."

Still, in Ann Arbor, the lack of authority and institutionalization do not appear to prevent the development and implementation of cohesive environmental sustainability initiatives. Environmental quality is a long-term, overriding value in the community, and most city leaders and staff are likewise perceived as holding it as a personal value. For the most part, therefore, Systems Planning staff do not have to convince relevant actors about the importance of sustainability, and Ann Arbor's engaged and demanding public helps ensure that it does not fall to the back burner. The significant reduction of city staff in the early 2000s has resulted in a staff that interviewees still consider "extremely lean." On one hand, this can make it more difficult for Systems Planning to direct overall sustainability efforts because staff is already stretched thin. On the other hand, that thinness is pointed to as essentially forcing collaboration. One interviewee described a "formula" for why collaboration around sustainability occurs in the city: "Complex issues plus a lean organization plus an engaged community equals collaboration."

Integration Mechanisms

Integration challenges in Ann Arbor occur primarily at two levels. The first is within Systems Planning itself. Although the unit contains many of the individuals responsible for overseeing projects that collectively contribute to environmental sustainability, they tend to function in a relatively siloed manner because of their narrow and deep expertise. At the second level, the integration challenge involves the need to expand proactive consideration of environmental sustainability from Systems Planning to relevant units in other service areas. Although the Ann Arbor ethos and broad acceptance of sustainability as a value mitigates much of the explicit pushback observed in some other cities from partner departments, some instances of friction remain. For example, Systems Planning staff would like to be engaged by

TABLE 6.2: CITY OF ANN ARBOR INTEGRATION MECHANISMS

Citywide integration	Systems Planning integration
Formal	
• Systems Planning Division	• Planning Area Theme (PATh) Framework
• Sustainability Framework	• Weekly staff meetings
• Sustainability Action Plan	
• Capital Improvements Plan process	
• Citywide agenda session meetings	
Informal	
• Relationships	• Relationships
• Shared space	• Shared space
• Request for proposal processes	• Request for proposal processes

other units on relevant projects early on, but that is not systematized and, as a result, is often overlooked. Also, as is seemingly the case everywhere, departments often bristle at the idea of changing their standard operations in the name of an external goal.

Table 6.2 lists the mechanisms in place in Ann Arbor that facilitate integration around the development and implementation of sustainability initiatives. The formal mechanisms are institutionalized, and they establish the basic structure for the city's efforts and provide guidance for what they should look like. However, as with the other cities highlighted in this chapter, they do not endow the sustainability lead with much authority, resulting in a high reliance on informal mechanisms for actually getting things done.

Formal Mechanisms

Several institutionalized structures, plans, and practices act as formal mechanisms facilitating functional integration around sustainability, both between the specialized staff members working in Systems Planning and across the city government. As the division that generally leads relevant efforts, the presence and structure of Systems Planning itself is key among these mechanisms.

Systems Planning Division

The Systems Planning Division is characterized as comprising staff that "liaison out" across the city, with Systems Planning being described by its manager as the "connective tissue" among the units. The units that comprise Systems Planning include offices that directly affect environmental sustainability, including those dealing with water, solid waste, and transportation. Environmental sustainability was not an overt consideration when the city's administrative reorganization positioned Systems Planning within the newly created Public Services Area. Rather, over time Systems Planning has taken the lead role in the city's sustainability initiatives because of the expertise of the offices and staff that comprise this division. One staff member explained that Ann Arbor does not have an explicit sustainability office or staff because "once sustainability became a thing, the environmental coordinator assumed the informal role of the sustainability point person within Systems Planning." Neither a new position nor a change in title for the environmental coordinator one is perceived as necessary.

Interviewees describe the division as operating something like a long-range planning department with an infrastructure focus. Compared with staff in many other departments, the job responsibilities of Systems Planning staff are less constrained, which enables them to think more outside the box and on longer-term time horizons. Although they take the lead on certain projects, their integrative role comes by linking the staff working on implementation in other departments across the city with the bigger-picture plan. For example, the city has a larger forestry staff in the Public Works Department as well as an urban forestry and natural resources manager in Systems Planning. That job involves developing forestry-related plans, conducting tree inventories, and interacting with the city council. The manager also works regularly with the forestry staff in Public Works to help implement relevant plans on the ground. The manager's interactions with colleagues in Public Works are horizontal, and she cannot compel them to follow suggestions. The manager at the time explained, "Forestry has its own supervisor. I am not the forestry supervisor's supervisor. . . . We are at the same level, but we have completely different jobs." In sum, the Systems Planning Division houses staff with considerable expertise across a variety of areas, promotes interdepartmental outreach, and enables long-term thinking. The staff are thus able to provide assistance to frontline functional departments across the city and influence their efforts, so they remain consistent with the city's larger environmental goals.

Sustainability Framework

The Ann Arbor Sustainability Framework brings together, in a single document, the goals and policy statements relative to promoting sustainability contained within twenty-two stand-alone plans adopted by the city over a twenty-year period. Thus, it serves as an important and overarching integrative mechanism. The framework does not develop any new objectives but instead organizes the large number of existing objectives around sixteen sustainability goals and attempts to clarify their impact and relationships. In 2013 the city council adopted it as an element in the city's master plan (City of Ann Arbor, n.d.c).

The framework functions as a relatively high-level document that sets aspirations but does not shape people's daily work. Its most tangible impact is seen in its link to the budget: every budget request and proposal to the city council must reference this framework and show how it advances at least one of the goals. In this way, it forces the consideration of sustainability at some point in the development of every major project or program. It is unclear, however, how much more sustainable projects are as a result than they otherwise would have been.

Sustainability Action Plan

The Sustainability Action Plan builds from the Sustainability Framework and provides additional structure to facilitate integration around sustainability. The Sustainability Action Plan includes quantifiable targets and implementation steps along with thirty-eight indicators to measure progress toward the sixteen goals outlined in the framework. It also indicates the primary unit responsible for leading relevant actions. The plan is reviewed every two years in conjunction with the budget cycle. At this time, up-to-date progress reports are made public through a web-based Sustainability Dashboard that gauges achievement toward framework goals. The plan and associated dashboard require that the multiple offices within and outside of Systems Planning that are responsible for the implementation communicate and share information on the nature of their activities with one another and the broader community.

Capital Improvements Plan and Planning Process

The CIP process links both to the framework and the Sustainability Action Plan and is a second mechanism that, through its tie to the budget, pushes broad sustainability goals through the city government. The CIP outlines the city's capital spending plans for five years, and sustainability is one of several criteria on which capital project proposal are graded. The metrics for its grading come from the Sustainability Action Plan. Systems Planning leads the city's CIP process on an annual basis, although it is a major exercise only every other year, coinciding with the city's two-year budget cycle. The process includes representatives from all different service areas, and the widespread involvement of many Systems Planning staff means they have an early voice in shaping many capital projects.

Citywide Agenda Session Meetings

Agenda session meetings occur twice a month and are attended by all unit and area managers in the city government. This provides a venue for the mid-level managers who are overseeing specific programs or functions to share new ideas and upcoming projects. Systems Planning has two representatives attend these meetings, which enables them to keep current on the initiatives being pursued elsewhere in the city. They are then able to inform relevant Systems Planning staff and encourage connections to be made.

Planning Area Theme Framework and Staff Meetings
Whereas the preceding mechanism provides a formal path to integration across the city, the Planning Area Theme (PATh) Framework is internal to Systems Planning. PATh represents a new, intentional approach spearheaded by Cresson Slotten, the systems planning unit manager at the time of interviews. Recognizing that Systems Planning staff all have specialized expertise, PATh is based on the identification of areas of overlap and the formation of subgroups around them. These subgroups—structured around issues of transportation, utilities, water resources, and sustainability and energy and resource management—hold regularly scheduled meetings outside of general Systems Planning staff meetings.

Associated with the PATh Framework is a matrix that shows the relationship between the primary planning area in which efforts fall and the staff members who are responsible for its management (see Table 6.3). Importantly, the PATh matrix also explicitly links the appropriate staff and planning offices to the city's Sustainability Framework. The entire Systems Planning staff was involved in the PATh's development, so the act of creating it and updating it is itself an integrative exercise. The hope is that the structured subgroup meetings will lead to increased synergies between Systems Planning staff.

Weekly staff meetings are a final important, albeit quite standard, mechanism for integration within Systems Planning. They provide opportunity for individuals and PATh subgroups to share their projects with the larger group. During these meetings, staff members are encouraged to consider one another's projects from different sustainability angles that might not otherwise be considered; for example, the energy specialist may provide insight on the energy implications of a particular solid waste project.

Informal Mechanisms

The formal arrangements, plans, and regular meetings described above provide the structure underlying collective action around sustainability efforts in Ann Arbor. Other than a few small exceptions, in which considering sustainability outcomes is a required part of the budget process, the mechanisms lack authoritative backing. However, given the city's overall collaborative dynamic and the fact that environmental sustainability is part of the Ann Arbor ethos, this scaffolding appears to be sufficient to support the

TABLE 6.3: EXAMPLE PATH WORKSHEET

PATh (Planning Area Theme)	Sustainability and energy and resource management			Transportation	Utilities	Water resources		All
Planning areas	**Environmental protection:** Air quality, Landfills, Brownfields, Emissions	**Climate and sustainability:** Municipal energy, Community energy, Adaptation, Framework/action plan	**Resource recovery and solid waste:** Recycling, Solid waste, Composting, Waste to energy	**Transportation:** Nonmotorized vehicles, Transit, Street system, Streetlights	**Utilities:** Water, Wastewater, Stormwater, Capital costs recovery, Master planning	**Water resources:** Floodplains, Creeksheds, Water quality	**Urban forestry:** Street trees, Park trees, Volunteer programs, Wood utilization, Natural features ordinance	**Economic vitality:** Brownfields, University of Michigan Development review, Economic development, Utilities master plan
Staff	Environmental coordinator, Solid waste and recycling program coordinator, Water quality manager, Senior project engineer, GIS analyst	Energy program manager, Environment coordinator	Solid waste and recycling program coordinator, Energy program manager, Systems planning analyst	Transportation program manager, Energy program manager, GIS specialist, GIS analyst, Systems planning engineer, Systems planner, Systems planning analyst	Senior project engineer, Water quality manager, Systems planning engineer, GIS analyst, GIS specialist, Stormwater and floodplain program manager, Systems planner	Water quality manager, Stormwater and floodplain program manager, Systems planning engineer, Senior project engineer, GIS specialist, GIS analyst, Systems planner, Systems planning analyst	Urban forestry and natural resources coordinator, Systems planner, GIS analyst	Private development coordinator, Senior project engineer, Development services inspector, Systems planner, Systems planner and analyst, Solid waste and recycling program coordinator, Urban forestry and natural resources coordinator, GIS specialist, Environmental coordinator

Asset management	X	X	X	X	X	X	X
Capital Improvement Plan	X	X	X	X	X	X	X
City council and commissions	X	X	X		X	X	X
Community engagement and process	X	X	X	X	X	X	X
Compliance and enforcement	X	X	X	X	X	X	X
Emergency response	X	X			X	X	X
GIS, infrastructure data	X	X	X	X	X	X	X
Grant procurement	X	X	X		X	X	X
Plan review	X	X	X	X	X	X	
Standards and specifications	X	X	X	X	X	X	X

informal dynamics that more directly shape collective action. In particular, the fact that sustainability is a widely shared value in the city government enables informal mechanisms to be effective. The same basic set of informal mechanisms facilitate integration both within Systems Planning and across the larger city government.

Relationships

Productive interpersonal relationships provide the single most important means of getting around potential FCA challenges in Ann Arbor. Because the individuals in Systems Planning cannot effectively require one another or units in other divisions to cooperate around "big umbrella" sustainability goals, cooperation must be encouraged in other ways. The primary way that this is done is through the nurturing of relationships and networks across the city government, which increases the likelihood that staff will share relevant information and will agree to and follow through on collaborations that may extend beyond their normal responsibilities. Along these lines, relationship building is considered a skill important to Systems Planning employees. One staff member explained, "We are people and relationships based. Personality analysis is a part of the hiring process. The people in Systems Planning are collaborative, extroverts, a little outspoken. We make the connections." Across several interviews, being a proactive "connector" was pointed to as fundamental to accomplishing the work of Systems Planning. The outsized importance of interpersonal relationships might be a result of Systems Planning and sustainability leaders not having much authority over other units (i.e., it is the only way things can get done); or, Systems Planning and sustainability leaders might not have much authority over other departments because the good relationships and collaborative culture make it unnecessary. Both seem to be true.

Shared Space

Shared space is a mechanism that facilitates integration around sustainability insofar as it enables, enhances, and expands the scope of the relationships that exist among city staff members. Most of the Systems Planning staff are colocated, which enables their regular ad hoc communication, but a few have offices strategically located within different departments. For example, the Systems Planning soil erosion expert sits with Community Services, which helps with coordination across service areas.

Requests for Proposals and Grant Seeking

Finally, the act of writing proposals for external funding regularly brings staff from across the city together around issues related to sustainability. Whether or not the project being proposed is directly about sustainability, other service areas frequently tap the expertise of Systems Planning staff when writing grants. This provides an opportunity for substantive connections to be made and enables comprehensive perspectives on sustainability to influence thought around particular projects. Proposal writing also provides actionable means for the subject-area experts within Systems Planning to enhance the dimensionality of their own projects. For example, at a Systems Planning staff meeting, the floodplain coordinator shared that he was responding to a request for proposal to remove an old rail berm near the Huron River to allow better water drainage. The transport coordinator had been considering trying to make a pedestrian bridge in that same area. They merged their plans and submitted proposals for a joint project, eventually receiving over $4.4 million in funding for it. This positive experience set a precedent for earlier and more proactive conversations across subject-area experts.

Overview of Sustainability Efforts in Oakland, California

"Oakland is a story of two communities," explains Daniel Hamilton, the city's sustainability coordinator, during our interview. "What Oakland is to you depends on where you live or spend your time." Parts of Oakland are green, lush, and extremely affluent with highly educated residents and high levels of investment. The city is also characterized by high rates of violent crime, community tensions with police, and areas of extreme poverty. Moreover, a racialized geography from years of urban renewal and home lending practices that systematically disadvantaged minority communities continues to limit their access to housing, jobs, and services. Ameliorating historic and racial inequities is the goal that underlies Oakland's sustainability efforts. One interviewee noted, "We don't view sustainability as a three-legged stool the way most cities or businesses do. We view equity as the primary lens."

Although it has gone through several iterations, sustainability has been a formal program in Oakland for over twenty years, which makes it one of the oldest in the nation. Since 2006, these efforts have been led by the Sustainable Oakland program, which is located in the city's Public Works Department. Reflecting the political priorities of the city as a whole, Sustainable Oakland uses sustainability as a vehicle to achieve greater social equity. This manifests in its energy efficiency and climate protection initiatives, which are Sustainable Oakland's programmatic priorities. The sustainability coordinator explained that, functionally, "this means we don't pursue deep energy efficiency programs in affluent neighborhoods, even though it may be low-hanging fruit and may reduce GHG emissions. It is less valuable from a social perspective than targeting a little bit more difficult emission reductions in low-income neighborhoods."

Oakland is also particularly vulnerable to the effects of climate change and sea level rise that will affect the city's infrastructure. The California Energy Commission projects that the mean sea level rise in the San Francisco Bay area is "likely" to be 2.4 to 3.4 feet by 2100, with extreme case projections of over 10.0 feet (State of California 2018). Thus, floods are expected to be almost inevitable in many low-lying areas in Oakland. This links back to equity considerations: Oakland's more affluent neighborhoods are generally located in the city's hills, whereas its lower-income communities are disproportionately located in low-lying areas. Mitigating the impacts of sea level rise is key to both the city's sustainability and resiliency efforts. In 2013 Oakland was selected into the Rockefeller Foundation's 100 Resilient Cities program and subsequently established Resilient Oakland—a citywide initiative led by a chief resilience officer—to improve its ability to adapt to stresses on infrastructure caused by environmental events such as sea level rise and to promote and integrate environmental justice initiatives into capital improvement projects.

Oakland has a mayor-council form of government, and interviewees describe the city as having three power bases: the strong mayor, the city council and council president, and the bureaucracy and city administrator. Of the three, the city council is perceived as least likely to prioritize sustainability, given Oakland's other challenges. As one interviewee explained, "None of the council members are against sustainability, but many have more pressing issues like crime and policing to worry about. Crime and policing take all the air out of the room." Another stated, "If I could wave my wand, I'd make it so the police and crime issues in the city were resolved. Sustainability could then get more attention." In addition to competing political priorities, Oakland faces significant resource and staffing shortages. As illustration of this point, an interviewee noted that Oakland has half the population of San Francisco but only one-eighth of the budget. Thus, despite its long history and ambitious objectives, particularly surrounding GHG mitigation and equity, Oakland's sustainability efforts face considerable challenges.

Sustainability Administration: Description, History, and Rationale

Oakland's city council adopted sustainability as a formal programmatic objective in 1997, making it one of first cities in the country to do so. It was also one of the first twenty cities globally to partake in ICLEI's Cities for Climate Protection program and inventory its GHG emissions. As a result of Oakland's early engagement with the issue, sustainability programming has had considerable time to evolve and change and is in its fourth iteration. Initial efforts were led by the city's Community and Economic Development and Public Works Agencies. Shortly thereafter, a sustainability analyst position was established within the city administrator's office. Although a relatively low-level position, the analyst was the first to confront the collective action challenges associated with the citywide pursuit of sustainability. In 2003, the sustainability analyst position was elevated to a sustainability program manager and was transferred to the city's Planning Division. For a short period, during then Mayor Jerry Brown's second administration, a second sustainability administrator was added as part of the mayor's cabinet. In 2006, both these positions were relocated to the Environmental Services Division, where the administrative responsibility for sustainability remains.

Sustainable Oakland spearheads the city's ongoing sustainability efforts. It is one of four sections in the Environmental Services Division, which is a part of the larger Public Works. Figure 6.3 shows the city's organizational structure. Environmental Services has approximately thirty full-time-equivalent staff and, in addition to Sustainable Oakland, it includes recycling and solid waste, environmental compliance, an energy group focused on governmental operations, and an environmental stewardship volunteer program. Sustainable Oakland has two core staff, a sustainable program

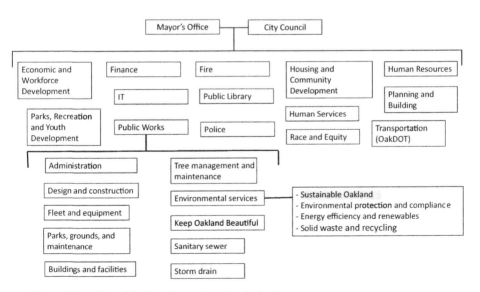

Figure 6.3 City of Oakland organizational chart

manager and an energy policy analyst, and six focus areas: (1) buildings, energy, and climate; (2) economic prosperity; (3) education, culture, and community; (4) health, safety, and well-being; (5) housing, land use, and transportation; and (6) natural resources, waste, and environmental health. Although they have a broad scope, the focus areas all link to energy conservation and climate change and are pursued with an explicit eye toward equity. Sustainable Oakland coordinates the implementation of the citywide Energy and Climate Action Plan (ECAP) and leads efforts to achieve its stated GHG reduction goals.

Although the staff across the five sections of Environmental Services regularly work together on joint objectives, Sustainable Oakland and the sustainability program manager have little authority by which to directly shape their actions and priorities. A variety of documents and frameworks help give sustainability gravitas, the ECAP chief among them, but in the absence of formal authority or an explicit and sustained push from the city's top leadership, the sustainability manager largely relies on relationships, goodwill, and voluntary cooperation to overcome FCA challenges and advance citywide goals. The challenge of this dynamic is intensified for interactions with units outside of Environmental Services.

Sustainability Priorities

Mitigating GHG emissions in a way that addresses historic inequities is Sustainable Oakland's overarching programmatic priority. The specific projects and policies it pursues all link back to that objective. The city of Oakland is aiming for "deep decarbonization." In 2009, the city council adopted the goals of reducing community-wide GHG emissions by 36 percent below 2005 baseline levels by 2020 and 83 percent below by 2050. The city's 2012 ECAP identifies 175 action items to achieve these mitigation goals (City of Oakland 2012). As of the plan's 2017 update, 32 of these action items were complete or "fully underway," another 56 were designated as priorities, and the remainder had yet to be started. The description of each priority action item includes the departments or divisions responsible, its implementation status, its anticipated cost, and whether it is supported by current resources (16 of the 56 priority actions) or if it requires new resources to be completed (40 of the 56) (City of Oakland 2018a). The "creation of significant social equity benefits" is one of the criteria used to determine the prioritization of action items. Specifically, these benefits are characterized in the ECAP as (1) providing "benefits to disadvantaged residents in the form of jobs, cost savings, and other opportunities; (2) reducing pollution in heavily impacted neighborhoods; and (3) achieving equity in protection from impacts of climate change" (City of Oakland 2018a).

In addition to measuring core GHG emissions, which are released within the city limits, Oakland also inventories consumption-based emissions to more comprehensively account for GHGs associated with the production, transport, and eventual disposal of goods used within the city. The consumption-based accounting approach has resulted in some revision of programmatic priorities. For example, it has led to an increased focus on minimizing natural gas use because of downstream problems with methane leakage. An assessment of 2015 data shows that consumption-based emissions have been reduced 16 percent below the 2005 baseline, which, while significant, is not on track to achieve the 2020 goal (City of Oakland 2018b).

Addressing infrastructure deficiencies, and investing in infrastructure improvements in a manner that enhances both environmental sustainability and social equity, is another of Oakland's relevant priorities. In 2016, Oakland residents approved Measure KK, known as the Infrastructure Bond, with 82 percent of the vote (City of Oakland 2017b). This general obligation bond provides $600 million to fund citywide transportation projects, improve city streets, fund antidisplacement and affordable housing projects, and invest in public facilities including libraries, parks, and public safety facilities. While not explicitly tied to sustainability, how this money is used will meaningfully shape the city's physical, environmental, social, and economic landscape for the next several decades. Working to ensure that the capital projects funded with this money incorporate life-cycle assessments and reflect sea level rise adaptation strategies is a priority for the sustainability manager.

Vehicle electrification has received considerable recent attention in Oakland and is an example of a specific issue that links infrastructure, GHG mitigation, and (somewhat surprisingly) equity considerations. The city's consumption-based GHG inventory identifies automotive fuels as a primary contributor of emissions, whereas electricity in California is quite clean. This provides an important climate-based rationale for developing local infrastructure to support electric vehicles. At the time of interviews, approximately 5 percent of all new cars sold in the Bay Area had electric powertrains. This relatively high number suggests that, regionally, the new car market for electric vehicles is healthy. However, the sustainability manager observed that the market for used electric vehicles is lacking, in part because many used-car buyers live in rented multifamily units where they do not have the authority to put in electric charging infrastructure. Approximately 60 percent of Oakland's housing units are renter occupied (U.S. Census Bureau 2019f), and this segment of the population is largely precluded from electric vehicle ownership. Reflecting its equity orientation, Sustainable Oakland is working to enable a secondary market for electric vehicles. Along these lines, in 2017, the city council unanimously passed an ordinance changing city code to require that all newly constructed multifamily buildings install chargers in 10 percent of parking spaces and make another 10 percent ready for electric vehicles by having wiring in place so that changing technology can be added easily when and if needed.

Sustainability and the Elevation of Complementary Priorities

Several new specialized departments have been created around certain issues that are complementary to sustainability. Specifically, in 2016 the Oakland Department of Transportation (OakDOT) was formed with the mission to "envision, plan, build, operate and maintain a transportation system for the City of Oakland and assure safe, equitable, and sustainable access and mobility" (City of Oakland, n.d.b). This new three-hundred-person unit pulled together transportation-related functions that were previously parts of the city's Planning, Public Works, and Police Departments. OakDOT has responsibility for street and bikeway design, sidewalks and pedestrian safety programs, parking management, mobility services, and street maintenance. Thus, its policy decisions will have significant implications for GHG emissions and the goals outlined in the ECAP. The same year, the city launched a new Department of Race and Equity. This two-person department is aimed at creating a city where "diversity is maintained, racial disparities have been eliminated and racial equity has been achieved" (City of Oakland, n.d.a). Given Sustainable Oakland's equity orientation, their missions are closely aligned. Still, the city's decision to departmentalize and elevate particular sustainability dimensions affects how the broader objective is managed.

The 2014 creation and location of Resilient Oakland offers a comparison and provides some insight into the implication of organizational placement within the city government. Like Sustainable Oakland, Resilient Oakland is a two-person unit. However, as a condition of the city's acceptance into the Rockefeller Foundation's 100 Resilient Cities program, it is located within the Chief Administrator's Office (CAO). The resiliency initiative focuses on community issues such as gentrification, housing and rent stabilization, and infrastructure improvements related to climate adaptation and sea level rise. The deputy resiliency officer described the initiative as largely driven by the broad goal of "making it so the people who live here can stay here and thrive long-term." This objective is not unlike that of Sustainable Oakland, and several interviewees did not see a clear distinction between the city's sustainability efforts and its resiliency efforts.

Placement in the CAO provides Resilient Oakland with several advantages. Key among these is regular access to department heads: the chief resiliency officer has a seat at the weekly citywide directors' meeting. Neither the sustainability manager nor his direct supervisor, the environmental services division manager, attends these meetings. Being a consistent part of high-level conversations enables resiliency issues to be injected into big-picture considerations. A second benefit of being located in the CAO is the authority it confers when communicating new initiatives and actions. Line staff are used to getting guidance and requests from the CAO, so such communications are perceived as relatively standard. Conversely, Resilient Oakland's location in the CAO contributes to perceptions that it may be a temporary or transitioning initiative. According to the deputy resiliency officer, "I am not the first person who has been in the CAO . . . telling people in the government that they need to change things. I might be gone in three years when a new [chief administrator] comes in. They will still be there." As explained by the officer, Sustainable Oakland's integration into a line department may be both a cause ("We are buffered from political winds") and a consequence ("Where we are speaks to how long we've been doing this. . . . We started when sustainability programs were an outgrowth of recycling") of its longevity as an initiative in the city.

OakDOT, the Department of Race and Equity, and Resilient Oakland—along with the longer-standing departments of Planning and Public Works—are key partners assisting Sustainable Oakland's mission. There is not a perception of competition between them, and the sustainability manager described them all as sharing Sustainable Oakland's "zeal for GHG reduction and service to the community through environmental programs." Yet, reflecting on the recent organizational changes and Sustainable Oakland's location still several layers deep within Public Works, one interviewee noted that "there is the recognition that if you take something seriously in the city, you dedicate a director to it." The sustainability manager noted that the current structure may "limit the perceived status of the program relative to other priorities. That being said, all that really matters is the implementation and how people take you when you show up at their door and ask them to do something." Although their reactions have not been uniform, both directors and line staff across the city have tended to be responsive to requests that originate from Sustainable Oakland.

Approaches to Integration

Sustainable Oakland relies heavily on relationships and the idea that sustainability is a shared value in order to get cross-departmental assistance on its initiatives. Consistent support from top city officials—particularly the last several mayors and city administrators—and institutionalized plans, procedures, and structures developed around sustainability objectives enhance the efficacy of relationships and values-based approaches. Table 6.4 shows the mechanisms identified as most important.

TABLE 6.4: CITY OF OAKLAND INTEGRATION MECHANISMS

Formal
- The sustainability manager position and location in Environmental Services
- Energy and Climate Action Plan (ECAP)
- Finance flowchart
- Environmental Services paying for positions in other departments
- Council agenda reports

Informal
- The person of sustainability manager
- Relationships

Formal Mechanisms

In some respects, the approaches used to administer sustainability in Oakland appear to be moving in an increasingly informal direction, with the abandonment of certain formal mechanisms. Notably, under a previous sustainability manager, interdepartmental sustainability teams met regularly and provided an important venue for coordination. They have since been disbanded. The leadership change was a primary reason cited for this, along with a lack of staff enthusiasm over the extra work that the teams entailed. At the same time, a main initial task of the teams was to help develop the ECAP, so its completion provided a natural stopping point. Finally, Oakland also received its grant from 100 Resilient Cities at about this time, and some interviewees noted that resiliency began to replace sustainability as an organizing principle and may have co-opted some of the formal structure that had previously been used for sustainability. In particular, the creation of resilience delivery teams, involving many of the same players, called into question the value of multiple sets of standing meetings.

A considerable number of formal mechanisms continue to support Oakland's sustainability efforts. Although they do not bestow Sustainable Oakland or its manager with much authority, they give the program standing and provide regular channels of communication across the city government. In and of themselves, the formal mechanisms appear to play a modest role limiting FCA challenges, but they enable the informal mechanisms to work effectively. Of the formal mechanisms that facilitate cross-departmental cooperation around sustainability, the position of the sustainability manager and the ECAP appear central. Others, like the Finance Flowchart and council agenda reports, play important background roles.

The Sustainability Manager Position and Location in Environmental Services

The sustainability manager, as opposed to the position's analyst precursor, has a broad mandate to work across the city government in the pursuit of sustainability—which is currently operationalized as mitigating GHG emissions in a manner that reduces historic and racial inequities. Although the position's specific focus has occasionally been refined to reflect political priorities, the longevity of the position gives its overall mission gravitas. Being located few layers deep within a line department means the sustainability manager is not able to direct the actions of other units; however, the fact that the position has been embedded within Public Works for over a decade facilitates a smooth integration of its efforts with those of several key partners. As Figure 6.3 shows, the four different teams within Environmental Services all have sustainability-related responsibilities, as do a majority of the other divisions within Public Works. Although the Sustainable Oakland staff work across virtually all city departments, having the individuals who design and implement a large portion of relevant activities as day-to-day colleagues makes communication relatively easy.

Energy and Climate Action Plan
The Oakland ECAP is arguably the most important organizing principle for Sustainable Oakland. As previously described, it identifies and prioritizes 175 actions the city can take to reduce energy consumption and GHG emissions and establishes processes for coordinating their implementation and reporting on progress. It outlines three broad policy areas for mitigation actions to reduce GHG emissions: transportation and land use, building and energy use, and material consumption and waste—and, thus, directly incorporates OakDOT, the Planning and Building Department, and the Public Works Department. As shown in Table 6.5, the ECAP matches the responsible divisions with each priority action and, in so doing, often prescribes working partnerships. The responsible units are expected to provide regular updates on the status of their action(s). The actual impact of the ECAP in shaping departmental actions varies considerably by unit, with

TABLE 6.5: EXAMPLES OF ECAP PRIORITY ACTIONS AND IMPLEMENTING ADMINISTRATIVE UNITS

Priority action	Responsible departments/divisions
Identify and adopt priority development areas	Transportation Services; Strategic Planning; Redevelopment
Offer property-based energy financing	Environmental Services; Planning; Building Services
Launch a residential green retrofit program	Environmental Services; Planning; Housing and Community Development
Develop regulations enabling urban food production	Strategic Planning; Economic Development

some using it as a guiding principle and others acting in ways that are directly contradictory to it because they do not know it exists. One interviewee noted that the latter occurs in part because "there is no new employee orientation that tells people about our climate action strategy." Fortunately, all the senior-level managers in the city government are familiar with the ECAP, so they can act as a stopgap.

Finance Flowchart

The Finance Flowchart is an internal document that explicitly shows how sustainability is paid for in Oakland. It graphically links every one of the 175 action items in the ECAP with its source of funding and presents the estimated cost of each action, how much money has already been spent on each, and how much more needs to be spent to reach stated goals. The flowchart was created as an outgrowth of an Innovation Fund project sponsored by the USDN examining how cities finance sustainability. The sustainability manager described its motivation as the observation that cities "largely write climate action plans without including any budget numbers whatsoever—and then we hope we can find a way to pay for them, which is not a very robust or defensible strategy." Oakland's Finance Flowchart shows the shared responsibility of paying for sustainability across the city and illustrates, he explained, that "sustainability is not simply [that] you have a tax, you implement it, and it's done. . . . We do regional programs, we do grants, we do franchise fees, we do solid waste hauling, we do building permit fees, we have a port that has its own revenue stream. . . . There is just a tremendous number of inputs required to pay for these disparate strategies because they touch literally every part of municipal operations."

Environmental Services Positions in Other Departments

To create "intentional connectivity," Environmental Services sponsors positions in other departments to ensure that environmental issues are being considered. The environmental services director noted, "We don't really have a hammer, so in some cases we have to implement things ourselves." For example, Environmental Services pays for the green industry specialist in the Economic and Workforce Development Department. This position began in 1999 with the intent to develop an economy to use recycled goods in the region and has transitioned to work with the variety of explicitly green companies in Oakland. Although all of the reporting and evaluation associated with this position goes through Economic Development, it works closely, but informally, with the sustainability manager. This position and its structure are evaluated as successfully linking missions.

Council Agenda Reports

A triple-bottom-line analysis is included as part of the report form that staff complete when proposing new policies or initiatives to city leadership. It requires that any social, environmental, and economic impact be identified and described. The expectation is that going through this process will encourage reflection and adjustments to improve relevant outcomes. However, the actual impact of the triple-bottom-line inclusion in council agenda reports is unclear. Several interviewees noted a tendency of units to take a "cut and paste" approach to their responses, and city leadership does not often push them to be more thoughtful or comprehensive.

Informal Mechanisms

Whereas the formal mechanisms described above institutionalize linkages and provide the structures around which collective action for sustainability can be built, informal mechanisms—which depend heavily on specific people and relationships—serve as the actual means of integration. Although this reliance on informality does present a risk of instability, particularly as personnel change, these concerns have largely not materialized because of consistent support from top-level administrators and because members of the Oakland public provide a meaningful check on efforts. In addition, many of the leadership staff in the Environmental Services Division have worked within it or other departments in the city for many years and, as a result, have accumulated robust interpersonal ties with staff across the city government. They have also acquired significant institutional knowledge of past sustainability-related practices and a history of the policy issues in Oakland. This "soft infrastructure" strengthens personal ties and is a particular asset when working across departments to launch new initiatives.

The Person of the Sustainability Manager

The position of Oakland's sustainability manager—its responsibilities and location in the government hierarchy—was previously discussed as a formal mechanism. However, the importance of the specific *persons* who have held that position—and their particular skills, visions, and abilities to effectively operate within the city government—has also been emphasized. Since its current incarnation in Environmental Services, two people have held the position: Garrett Fitzgerald (2008–2013), who moved to the USDN, and Daniel Hamilton (2014–present). Both were described by interviewees as having developed strong credibility with city leaders and the staff responsible for policy implementation. They were also noted as doing a particularly good job managing relationships and as being necessarily proactive in reaching out to relevant people to get things done. Reflecting on Daniel Hamilton, one interviewee stated, "If we lost Daniel, it would be devastating. He has learned to navigate the system so well."

Relationships
Interpersonal relationships, many forged by the sustainability manager, are key to getting things done. One interviewee stated that sustainability gets done because "we generally don't disagree that it's important, and are usually willing go a little out of our way to help each other out." Often this quid pro quo interpersonal approach works, but reliance on it can mean that when obstacles emerge, there are few mechanisms available to overcome them. For example, Oakland's Environmentally Preferred Purchasing Policy has been touted as a success in incorporating ECAP goals widely across government operations. However, its achievement was delayed significantly because of one person's resistance. An interviewee noted that a downside of reliance on relationships and goodwill means that if they cannot be forged, "sometimes you just have to wait until people retire."

In sum, a two-person unit buried deep within Public Works is able to overcome a majority of FCA challenges around sustainability in Oakland because of its long history and general alignment with community and political priorities and because its leaders have been able to establish broad credibility and develop effective relationships to leverage formal structures and plans.

Comparative Assessment of Providence, Ann Arbor, and Oakland

This chapter overviews three city governments that use relationships and bargaining as a primary administrative approach to overcome interdepartmental FCA in order to implement sustainability initiatives. This approach is necessary because the unit designated as the sustainability lead lacks the ability to require or meaningfully incentivize cooperation, so it must achieve cooperation by appealing to colleagues' goodwill. Across these three cities, generally speaking, the reliance on relationships and other informal mechanisms to facilitate sustainability works fine; although efforts in Providence face notably more resistance. All are making meaningful advancements toward their particular operationalization of sustainability. Taken together, these case studies suggest the importance of four attributes enabling the successful functioning of relationship-based intracity sustainability administration: (1) skilled point people able to navigate the system,

(2) sustainability being shared as a value by a majority of city staff, (3) an active and supportive community that serves as a check on city action, and (4) sufficient formal mechanisms to serve as a scaffolding around informal efforts.

The sustainability leads in Providence, Ann Arbor, and Oakland play a particularly important and ongoing role forging paths for sustainability initiatives in their city governments. Much of this is done by developing productive relationships with key actors across the city and, as necessary, educating them about what sustainability is and clarifying their role in working toward it. Direct lines of cross-city communication are not always available, and because of their relatively low placement in their respective cities' organizational hierarchies, there are often multiple "filters" or intermediaries that information must pass through before reaching the intended recipient. For example, none of the sustainability leads in these cities have a regular seat at directors' meetings, so cultivating the support of those higher in the hierarchy can be important to ensure that their interests are represented. One way that this has effectively been done is by selecting and tactfully framing sustainability efforts so they match leaders' political priorities. The equity emphasis in Providence and Oakland reflects such an approach. When working from a position embedded within the organization, horizontal requests also must be navigated carefully and in such a way that the directors and managers of other units see them as complementing their own core responsibilities. The Providence sustainability officer's previously described "small wins" strategy is an example of this. Decisions in these cities, some made long ago, about where to place sustainability amplifies the importance of the sustainability leads' savvy and their ability to communicate with and cultivate support from relevant actors across the city.

Convincing city government staff to engage in collective action to support sustainability—particularly if it involves some extra work and/or is not immediately linked to core responsibilities—is easier to do if people personally believe it is a worthy and relevant objective. Of these three cities, a broad "sustainability ethos" was most apparent in Ann Arbor, where several interviewees noted that virtually all city staff are onboard in principle. Oakland's efforts are also facilitated by broad buy-in. In both of these cities, sustainability initiatives have been pursued for twenty-plus years, which is likely both a cause and an effect of its broad acceptance as a value. In the Providence city government, sustainability does not benefit from the same level of widespread acceptance, which increases the importance of relationship-building, education, and framing as described above.

Active community support is a third feature that, based on these case studies, appears particularly important in enabling low-authority units to lead effective government-wide sustainability initiatives. Specifically, when advocacy or neighborhood groups contact elected leaders to encourage action on sustainability issues and/or ask for status updates on the implementation of related plans, they often result in additional attention from city leaders who then charge staff to act. Moreover, when the larger public *expects* its city to be, for example, a progressive climate leader, as is the case in Ann Arbor and Oakland, the objective of sustainability is bestowed with authority even if the unit leading it is not. Being able to point to community demands helps generate cooperation for sustainability initiatives.

It is also possible to formalize community engagement around sustainability by appointing community members to official city tasks forces, boards, and/or commissions. Ann Arbor and Providence have convened standing citizen groups around relevant issues. Particularly in Providence, the Environmental Sustainability Task Force provides a mechanism through which the Office of Sustainability can raise the profile of sustainability issues throughout the community. Moreover, because the task force is composed of citizens appointed by the city council and the mayor, proposals originating from the task force have legitimacy and thus generate political responsiveness. Moreover, the task force serves as a buffer between the Office of Sustainability and the city council, particularly with the members who may not fully endorse sustainability principles or view the concept as not being applicable to how a city should function. Active community engagement is presumably helpful across administrative arrangements, but it appears to have particular effect when the sustainability lead lacks its own authority and maneuvers horizontally through the government.

Finally, although the cities in this chapter have designated lead units that rely on relationships and informal mechanisms to achieve FCA on sustainability, they also employ a reasonable number of formal mechanisms that provide structure, direction, and standing. All have formal plans, which set out goals and assign responsibility for the accomplishment of identified activities to specific departments. They are generally assessed as having modest direct impact but provide an organizing principle and framework for action. They also serve as something for sustainability leads to point to when making requests of other units. "Sustainable Providence," the Sustainability and Climate Action Plans in Ann Arbor, and the ECAP in Oakland give legitimacy and gravitas to the initiatives undertaken in pursuit of the goals they line out.

While the aforementioned attributes in Providence, Ann Arbor, and Oakland support integration, the struggle for resources in each city shapes its tendencies toward collaboration. Their differential reaction to resource scarcity is interesting in and of itself and shows how some of the attributes described above interact. Interviewees across all three cities share the perception that they are understaffed and that the staff they do have are stretched thin. However, the responses to this shared condition differ. Most notably, in Providence, where the fiscal situation is arguably most severe, the lack of resources exacerbates FCA challenges by causing staff to cling more closely to their core responsibilities. At the other end of the spectrum, in Ann Arbor, similar resource pressures appear to have a stimulating effect on cross-departmental collaboration; it is done out of perceived necessity. The FCA-relevant reactions in Oakland to being underresourced fall somewhere in the middle of the other two cities.

In each city, the sustainability lead is faced with figuring out how to effectively respond to (i.e., minimize or leverage) the reactions of potential partners across the city government who are facing their own financial and staffing burdens. The Office of Sustainability in Providence has adopted a strategy of identifying projects that generate resources for other departments or that enable departments to achieve their goals without siphoning resources or significantly detracting from their day-to-day responsibilities. The relative newness of sustainability as an explicit objective increases the challenge of doing this effectively—the city has been lacking resources for decades, and sustainability is viewed by some as a recent add-on that absorbs staff time and resources with no additional compensation. In Ann Arbor, the long history of environmental management, and the active local environmental groups and neighborhood associations that provide regular checks on the city's actions, means that environmental sustainability is an expectation, not an ambition. Thus, in the face of resource constraints, the question is not if but how it will be pursued. The Systems Planning Division is the proactive driver of relevant collaborations, but its efforts are generally well received.

Conclusion

The three cities considered in this chapter are unlike each other in many ways—including history, size, and governmental form—yet they share striking similarities in how they operate to mitigate the potential of FCA around sustainability initiatives. In each, informal mechanisms—relationships—are key. Formal mechanisms provide scaffolding and, on occasion, some modest requirements that sustainability implications be considered. The organization of the lead units is similar—more so in Oakland and Ann Arbor, where they are both subunits of much larger line departments. In Providence, although the lead unit is nominally in the Mayor's Office (which led us originally to hypothesize it would function via lead agency coordination; see the left side of Figure 3.3), in practice it is buried several layers deep in the hierarchy and operates much like the others.

Compared to Providence, Oakland and Ann Arbor have much older sustainability programs. Perhaps because of this, or perhaps because of consistent external pressure from the community shaping both, sustainability is perceived as a shared value for a majority of city government employees in both cities. This enables informal negotiations and interpersonal relationships to more effectively overcome the FCA challenges that could otherwise hinder sustainability efforts. Formal mechanisms structure opportunity for collaboration, but by and large, they are weak and neither require nor meaningfully incentivize it. Although they are not without some struggles, in these two cities that approach is sufficient. In Providence, conversely, the reliance on informal mechanisms to facilitate FCA around sustainability is more problematic. For a variety of reasons, the Office of Sustainability and its director experience relatively more pushback from departments and employees across the city when they are asked to assist with particular initiatives. Sustainability is a newer initiative, and not as universally regarded as a priority, so the informal and weak formal mechanisms available are less consistently able to achieve the buy-in necessary. Instead, small wins are the goal.

7

Decentralized Networks

El Paso, Texas, and Gainesville, Florida

> We don't have an office of sustainability or a centralized place
> for information and for programs. And so because of that . . .
> it's embedded in these various areas and units, but we may not
> necessarily have a consistent definition of sustainability.
>
> —CARRIE BUSH
> (former director of strategic initiatives, Gainesville, Florida),
> interview by the authors, June 2019

The final organizational arrangement available as a means to mitigate functional collective action (FCA) challenges related to sustainability is characterized as a decentralized network. Reflecting on the FCA framework introduced in Chapter 3, general arrangements for overcoming intraorganizational fragmentation around a given issue vary on two dimensions. The first involves whether there is a designated lead agency and the degree of authority it has over other units in the government. The second dimension captures the number of independent entities within a government that share some responsibility for implementing relevant initiatives. In decentralized networks, responsibility for a particular objective is spread across multiple units in an organization, with none empowered to direct overall efforts. Of the three organizational arrangements illustrated in preceding chapters, the decentralized network shares key features with the relationship and bargaining approach but has less of a nucleus. Whereas, under a relationship-and-bargaining-based arrangement, the lead unit lacks authority to require or meaningfully incentivize cooperation from other units across the city; working to do so using other, softer means is part of its mandate. In decentralized networks, conversely, there is not a clear lead unit responsible for engaging others around the pursuit of an overarching objective. In this situation, if integration is achieved, it is through a self-organizing network or communication and coordination among individual units. Although within decentralized networks a policy champion or entrepreneur may emerge, he or she lacks the formal ability to direct the actions of other units.

This chapter examines two cities whose sustainability efforts are characterized as decentralized networks: El Paso, Texas, and Gainesville, Florida. Sustainability efforts in El Paso started in the early 2000s and have been reorganized several times since. At times it has reflected more of a "relationship and bargaining" arrangement led by a sustainability office. However, as a result of political and personnel changes, it has recently shifted in the direction of a decentralized network. A reasonable amount of coordination continues between departments and is generally organized around specific programs as part of the city's implementation of its strategic plan. Gainesville has been actively pursuing sustainable energy initiatives for decades through its municipal utility. Between approximately 2005 and 2015, its issue scope expanded, and coordination around more-encompassing sustainability initiatives was aided by the action of several informal teams. More recently, after leadership changes and significant government restructuring, Gainesville reduced its focus on sustainability to prioritize economic development and customer service.

Unlike in some of the cities profiled in previous chapters, sustainability is not an overriding community ethos in either El Paso or Gainesville. Its absence as a widely shared value means there is not a consistent external check on governmental efforts whereby citizens hold the city accountable to ensure follow-through on plans and commitments. This can create challenges for effort continuity, particularly when an issue champion leaves. Both cities experienced political and administrative flux in the several years preceding our examination. As a result, their sustainability programs appeared to be weaker and less organized than they had been shortly before.

The information for this chapter comes from fifteen semistructured interviews conducted either in person or over the phone with current and former staff from each city. El Paso staff include the following people:

- Sustainability program specialist
- Senior economic development specialist
- Former sustainability director
- Performance systems administrator
- Former sustainability program engineer
- Former city manager
- Director of environmental services

Gainesville staff include the following people:

- Public works director
- Gainesville Regional Utilities supervising utility engineer
- Director of facilities management

- Interim director of Department of Doing
- Former city manager
- Director of economic development and innovation
- Former director of strategic initiatives
- Community Redevelopment Agency director

Appendix C provides the interview template. Additional information supplementing these interviews was gathered from the cities' websites, policy and budget documents, and local newspaper stories. The rest of this chapter provides background about sustainability efforts in El Paso and Gainesville, including how the arrangements evolved and the priority issues that they are addressing. It also offers descriptions of the specific mechanisms used by each city to implement and integrate sustainability.[1] The chapter concludes with a comparison of the cities' approaches to overcoming FCA dilemmas in the absence of a clear lead and assesses their relative successes. Appendixes J and K offer narrative profile of El Paso and Gainesville, respectively.

Overview of Sustainability Efforts in El Paso, Texas

As a large city in a major binational urban center on the Texas-Mexico border, El Paso faces a unique set of dynamics around sustainability. Some challenges, most notably those having to do with water scarcity and poverty, present obvious and immediate needs. Others, such as land contamination, are remnants of past economic activity; they are less visible but still very real concerns. At the same time, El Paso has unique opportunities; its average 320 days of sunshine a year give it the natural resource potential to be a solar energy hub (City of El Paso 2013), and its approximately 680,000 residents—the majority of whom are bilingual and 27 percent of whom are under eighteen—are poised to provide a productive workforce for the modern economy (U.S. Census Bureau 2019b). The city's economic needs have given rise to a local policy agenda that is generally characterized as "pro-growth," although its ongoing sustainability efforts have attempted to steer it in the direction of sustainable development.

El Paso has had an explicit sustainability objective since 2008. During the ten years between its initiation and late 2017, when the data informing this case study were collected, the city's sustainability initiative experienced considerable change. Initially this change was structural. Between 2008 and 2014, the lead sustainability unit was housed within three different city

---

1. These are point-in-time descriptions of the cities' goals and mechanisms as they were in 2019, when data were collected.

departments: the City Managers' Office, the Economic Development Department, and the Environmental Services Department. More recently there have also been changes in relevant personnel, including the departure of a key sustainability champion. After several years, the role of sustainability champion remains unfilled; staff in positions most likely to take up the mantle of sustainability are occupied in the pursuit of other pressing priorities, notably economic development and resiliency. From some perspectives, El Paso has lost a clear direction for its sustainability initiatives. However, a new strategic-plan-based approach, which at the time of our study had not been fully implemented, promises to achieve the dual objectives of embedding sustainability into the functions of all city departments and increasing the efficiency of sustainability implementation.

Background, History, and Current Context of Sustainability

Sustainability efforts undertaken by the El Paso city government can be broken down into three eras. The first extends from approximately 2008 to 2014 and represents the time of clearest sustained direction for sustainability. At the initiative of its then city manager, Joyce Wilson, a sustainability unit was created, and the first sustainability officer was hired in 2008. The sustainability officer at the time, Marty Howell, was initially located in the City Manager's Office, where he benefited from both significant autonomy and significant support from leadership. The unit's initial accomplishments included creating "The Livable City Sustainability Plan," which specified priorities and actions to be implemented over the next five years. This was an eight-month effort to assess current conditions and establish specific goals and strategic action items. As one interviewee explained, it was primarily developed with a team of "middle-management folks . . . because the top end wouldn't show up, and the bottom-up end didn't know how decisions were made." The plan's substantive priorities included improving regional air quality, taking advantage of renewable energy resources, sustainable development and sprawl reduction, developing a regional transport system, establishing a green procurement process for the city government, and messaging to the community the value of a sustainable lifestyle (City of El Paso 2009). The five-year plan was adopted in 2009 and retired in 2014.

Despite its organizational location changing three times during this period, the sustainability office continued to function with little disruption to its operations. A deputy sustainability officer was also hired during this time, and the city's two sustainability staff functioned using an administrative approach based on relationships and bargaining. As is standard under this arrangement, the designated lead unit encouraged, organized, and coordinated citywide sustainability efforts but relied on others in the government to implement them. Moreover, because it lacked the authority to *require* their cooperation, collective action was pursued through informal means (see Chapter 6 for more detail on relationship-and-bargaining-based arrangements).

In 2014, a number of significant changes occurred and ushered in the second "era," characterized by a new focus on resiliency. The first set of changes involved the turnover of a majority of the city's original sustainability-relevant leaders. Precipitated by an election that resulted in a new mayor and four new council members, the city manager, Joyce Wilson, left the position after having served in it for ten years. Shortly thereafter, after six years as sustainability officer, Marty Howell also left. The deputy sustainability officer temporarily took over his position, the sustainability office was moved into the General Services Department, and its budget was reduced. Soon the deputy sustainability officer, who by then had worked in the sustainability office for six years, also left to assume a similar position in another city. Although one sustainability employee remained, the vast majority of institutional knowledge about the previous decade of El Paso's sustainability efforts was lost in a year.

The decline in the city's sustainability efforts also coincided with a new focus on community resiliency. Prior to their departure, the sustainability leadership applied for and the city was accepted into the Rockefeller Foundation's 100 Resilient Cities Program. The resources received from the foundation included money to hire a chief resilience officer (CRO), which by program requirement reports directly to the city manager. The new city manager was not a part of the original application to 100 Resilient Cities and initially described the CRO position as "very ethereal and hard to put substance next to it" (Crowder 2014). In December 2014, the city hired Nicole Ferrini as the city's CRO and shortly thereafter created the Office of Resilience and Sustainability. In addition to the CRO, the office housed a sustainability program specialist who managed program implementation, outreach, and education. It also hosted two full-time AmeriCorps VISTA members who were responsible for working with community groups, neighborhood organizations, and businesses to determine the risks associated with climate change and to enhance local capacity for resiliency.

The establishment of the Office of Resilience and Sustainability, and the hiring of the CRO, provided a launchpad for an extensive formal community engagement process to identify priority areas where action was needed to build long-term community resilience. Two weather-related shocks, in particular, motivated the city's resiliency initiative: in 2006 the city received the equivalent of two years of annual rainfall over a few days, causing more than $700 million in damages to public and private property; and in 2011 the city suffered from extreme cold that resulted in significant infrastructure failures (City of El Paso 2018). Extreme climate conditions have become chronic stresses on El Paso and have negatively affected a wide range of public services. They have also exacerbated the city's social, environmental, and economic vulnerabilities, which carry a particular weight given its location as a geographically isolated border city in an arid climate. The office and the CRO served as the pivot for resilience building across El Paso and for coordinating efforts across city government departments to more effectively address the city's vulnerabilities.

To guide the city's actions, the office developed "Resilient El Paso," a plan aimed at addressing the challenges of poverty, energy affordability, transportation, health, food access, extreme heat, flash floods, drought, workforce development, and the "challenges of building a border metroplex" (City of El Paso 2018). These, in turn, led the city to create a resilience strategy around four pillars: a vibrant desert city, a thriving binational economy, empowered El Pasoans, and resilient governance. Although they are approached from a different angle, some of the issues included in the resiliency plan's wide scope are substantively related to those in the 2009 "The Livable City Sustainability Plan." The administrative structure used to manage these efforts lasted for about three years, at which point the Office of Resilience and Sustainability was absorbed into the Department of Community and Human Development. Nicole Ferrini became the director of this department and continued to hold the title of CRO.

In this third era, sustainability administration in El Paso transitioned fully into a decentralized network structure, whereby efforts that require the cooperation of numerous departments do not have a formal leader. Although it has assumed an explicit efficiency orientation, sustainability remains a goal in the city's Strategic Plan, which now provides the primary structure for its administration. "Goal teams," composed of representatives from relevant departments, are organized around each of eight Strategic Plan goals. They are intended to "ensure cross-functional collaboration" (City of El Paso 2017a, 17). These teams are expected to take meaningful action in pursuit of their goals and are held accountable via performance measures and regular public presentations. This formal, but still decentralized, approach is considered by city leadership as an efficient way of baking sustainability into all relevant city functions. Representatives of seven different city departments, including the CRO, are assigned to Goal 8: "Nurture and Promote a Healthy, Sustainable Community." Figure 7.1 presents these units within the formal organizational structure of the city.

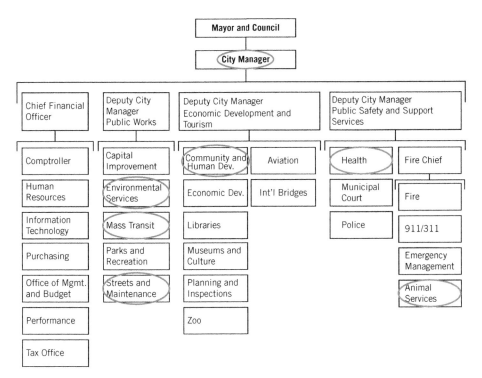

Figure 7.1 City of El Paso organizational chart and Goal Team 8 departmental participants

Foundations for Decentralized Administration of Sustainability

Current integration and FCA around sustainability in El Paso can be characterized as operating as a two-level decentralized network. The first level is more formal: the existence of citywide goal teams, including one centered on creating a heathy, sustainable community, are specified in the Strategic Plan, and departmental participants are identified by the performance systems administrator in the City Manager's Office. However, the interactions that occur within each goal team and the initiatives they pursue are determined internally by its members. The first level rests on three primary documents: "The Livable City Sustainability Plan," "Resilient El Paso," and the city's Strategic Plan. Although the Sustainability Plan is no longer active, it folds into the others and they retain some of its focus (see Figure 7.2).

El Paso's Strategic Plan 2.0 includes elements of the other plans and is tied directly to the budget (City of El Paso 2019). It operates as the preeminent policy document and integration mechanism in the city. The first version of the Strategic Plan was formally adopted in 2015 and comprised eight

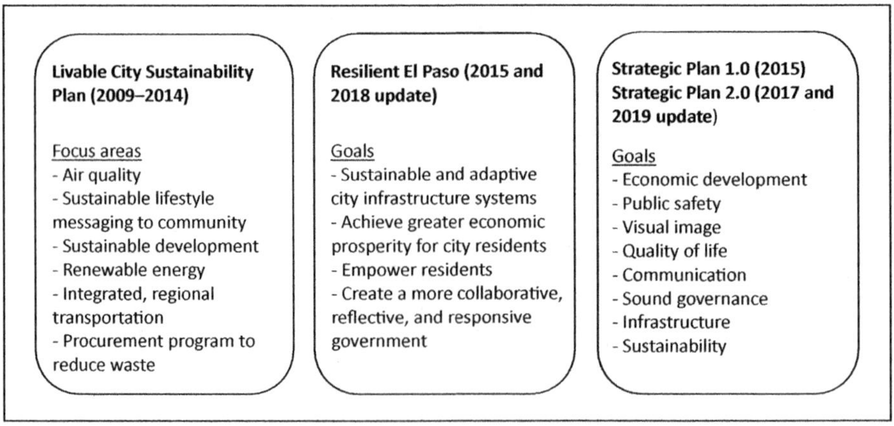

Figure 7.2 Foundational plans underlying sustainability efforts in El Paso

goals, set forth by the city council. The goals serve as pillars around which relevant functional units across the city organize. Specifically, goal teams, which consist of approximately ten staff members, are assigned to lead the implementation of strategies associated with each goal. Goal team members act as liaisons with their home departments, working with their department to identify deliverables and performance indicators. They are also expected to serve as "champions" for the goal within their departments. The Strategic Plan was updated in 2017 and again in 2019. Although the eight goals remained the same, changes were made to several specific strategies, and twenty "visionary initiatives" to be achieved by 2020 were added in 2017, followed by the 2019 addition of another five by 2025. Importantly, several of the Strategic Plan's updates explicitly incorporated strategies from "Resilient El Paso."

The implementation of the strategic planning process is ongoing and managed by a performance system administrator, who is part of the city manager's executive team. The administrator works with each goal team to specify a team leader who serves in a coordinator capacity by organizing meetings and following up with team members. Every goal team is responsible for identifying specific actions and measurement strategies to assess outcomes. Team leaders work with the performance system administrator to develop presentations of progress, which are provided quarterly to the city manager and annually to city council, prior to budget discussions. The city budget is explicitly linked to the Strategic Plan and is presented by goal rather than by department (City of El Paso 2017b).

As its name suggests, Goal 8 provides the structure for most of the city's actions related to sustainability. Seven city units are designated as participants around this goal: the City Manager's Office, Public Health, Streets and

Maintenance, Environmental Services, the Sun Metro transit service, Animal Services, and Community and Human Development—which has absorbed the previous Office of Resilience and Sustainability. Other potentially related departments such as water utilities, desalination, economic development, and parks and recreation are notably not included in the Goal 8 team. Representatives from each included department serve on the goal team and work with their home departments to achieve progress on the following nine specific strategies:

8.1 Deliver prevention, intervention, and mobilization services to promote a healthy, productive, and safe community.
8.2 Stabilize neighborhoods through community, housing, and Americans with Disabilities Act improvements.
8.3 Enhance animal services to ensure that El Paso's pets are provided a safe and healthy environment.
8.4 Reduce operational energy consumption.
8.5 Improve air quality throughout El Paso.
8.6 Provide long-term, cost-effective, sustainable, regional solid waste solutions.
8.7 Ensure community compliance with environmental regulatory requirements.
8.8 Improve community resilience through education, outreach, and the development of resilience strategy.
8.9 Enhance vector control and environmental education to provide a safe and healthy environment (City of El Paso 2017b).

In the 2018 adopted budget, $108 million, or 12 percent of the budget, was allocated to efforts and staff associated with Goal 8.

Strategic Plan Implementation as Integration

FCA problems associated with fuzzy boundaries, externalities, and the lack of overall accountability can be mitigated through the successful integration of government units. The "Resilient El Paso" plan sets forth goals and outlines strategic interventions to achieve the city's resiliency and sustainability objectives. However, it is a stand-alone document and was initially not linked to the city's Strategic Plan. Of the many plans that exist in the city of El Paso, it is the Strategic Plan that carries the most clout. It is the primary document that outlines city priorities, guides the city council and city manager's decisions on resource allocation, and shapes departments' functional activities. To better activate the "Resilient El Paso" plan, its strategies were folded into the city's Strategic Plan as part of the latter's 2017 update. In this regard, "Resilient El Paso" now lives within the Strategic Plan. "Resilient El Paso" goals have been embedded in five of the Strategic Plan's eight goals. The majority of sustainability-focused initiatives are positioned under Goal 8. Concurrently with the update of the Strategic Plan, "Resilient El Paso" was also amended to include the strategic planning goal teams designated to act as the lead for each of its initiatives. Thus, in their updates, these two documents have been made complementary.

There were multiple objectives behind this content integration. First, because many of the Strategic Plan's strategies focus on growth, this integration better ensures that resiliency is used as a framework for how El Paso views the relationship between economic development and environmental issues. Second, folding the resiliency strategies into the Strategic Plan also is intended to improve the efficiency of their implementation by providing a structure that reduces the transaction costs of bringing relevant parties together. Ensuring that resiliency—and, less directly, sustainability—is included in multiple areas across the Strategic Plan is itself a means to reduce challenges associated with achieving FCA.

Several features of the strategic planning process described in the previous section serve as mechanisms for reducing FCA challenges in the pursuit of the nine strategies associated with the "healthy, sustainable community" goal. First, by virtue of its cross-departmental membership, the goal team acts as a conduit for boundary-spanning conversations around sustainability. The requirement that team members work together to develop reports for the city manager and city council provides opportunity for substantive dialogue between engaged staff. Second, the fact that the Strategic Plan is tied to the budget process ensures that it is taken seriously. Four city departments are funded under Goal 8: Animal Services, Community and Human Development, Environmental Services, and Public Health (City of El Paso 2017b). These departments must, together, show progress in achieving a healthy, sustainable community, as operationalized by the underlying strategies, to justify their next year's budget allocation. Finally, the performance system administrator's engagement in the process may further reduce FCA challenges within the goal team while also serving as a link to the larger city organization.

Assessing Network-Based Sustainability Administration in El Paso

The use of a Strategic Plan–based network structure in El Paso is relatively new. For the majority of the years El Paso has been pursuing sustainability as a goal, a lead unit was in place and used a relationship-and-bargaining-based approach to work toward citywide buy-in around sustainability. As described by the former chief sustainability officer, "I would approach a department head with an idea and say, 'It's something other cities have been doing. What do you think?' If they gave me the cold shoulder, I would move on. But if they were interested, we continued. We spearheaded energy retrofits only with the blessing of the department manager in charge." Although this yielded mixed results across departments, there was sufficient buy-in to make substantial progress. Additionally, the chief sustainability officer was a clear policy champion for sustainability in the city who used his platform to promote related efforts: "A lot of my job was cheerleading. I bragged about sustainability. I had fifteen minutes in new employee training where I bragged about sustainability in El Paso and then asked them to help to do more."

Although this earlier approach appeared, by and large, to be effective, three dynamics contributed to the change. The first was the loss of the long-term and well-respected sustainability champion in the city government and his replacement by someone who was both new to the organization and whose primary focus was on a different issue (resiliency). The second was the election of a city council and the selection of a new city manager who prioritized efficiency as a primary public value. The third and related dynamic is that, on the whole, the El Paso public appears ambivalent to sustainability and does not provide an external check on the government to ensure that it is following through on stated plans. Thus, there was little community outcry when the sustainability office was first absorbed and later dissolved.

That said, although there is no longer a dedicated unit for sustainability, efforts in its pursuit have not altogether stopped. Whether a Strategic Plan–based network structure is effective in resolving FCA challenges around sustainability, and whether the resulting efforts are more or less successful under this arrangement, are pivotal and open questions. Although it is too soon to answer definitively, there is reason to think that the changes to El Paso's administrative structure have diluted its sustainability efforts and resulted in them being less about the big picture. Early on, as articulated in "The Livable City Sustainability Plan," El Paso's sustainability initiatives focused on long-term, community-wide and region-wide issues. In more recent years, which saw the establishment of the Office of Resilience and Sustainability and the appointment of a CRO, broad sustainability principles continued to underpin initiatives and served as guideposts for their evaluation. However, with the latest round of changes including the absorption of resiliency into the Department of Community and Human Development, sustainability is less front and center than it once was. The current initiatives tied to the Strategic Plan also reflect a more operational and less ambitious stance.

A decentralized network structure with no clear lead may offer some advantages to implementation in El Paso. It necessitates high levels of horizontal dialogue among government units and may result in greater buy-in and support. The idea that, via a decentralized network, collective action can be achieved by embedding the principle of sustainability across all city units is compelling. However, caution is warranted to hedge against the possibility that coherent and comprehensive efforts are not simply replaced by a series of uncoordinated operational tweaks undertaken by departments.

Overview of Sustainability Efforts in Gainesville, Florida

Since the 1970s, Gainesville Regional Utilities (GRU), the city's municipally owned electric and water utility, has established itself as a leader in renewable energy generation and energy conservation. In the early 2000s, with the backing of a "sustainability-minded" city commission and manager, the larger city government also became involved in complementary climate protection and environmental sustainability efforts. Gainesville was an early member of ICLEI's Cities for Climate Protection campaign, and in 2005 the city pledged to reduce greenhouse gas emissions (GHG) by signing the U.S. Conference of Mayors' Climate Protection Agreement. It subsequently established a sustainability goal of reducing community-wide GHG emissions to 7 percent below 1990 levels by 2012. This goal was achieved by 2013, largely by increasing the use of renewable energy and by improving energy, water, and power generation efficiency (City of Gainesville 2012).

The city's largest employer—the University of Florida—has complemented the city's efforts by becoming a hub of science and engineering innovation to tackle energy- and sustainability-related issues. In 2016 the university signed a memorandum of understanding with the city to improve collaboration on environmental stewardship and the application of "smart city" technologies. The agreement includes other quality-of-life improvements for city residents, particularly those of poorer neighborhoods with fewer amenities and services.

Although sustainability was pursued using a decentralized team-based approach that rested on the idea that everybody should own the value, in practice GRU largely carried the mantle of environmental sustainability in Gainesville for the past few decades. It acted as a policy champion and was the de facto entity responsible for designing and implementing a majority of the city's renewable energy and efficiency programs. In recent years, however, GRU has stepped back from its leadership role and the city government as a whole is pursuing sustainability with less gusto. Since about 2015, the policy direction of the city commission and city manager has been oriented toward achieving development, economic growth, and cost saving. This, in turn, has crowded out some of the previous sustainability initiatives aimed at energy efficiency and conservation and has chipped away at the shared understanding of sustainability across the city government.

As with El Paso, however, changes in priorities and leadership structure do not necessarily mean relevant efforts have altogether stopped. For example, recent initiatives to define Gainesville as a "New American City" are aimed at encouraging greater collaboration across units within city government itself (City of Gainesville 2019, 3). The initiative has resulted in a reorganization of departments and the city commission's adoption of a strategic planning framework that places citizens more at the center of budget and policy decisions. This has elevated discussions around how to best to deliver services and address pressing environmental, social, and economic issues of the community. Additionally, at the time of our research, Gainesville was in the process of hiring its first ever sustainability manager. This position was intended to be located in the Public Works Department and its responsibilities relatively narrow in scope, generally overseeing waste management and recycling programs. As a result, the new position did not suggest an immediate shift away from a decentralized network approach; rather, it would likely be left to individual departments to define sustainability and carry it out through their daily administrative functions. Figure 7.3 illustrates Gainesville's organizational structure, and Appendix K offers a more detailed overview of the community context.

Municipal Utility as a Sustainability Leader

Before 2005, sustainability and energy conservation was the exclusive responsibility of the utility. Thus, for many years, sustainability was pursued by this single functional unit and generating broader collective action around it was not a consideration. GRU was established in 1912 and is now the fifth largest municipally owned utility in Florida. It serves approximately ninety-three thousand customers with electric, natural gas, water, wastewater, and telecommunications services. In addition to being a direct service provider to city residents and businesses, GRU is also a significant financial contributor to the city of Gainesville. It provides nearly $37 million annually to the city's general fund and also helps pay costs associated with the city's vehicle fleet and human resources and legal services departments. This means the city's long-term financial stability is inexorably tied to GRU's financial prospects (City of Gainesville 2015; Anderson 2016).

Organizationally, in accordance with the city of Gainesville charter, GRU reports directly to the Gainesville city commission. GRU's general manager for utilities is appointed by and serves at the will of the commission.

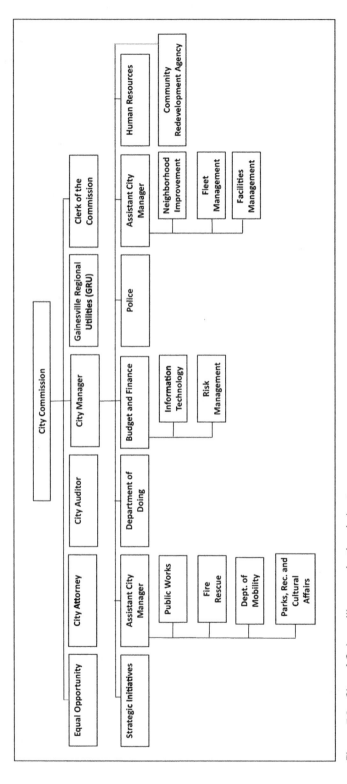

Figure 7.3 City of Gainesville organizational chart

To more fully engage the community at large, the city commission established a seven-member utility advisory board in 2016. The board advises the commissioners on policy and governance decisions related to the utility services. In 2018, a local ballot measure that would have changed GRU's governance from being overseen by the city commission to a newly created Gainesville Regional Utilities Authority, with five members appointed by the city commission, was defeated by 60 percent of the vote. As a result, the direct link between the GRU and city commission was reinforced. Since GRU reports directly to the city commission and is not under the control of the city manager, coordination with the majority of other city government units, which are under manager control, is more complicated.

Both because of the reporting structure and the strong financial link between GRU and the city, GRU's policies related to promoting sustainability are highly intertwined with political decision making. One example of this was experienced in 2003, when utility staff recommended the construction of a new 220-megawatt coal power plant to meet the region's growing electricity demand. This recommendation was met with public opposition and initiated a community conversation about ways to diversify the utility's energy generation portfolio and reduce the city's overall GHG emissions (Queiroz, Najafi, and Hanrahan 2017). One outcome has been a significant increase in GRU's energy efficiency and conservation-oriented programing. With urging from the city commission, between 2006 and 2013, GRU spent approximately $32 million on rebates, marketing, personnel, and maintenance, all related to efficiency. The conversation eventually culminated in the city commission voting down the proposed power plant and, in 2009, adopting the first feed-in-tariff policy in the United States. The feed-in tariff allowed the GRU to purchase renewable electric energy from distributed generators. Specifically, GRU electric customers could invest in solar photovoltaic systems and sell the electricity that they produced directly to the utility under a contract for twenty years at a fixed price (Queiroz, Najafi, and Hanrahan 2017). The feed-in tariff was adopted in addition to an already existing net metering policy and was paid for by a small increment added to electricity bills. The GRU saw a 2,600 percent increase in solar capacity during the first two years of this policy (Queiroz, Najafi, and Hanrahan 2017).

One of the city's most important—and controversial—decisions to increase its use of renewable energy and achieve greater diversity in its fuel mix was entering into a long-term contractual commitment to the Gainesville Renewable Energy Center (GREC) biomass generation facility. The $2.1 billion 102.5-megawatt facility is fueled by "a plentiful supply" of local wood waste generated by paper and timber industries and urban users (Gainesville Regional Utilities, n.d.). Critics argued that the city's single-minded focus on sustainability resulted in poorly planned and costly investment decisions. The thirty-year contract GRU signed with GREC has been assessed as one of the worst biomass deals in the nation (Caplan 2018). Approximately 30 percent of GRU's energy now comes from the facility, but part of the community's pullback of support for sustainability can be traced to this controversial decision.

Construction on the facility began in 2011, and the plant began commercial operations in December 2013. The city's long-term commitment to biofuel was poorly timed, as it occurred just before the costs of fossil-fuel-based energy plummeted. The result was a long-term commitment for the city to purchase energy from the GREC biomass facility at a cost much higher than energy produced by conventional fuels. Because the city locked in to energy purchases at high costs, energy bills for customers have been some of the highest in the state; residential electricity rate in Gainesville as of 2019 was 12.93 cents per kilowatt-hour, which was 13 percent greater than the Florida average rate, and the commercial electricity rate (14.07 cents per kilowatt-hour) was 46 percent higher than the state average. As a result, GRU managers identify reducing electricity costs for residents through, for example, cost-effective renewable energy alternatives like rooftop solar, as a main policy goal. The city's transition to alternative energy has been facilitated by the rapid decline in solar system costs and the feed-in tariff for solar energy production.

As the above examples show, for many years Gainesville's city-owned utility was the leader in the city's energy and environmental sustainability efforts. However, it proceeded in a narrow and functionally insular way. Although GRU regularly interacted with the city commission and administrative leaders, it did not assume the role typical to sustainability leads of trying to coordinate efforts or encourage participation from different units across the city government. The scope of Gainesville's sustainability did increase somewhat after the city signed the U.S. Mayors' Climate Protection Agreement; relevant efforts expanded outside of the confines of the utility. For example, traffic management and land conservation initiatives were led by other units under the umbrella of GHG reduction and were linked together through participation in informal sustainability teams.

Decentralized Administration of Sustainability in Gainesville

Although the city's strategic plan mentions three pillars of sustainability, the city has not adopted a stand-alone sustainability plan, and the city government does not have a sustainability unit or broadly focused sustainability coordinator. Outside of the renewable energy and energy efficiency measures managed by GRU, sustainability-related efforts are not coordinated by a single, centralized unit but rather are dispersed and housed under different roofs, including Parks, Recreation and Cultural Affairs, Public Works, Community Redevelopment Agency (CRA), Fleet Management, and the Department of Doing. One interviewee observed that sustainability is "considered as one of the key community values across city departments," and employees are described as generally sharing a common understanding about sustainability as a way to improve quality of life, livability, walkability, and quality of the natural environment.

In the absence of citywide or formalized sustainability coordination, attention to social and environmental sustainability varies tremendously across departments. Some departments, such as Public Works, have consistently held sustainability as a primary consideration. The new public works sustainability manager is tasked with planning, managing, and providing leadership for the solid waste program, zero waste initiative, recycling program, yard waste program, and commercial waste program. However, it is not a citywide or cross-department position. Other city departments whose actions can affect sustainability outcomes do not have supportive positions or mechanisms in place. As a result, even if sustainability is a value shared across employees, the attention and prioritization they give to it is inconsistent and often reflects the particular interests and preferences of division managers. This has led to community-wide sustainability initiatives being implemented on a case-by-case basis. For example, Gainesville's CRA does not maintain ongoing relationships with other city units around sustainability, but it makes connections with them as the need arises, such as when it helped build the city's Depot Park on a remediated brownfield site. During this process the CRA collaborated with other departments, including Parks, Recreation and Cultural Affairs, Economic Development, and Public Works. Although these units may not share a single articulated vision for Gainesville's overall sustainability, they coordinated and engaged in a process of learning and mutual adjustment during project implementation.

Empowered by a sustainability-minded commission, former city manager Russell Blackburn embarked on an aggressive sustainability agenda in the early 2000s. He worked to develop a culture of sustainability by tasking and resourcing a well-respected assistant city manager (ACM) to lead the sustainability effort and coordinate the city's functional agencies in pursuit of this goal. Through the ACM's office, the city's relevant departments and functional units were organized informally as teams. There was not a formal sustainability office or agency, yet under the ACM, a strong network of interdepartmental communication and reinforcement developed around initiatives related to reducing the city's carbon footprint. This process led to development of new efforts including a green building policy and residential solar incentives. Under this regime, the approach to sustainability was decentralized and team oriented, and external organizations were engaged through these informal teams. Although collaboration was emphasized, the ACM also encouraged interagency competition, which was seen as enhancing innovation and effort toward collective goals.

Following the Great Recession, there was a renewed promotion of economic interests in the city. With the election of a more pro-development commission, policy interests shifted to trying to balance sustainability and economic development goals. Policies that reduced energy costs remained in good favor, but sustainability actions that drew resources from other activities, or were considered overly regulatory or burdensome to businesses, were examined critically by the commission. Subsequently, although city managers and agency directors were described by interviewees as still generally supportive, consistent with the commission's preferences, they have not prioritized sustainability within the organization to the degree that it had been previously. The result has been less progress on sustainability objectives compared to the previous decade. The active involvement of economic development interests in the community, coupled with changes in elected city leadership, crowded out sustainability as a priority and constrained new initiatives from being developed. Gainesville has not necessarily lost its sustainability focus; the strong sustainability policies earlier enacted have not been significantly expanded in recent years, but, for the most part, they have not been rolled back significantly, either.

Citizen-Centered Government and Strategic Framing as Integration Mechanisms

Between 2015 and 2018, the city underwent changes in the executive office. The city manager, who had held this position for ten years, resigned in 2015, and Anthony Lyons, who was appointed interim and later city manager, resigned in 2018. As city manager, Lyons initiated, with the support from the mayor, a strategic planning process to define Gainesville as a "New American City."

The strategic planning process began in 2015 with the establishment of a twenty-three-member Blue Ribbon Advisory Committee for Economic Competitiveness, with the goal of making Gainesville "the most user friendly" and the "most citizen-centric city in the world" (City of Gainesville 2016, 7). To complement the committee's work, the city launched in early 2016 the Gainesville Creative Series, which engaged the community at large in the redesign of the city's strategic framework. Four guiding questions emerged from this process and formed the basis for a new citizen-centered approach to city service delivery: How can the city become a community model for the world, plan for a better future, foster greater equity, and support a strong economic environment?

As a result of this process, Lyons reorganized and renamed functional agencies throughout the city to reflect a customer-service orientation. For example, several existing departments were reconfigured to form the new Department of Doing. Reflecting the push for greater economic activity, the department is intended to facilitate development activity by housing together long-range planning, building services, and zoning, as well as a new strategic customer experience team. Collectively the department is expected to facilitate "a cooperative approach to helping citizens start or grow a business" (City of Gainesville, n.d.b). The city manager also created a new Strategic Initiatives Department, which brought together the divisions and offices of economic development and innovation, communications and marketing, intergovernmental affairs, strategic planning, and Citizen-Centered Gainesville. Since its inception, the Strategic Initiatives Department has largely focused on conducting outreach to the community and improving government responsiveness and accessibility.

Community development has become a more important player in the reconfigured governance arrangement, with the CRA now reporting directly to the city manager rather than being under one of the assistant managers. The CRA is funded by both the city and the county, and its work somewhat overlaps with the work of other city departments, such as Parks, Recreation, and Cultural Affairs and Public Works. Economic Development was subsequently moved from Strategic Initiatives in 2018 and is housed within the Department of Doing.

Sustainability is not an explicit part of the New American City initiative; however, its focus on economic development, some of which is aimed at addressing local economic disparities, taps into certain of its dimensions. Economic inequality in Gainesville falls along racial and geographic lines, which separate the city into clear east and west sides. The New American City initiative and the administrative reorganization that accompanied it may ultimately increase FCA around economic and equity-oriented objectives.

Concluding Assessment

Gainesville is not necessarily disadvantaged by its use of a decentralized sustainability structure and its lack of formal integration mechanisms. A decentralized structure can enhance the ability to deliver services in a timely and relevant fashion. This was especially true in the early 2000s when the GRU and select other units pursued actions associated with their own brand of sustainability. One interviewee identified a philosophy of Gaines-ville's decentralized approach as "attempting to solve more problems," whereby individual departments come up with diverse solutions and ideas, and they try to see "what works and what does not." This reflects a trial-and-error approach in learning and meeting the expectations of the community.

At the same time, some agency leaders recognized the city's decentral-ized approach to sustainability as a weakness that increases the difficulty of coherent messaging and acquiring and maintaining financial and relevant professional capacity. It was also described as a barrier to coordination and cooperation on sustainability initiatives, which are not consistent across the city government and absent for some units. When cooperative projects among units do proceed, they usually are ad hoc and/or grounded in the personal relationships that exist between certain department directors.

Although economic growth is the priority, social and environmental sustainability and enhancing community value were also identified as im-portant in Gainesville. Interviewees agreed that the city's sustainability pri-orities are often determined with input from residents, who place particular value on community authenticity, representation of their ethnic back-grounds, revitalizing urban areas, and the conservation of public parks.

Several interviewees noted that interest in sustainability from Gaines-ville's political and managerial leadership has been critical in shaping how it is administered. Past political support and the former city managers' ini-tiatives have resulted in sustainable practices being a routine part of opera-tions for certain units. However, compartmentalizing responsibility for sustainability means there is less room for interagency initiatives and more room for discretion about whether to pursue it as an objective at all. One interviewee noted, "All the general government units except the charter of-ficers are separately pursuing sustainability"; but another suggested that although "each department has specific [sustainability] projects, and de-partments share resources if they have a common project, there is not a lot of coordination and not an overarching approach." Within this decentral-ized structure, enthusiasm appears to have waned as priorities shifted and the customer-service approach supplanted the informal norms of govern-mental operation. Gainesville's administrative reorganization, most notably the focus on citizen-centered government, provided a basis for integration to occur, albeit without sustainability as an overarching theme or it being embedded in the administrative structure as occurred in El Paso.

One conclusion from examining the cases of El Paso and Gainesville together is that the success of a decentralized structure may be contingent on the prioritization of sustainability by city leadership. Where sustainabil-ity goals are salient, informal norms, expectations and incentives re-ward innovation and interagency collaboration. Informal norms are less constraining, yet they can be more powerful in influencing behavior than formal rules. Under the right set of circumstances, a self-organized approach to collective action through decentralized networks can enhance communication and enable participants to engage in meaningful development plans and actions, thereby facilitating mutual interests. Yet even self-organizing systems operate in the shadow of authority (McCabe and Feiock 2005; Feiock and Scholz 2010). Absent leadership, the informal rules, agreements, and norms that undergird sustainability are easily crowded out. Thus, a decentralized structure may not provide a stable and durable base for sustainability in the absence of a formalized sustainability unit.

8

A Closer Look at Interdepartmental
Relationships and Network Structures
around Sustainability in Select Cities

core objective of this book is to generate a better understanding of how local governments overcome barriers caused by institutional fragmentation to work toward integrative solutions for sustainability. This line of inquiry is driven by the broad observation that cities are assuming a greater policy-making role in a variety of complex and boundary-spanning public problems. Separate responses from individual governments or agencies is often no longer sufficient to address the issues most relevant to urban residents. The onus is now on cities to figure out how to work collectively across a range of jurisdictions and entities. This is true both across local organizations and across functional units within a single city government. The former has received considerable attention in the existing literature, whereas the latter is a newer area of inquiry and a focus of this book.

This chapter introduces social network analysis as a third methodological approach with which to examine the administrative responses to functional fragmentation within city governments. Network analysis augments the quantitative nationwide analysis (presented in Chapter 2) and the in-depth city case studies (presented in Chapters 4 through 7), and enables a triangulation of methods and data that helps ensure the validity of our findings. It also offers unique empirical insights. The network studies specify patterns of intracity relationships that exist between offices and departments around sustainability initiatives and provide quantitative evidence for some of the integrative dynamics described qualitatively in the case studies. Perhaps most notably, many of the case studies emphasize the role that the lead or headquarters unit plays in facilitating coordination between other units. Network analysis provides another way to assess and visualize the lead unit's impact as a connector within the city government.

The next section briefly introduces the concept of policy networks and the fundamental elements of their structure. This is followed by an overview of the relationship between the structural attributes of policy networks and functional collective action (FCA). The analytical portion of the chapter presents our data collection strategy and the results of the intracity network analyses conducted around the issue of sustainability in three cities: Fort Collins, Colorado; Kansas City, Missouri; and Orlando, Florida. The results we share are primarily descriptive. This descriptive approach enables examination and comparison of the three cities' networks on specific characteristics. Additionally, we use the descriptive network analysis to examine the relative importance of individual functional units in each city on this issue. This enables the identification of the most important actors, core partners, and peripheral players in each city government. The descriptive results provide a foundation for relating administrative structure to sustainability outcome. The chapter concludes with a discussion of the network analysis findings in the context of the case studies and identifies new insights available through their joint consideration.

The Role and Importance of Policy Networks

Policy making and governance occur in environments that are inherently relational, where the decisions and actions of relevant actors necessarily affect and are affected by others (McClurg and Young 2011). The term "policy network" is often used to describe the set of relationships that exist among interdependent actors whose policy actions are "knitted together to focus on common problems" and to achieve collective goals (Schneider et al. 2003, 143–144). Holistically, policy networks contain actors, the relationships between them, the rules that govern those relationships, and the resources that are exchanged (Scott and Ulibarri 2019). By providing a structural element to policy making, networks function as a mechanism to shape these exchanges (Hanf and Scharpf 1978; Knoke and Yang 2008).

Mark Lubell and colleagues describe policy networks as "meso-level arrangements" that hold a mediator position between higher-level institutions and lower-level individual behavior—shaping and being shaped by both (2012, 354). Within municipal governments, formal administrative arrangements often determine the units responsible for planning and delivering public goods and services. These arrangements—in combination with the rules and bureaucratic processes that guide how decisions are made and institutionalize certain channels of access or communication—play an important role in establishing the structural characteristics of a policy network. At the same time, actors in a policy network are embedded within a web of social relationships (Granovetter 1985), which are also important in shaping network structure. According to David Knoke and Song Yang, a key value-added quality of the network perspective is the fact that it "simultaneously encompasses both structures and entities, it provides conceptual and methodological tools for linking changes in microlevel choices and macrolevel structural alterations" (2008, 6).

As described throughout this book, cities use formal administrative structures to manage the daily activities of staff and organize their responsibilities. This is illustrated by local government organizational charts, most of which reveal a clear hierarchical governing system. Even if units share general objectives, the degree of power and autonomy they have to pursue the objectives may be quite uneven. Units also are likely to differ in their core responsibilities, organizational cultures, and the constituencies they must satisfy (O'Leary and Vij 2012). In this context, policy networks can assist in smoothing out differences that emerge during processes of implementation. The lines of communication and relationships that comprise them also assist in generating buy-in and support from units that may be wary of change or resistant to taking on new responsibilities for initiatives that do not fit within their core functions.

Networks are able to capture the complexity of institutional systems, and thus provide an important lens through which to study government and management. The network perspective shifts focus away from individual actors and organizations toward the relationships that exist between them (Scott and Ulibarri 2019). In this respect they are particularly well suited to capture the dynamics of collaboration and collective action and link neatly to related theories. Since most sustainability challenges span functional and geographic boundaries, they are often unable to be comprehensively addressed by a single organizational unit acting alone. Policy networks reflect theories and models of governance that situate responsibility for the resolution of complex policy issues within the overlapping relationships that exist among multiple actors—be they individuals, organizations, governments, or functional units. The structure of relations among actors is a central feature of policy networks and, in this chapter, it also serves as the basis for describing the resolution of FCA dilemmas.

An Overview of Network Structures

We present descriptive findings from a series of network analyses capturing patterns of interdepartmental interactions around sustainability as they occur within three U.S. city governments. The following overview of network fundamentals will assist in the interpretation of the results for readers unfamiliar with this methodological approach.

Networks are comprised of two main elements: actors, or "nodes," and the ties or links between them. Any pairs of actors in a network are known as "dyads," which may or may not be linked together. The links represent relationships, which can take many forms and serve, for example, as channels for communication and for the exchange of information and other policy-relevant resources (Kenis and Schneider 1991). The structure of these relationships—that is, regular patterns in their presence or absence—is of chief importance. Reflecting this, Knoke and Yang (2008) identify three assumptions that underlie network analysis. First, the structure of relationships that exist in a network offers primary insight to understanding observed behaviors and outcomes; even more than the attributes of particular actors. Second, the existing patterns of social relationships shape the thoughts and actions of actors. And third, these relationships are dynamic and so may change over time. From this perspective, the network that exists within a local government shapes the actions of particular units and may determine overall sustainability policy development, implementation, and outcomes.

Characteristics of the overall network structure, including its size and density, are often associated with particular outcomes. The size of the network—how many different actors it encompasses—affects the structure of social relations because of the limited capacity that each actor has for building and maintaining larger numbers of ties. Complexity also increases with size. Network density, or the percent of *possible* ties between all actors in a network for which *actual* ties exist, is another related characteristic. Network density can serve as a proxy for the breadth of integration within a network (Milward and Provan 1998) and provide clues to the speed at which information is likely to diffuse among the actors.

As part of the process of using social network analysis to conceptualize relational linkages and interpret their implications, it is also informative to consider the attributes of individual actors. For example, each actor can be characterized by a variety of centrality measures that consider their positions in the overall network and refer to how well connected each actor is, relative to other members of the network. Each centrality measure, in turn, is theoretically associated with particular characteristics or abilities, such as having a prominent reputation or control over information flow (Knoke and Yang 2008).

The simplest centrality measure is *degree centrality,* which is a count of the direct ties an actor has to all others in a network. Actors with high degree centrality tend to be viewed as prominent or visible in a network. *Betweenness centrality* is a second common centrality measure. Betweenness centrality measures how often an actor lies in the "geodesic path" or short-est distance between other actors who are themselves disconnected. Actors with high betweenness centrality link these less connected segments of the network with each other and often play an important role in information sharing and in introducing new ideas to different parts of the network (Knoke and Yang 2008). Actors with high betweenness tend to have the most holistic view of an issue (Prell, Hubacek, and Reed 2009). Although other centrality measures exist, we posit that degree and betweenness centrality have the most relevance for examining intracity relationships in the context of FCA. This case is made in more detail later in the chapter.

How a Network Approach Helps Explain Functional Collective Action

Both the horizontal and functional forms of the institutional collective action framework introduced in Chapter 3 evoke network perspectives and draw attention to theoretical explanations regarding their emergence and impact. Governance research often applies networks as a lens to study interactions between actors representing distinct organizations, agencies, jurisdictions, or stakeholder groups around a particular issue. We modify this conventional approach by applying network theory and methodology to look *within* individual city governments. The expectation is that, by capturing the full picture of interactions taking place between city departments around sustainability, patterns may emerge that will identify and enhance understanding of the specific ways cities confront FCA challenges.

In Chapter 3, we argue that externalities, transaction costs, and fuzzy boundaries inhibit the relevant functional units within a city government from working together to achieve comprehensive and integrated policy responses. Local governments—sometimes intentionally and other times by default—assume one of four organizational arrangements to mitigate this dynamic: lead agency consolidation, lead agency coordination, relationships and bargaining, and decentralized networks. Each of these is complemented by a variety of formal and informal mechanisms (i.e., discrete plans, procedures, structures, or norms) that also aid integration. Policy networks, and the set of structural relationships and exchanges they entail, can and do emerge across all four organizational arrangements.

Many of the challenges faced within city governments around the implementation of policy initiatives are "low-risk coordination" dilemmas (Feiock 2013, 408), in which there is underlying goal agreement on sustainability but a lack of relevant knowledge on how to proceed inhibits action.

This may be exacerbated by the presence of what Ronald Burt (1992, 2004) refers to as "structural holes" within the policy network, whereby actors who are endowed with a unique set of resources are disconnected from those who need these resources for completing a task. To mitigate these problems, a functional unit may serve as the go-between for pairs of actors and facilitate communication distribution by linking units that might otherwise be disconnected from the larger network. An actor in this position (i.e., a "broker") has significant information about the range of activities and resources of other units within the network and control over how that information is spread (Wasserman and Faust 1994). For example, in a city government, one group of actors may communicate regularly on transportation issues, whereas other sets of actors may engage on issues of social equity and energy efficiency, with minimal member overlap. In such a situation, a broker may serve as an effective bridge between these otherwise disconnected groups, enabling the development of more-comprehensive sustainability policy.

Finally, collaborations are embedded in a specific policy context, and the behavior of potential partners is influenced by that context (Isett et al. 2011). Understanding the characteristics of the network nodes complements the understanding of the overall network structure. Certain actors have outsized influence shaping the ongoing development of relationships and collaborative processes among others within the network. Within a local government, actors with a high degree of formal authority, such as the mayor, the manager, and directors of large departments, are obvious key actors. However, a network perspective enables us to identify other influential actors whose prominence is not based on their formal title or position in the hierarchy but is a result of their relationships to others in the organization. By linking formal administrative structures to the relationships that exist between functional units and collective action outcomes, the network lens offers insight into FCA that, until now, has largely been untapped.

Data Collection and Analysis

We use network analysis to examine the interactions that occur between functional units in three city governments around issues of sustainability: Fort Collins, Colorado; Kansas City, Missouri; and Orlando, Florida. As the following section describes in more detail, the data collection involved staff from every department across the city government completing a rather lengthy network survey. Although attempts were made to do this in all the cities highlighted as case studies, we were only successful in achieving a sufficiently high response rate in three of them. It is perhaps not a coincidence that these cities each have lead sustainability units with relatively high authority and reflect administrative arrangements characterized as lead agency consolidation and lead agency coordination. Although this results in a more limited picture than is ideal, it still provides a novel look at the structure of relations used in these cities to overcome FCA challenges.

Establishing Network Boundaries

Clearly specifying boundaries is essential for understanding the structural characteristics of relationships among a group of actors in a network analysis (Kenis and Schneider 1991). We define the boundaries of the potential policy network in each city as the universe of functional units within the city government. Functional units are the offices, divisions, or departments in a city government tasked with specific substantive service delivery responsibility; in other words, they are responsible for more than administration. Functional units serve as the actors or nodes in the network analyses presented in this chapter.

As a first step to identifying all functional units in the city governments, we reviewed the city's website, organization chart, and budget documents to create a list of units responsible for service delivery, regardless of whether the entity was involved in sustainability. Certain entities that may be listed in these documents that do not appear to be functional units according to our definition, such as "debt services" or "benefits," were excluded. Most of the functional units are located at the division or office level, but the extent to which we drilled down was determined on a case-by-case basis. The list of each city's functional units compiled from this review was provided to its sustainability contact, who was asked to verify the accuracy of the list and to make additions and deletions as necessary. The second column in Table 8.1 indicates the total number of functional units in each city. The sustainability contacts then identified any functional units that they determined were not in any way engaged in the city's sustainability efforts. These units did not receive the survey.

TABLE 8.1: NETWORK SURVEY DISTRIBUTION AND RESPONSE RATES

City	Total number of functional units	Functional units receiving the survey	Number of responding functional units	Percentage of responding functional units
Kansas City	72	63	44	69.8%
Fort Collins	41	41	26	63.5%
Orlando	56	39	20	51.2%

Data Collection and Assessment Approach

Data were collected via an online survey administered separately in each city. An invitation and link to an electronic survey was emailed directly to a representative, typically the manager or director, of each functional unit identified. The survey instruments were customized to reflect the functional units present in each of the three cities but were otherwise identical. The instruments started by asking each respondent which department, division, and/or office they represent. They then were provided with a fixed list of the city's functional units and were asked to identify those that their own unit had "worked with (e.g., shared information, data or advised) to advance the city's sustainability efforts in the past year." This "fixed list" approach allowed survey respondents to recognize rather than recall their relationships with other units in the city. As noted in Table 8.1, there is a difference between the total number of functional units in each city and the total number of units that received the survey. To account for the possibility that a survey respondent had worked with a unit not receiving the survey, the fixed list presented to the survey recipients included all functional units in the city. The length of the surveys varied considerably across the cities, reflecting the number of functional units identified in each.

City-level response rates range from 51.2 (Orlando) to 69.8 percent (Kansas City). Missing data from nonresponses is a concern in network analysis. These response rates are lower than desired and reflect a limitation to the research. However, reciprocity between nodes is assumed, which helps minimize potential gaps.

For each city, we aggregated data from the completed surveys into a binary matrix representing the relationships reported. In each matrix, a "1" in a cell represents a link from actor i to actor j, whereby i represents the "ego," or the respondent's own functional unit, and j represents the "alter," or the reported functional unit. A "0" in a cell represents the absence of a link. This directed relationship from ego to alter was converted to a nondirected matrix, so if either actor reports a link, it is represented as a "1." We used UCINET analytical software to examine the structural properties of the whole system of interactions around sustainability in each city as well as the positions of the individual functional units within these systems. This allowed us to assess how specific actors are embedded in exchange relationships and the characteristics of the network in its entirety.

Descriptive Network Results

Using the survey data described above, this section first presents descriptive findings associated with the entire network system and then focuses in on actor-specific, or "egocentric," measures. For the former, we focus on simple measures of network centralization and density to show the overall extent and pattern of node connectivity. We also present sociograms, or network maps, which are visualizations of the relationships between actors in a bounded system, or, in our case, functional units in a city government. For the latter, we use degree and betweenness centrality measures as means of identifying key actors in the system.

Overall Network Results

Complete network measures of density and centralization speak to the general level of a network's compactness. They are complementary measures whereby density indicates the overall cohesion of a network and centralization indicates the extent to which this cohesion is organized around a few certain nodes. More specifically, density is the ratio of the number of *observed* links to the number of *possible* links in a network. Table 8.2 shows the density associated with the intracity networks around sustainability for the three cities. Of them, Fort Collins exhibits the highest network density, whereby approximately one-third of the unit-to-unit working relationships that *could* exist around its sustainability efforts are realized. The overall network density in Orlando and Kansas City are below 20 percent. Empirical studies find that, because they require resources, there is a limit to the number of meaningful relationships that can be sustained (Gonçalves, Perra, and Vespignani 2011). As a result, larger networks—such as those in Orlando and Kansas City—are less likely to have dense connections than smaller ones (e.g., Fort Collins) because of practical limits in the number of functional relationships that each unit can maintain with others.

Centralization is calculated as the difference in the centrality score of the most central actor and those of all other actors. In general terms, network centralization indicates the extent to which a network has a structural center. Lower levels of centralization indicate that fewer network members hold highly central positions, or, alternatively, positions of brokerage are shared by a larger number of members. In more highly centralized networks, the one or few actors that have a broad range of contacts can play a crucial role in the distribution of information or coordination of activities across the entire network. Reflecting this, centralized network structures

TABLE 8.2: WHOLE NETWORK MEASURES

	Orlando	Kansas City	Fort Collins
Network density	19.30%	17.50%	33.70%
Network centralization	69.87%	63.54%	67.12%

have been found to yield greater efficiency in collaborations and information sharing (Milward and Provan 1998; O'Leary and Vij 2012). However, centralized networks may also be more vulnerable to disruption, such as when a key actor is removed or temporarily unavailable (Bienenstock and Bonacich 2003). As shown in Table 8.2, all three city networks appear moderate to highly centralized, with centralization scores ranging between 63.5 and 69.87.

Sociograms, or network maps, offer a way to visualize and visually compare networks on these overall measures. Figures 8.1, 8.2, and 8.3 depict the structure of relationships that exist between functional units around sustainability issues in Orlando, Kansas City, and Fort Collins, respectively. In general, they show fairly well-connected networks, despite their modest overall density scores. The sociograms also reveal which units are more central actors and which are more on the periphery. In these images, the nodes representing functional units are sized by degree centrality, which is a simple count of the number of each unit's direct ties to other units (more detail about degree centrality is provided in the next section).

Egocentric Network Measures

The term "egocentric" refers to any network measure for individual actors in the network. Centrality (distinct from network centralization) is a widely used approach to understand the structural sources of an actor's advantage and disadvantage relative to other nodes in the network. Actors who are more central to social structures are more likely to be influential or powerful. Centrality has been approached in network analysis in a variety of distinct but related ways. In this chapter we focus on the two centrality measures that have the most theoretical relevance to FCA: degree centrality, which indicates how well connected an actor is within its local neighborhood, and betweenness centrality, which speaks to an actor's ability to bridge gaps between otherwise disconnected alters. Both offer ways to operationalize the importance of functional units in a city's network, but they differ in how the unit's structural position is measured.

Degree centrality refers to the number of ties a node has to other nodes. In the context of sustainability policy networks, it provides a way to identify government units that are "in the thick of things" (Freeman 1978, 221) and, presumably, are very active within the network. A high degree centrality score signals that a unit occupies a position with relatively high prominence and that it serves as an important source or conduit of information and resources. In contrast, units with low degree centrality scores are likely peripheral actors that maintain relatively few connections with other units related to sustainability. They thus are located spatially at the margins of the

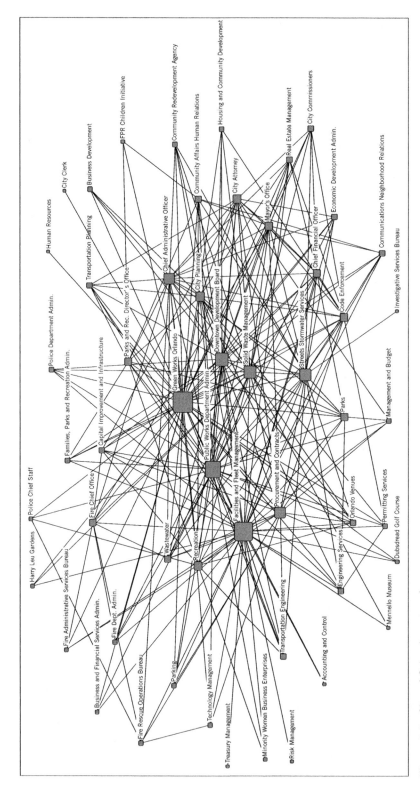

Figure 8.1 City of Orlando network map

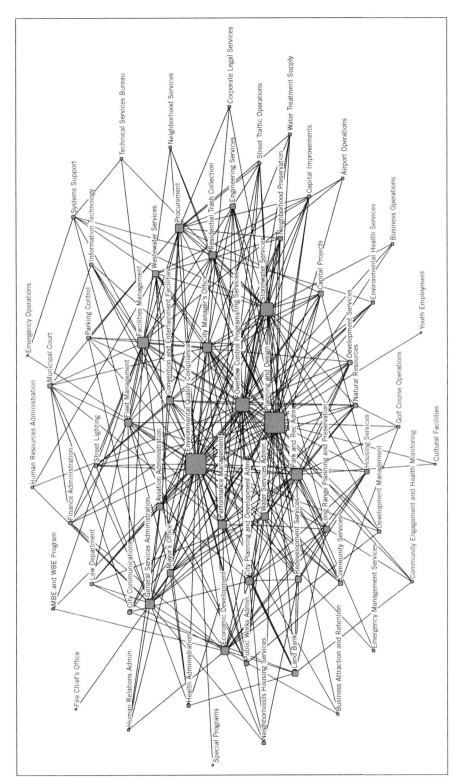

Figure 8.2 City of Kansas City network map

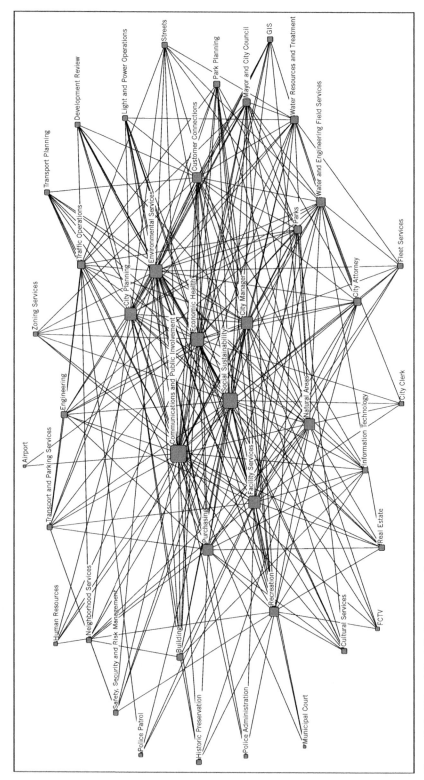

Figure 8.3 City of Fort Collins network map

policy network and are expected to have relatively little influence over other actors. Note that the centrality scores we employ can be compared between units within a single city. However, because the size of the networks differs for each city, the centrality scores cannot be compared across them. The sociograms provide a visual representation of each unit's relative degree centrality scores, and Appendix L provides the degree centrality score of each functional unit in the three policy networks.

We expect the lead sustainability unit in each city to have high degree centrality, since part of their core responsibilities include reaching out to other government units to encourage their involvement in relevant efforts. This expectation is supported by the results; in all three cities the sustainability lead has the highest or second highest degree centrality. Specifically, in Orlando, where the average number of direct ties a unit has to other units around sustainability is 12.5, Green Works Orlando has 45 ties to other units. The next most connected unit is Fleets and Facilities, with 40 direct ties. In Kansas City, the division of Planning and Design within the Parks and Recreation Department has the highest degree centrality score, with 49 direct links to other city units. The sustainability lead, the Office of Environmental Quality, has 48. Both of these are well above the citywide average of 10.8. In Fort Collins, when the three departments that comprise its consolidated lead are considered together, the Sustainability Services Area has the highest number of direct connections with other units. When its component departments are treated as separate units, the Communications and Public Involvement Office has the highest degree centrality (39), followed by Social Sustainability (35), Economic Health (30), and Environmental Services (30), respectively. The average degree centrality score for units in Fort Collins is 13.9.

The second measure we use, betweenness centrality, indicates the extent to which a node is connected to other nodes that are not directly connected to each other, measured as the number of times a node lies on the shortest path between other nodes. Actors with high betweenness centrality scores occupy important positions on communication paths and are thus seen as having influence over the flow of information within the network. Betweenness centrality tends to capture an actor's actual—rather than perceived— access to resources within the network (Freeman 1978). Work by Mark Granovetter (1973) and Burt (1992, 2004) demonstrates that by bridging ties between nodes and filling structural holes in the network, actors with high betweenness centrality assume positions that enable them to control the resources that move through the ties between nodes that they connect. Degree centrality and betweenness centrality are often highly correlated, and the lead sustainability unit in each city is expected to score relatively high on both measures. However, a unit's betweenness is not solely dependent on its own actions but is also shaped by the behaviors of its neighbors. If many units in a city work directly with one another on sustainability issues, rather than going through the lead, the betweenness centrality of even a well-connected lead will be reduced.

Betweenness scores are standardized and range from 0 to 100, with values closer to 100 indicating that the actor has relatively greater influence over what information and resources flow within the network (Wasserman and Faust 1994). The maximum value for betweenness is achieved when the focal actor is the center of a star network. In this scenario, no other nodes link directly with one another; rather, all directed communications between pairs of nodes go through the one positioned as the center of the network. Figures 8.4–8.6 show the betweenness centrality scores of the functional units in each city and their position within the city organizational structure.

In Orlando, as with degree centrality, results show two units—Green Works Orlando (27.316) and Facilities and Fleet Management (24.073)—with relatively high betweenness centrality scores. After these units, there is a significant drop-off. Solid Waste Management (4.814) and Streets and Stormwater Services (5.831), for instance, are two of a handful of marginal actors—that is, the set of nodes that cluster close to the center of the network based on a natural break in the distribution of the betweenness centrality score. Kansas City follows a similar pattern, wherein two units—Planning and Design (24.332) and the Office of Environmental Quality (22.468)—have betweenness scores that are much higher than all other units in the city. A handful of other units occupy a second tier with betweenness scores in the 5.0 to 7.0 range. In Fort Collins, the pattern is slightly different, with the Office of Communications and Public Involvement having, by a considerable margin, the highest betweenness score (16.898). It is followed by the Social Sustainability department (11.231). The other two Sustainability Services departments as well as Facility Services exhibit betweenness centrality scores in the range of 5.0 to 7.0.

Key Points from the Descriptive Network Analysis

The results of the two distinct approaches to network analysis—a whole network approach and an egocentric approach—provide insight into the structure of interactions between units, which serve as the building blocks for FCA. Since the presence of an influential lead agency characterizes the administrative arrangements used by the three cities examined, we expected those units to play prominent roles in each city's overall network. This expectation was largely borne out. In addition, the network analysis helps paint a more complete picture of how the units in each city are knitted together around sustainability.

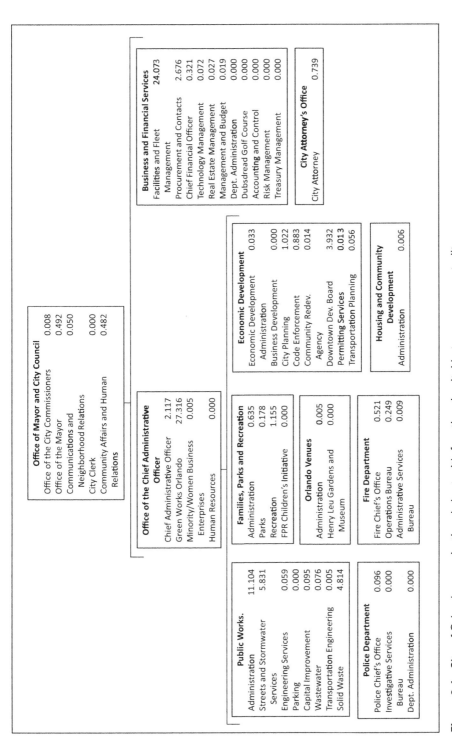

Office of Mayor and City Council

Office of the City Commissioners	0.008
Office of the Mayor	0.492
Communications and Neighborhood Relations	0.050
City Clerk	0.000
Community Affairs and Human Relations	0.482

Office of the Chief Administrative Officer

Chief Administrative Officer	2.117
Green Works Orlando	27.316
Minority/Women Business Enterprises	0.005
Human Resources	0.000

Families, Parks and Recreation

Administration	0.635
Parks	0.178
Recreation	1.155
FPR Children's Initiative	0.000

Orlando Venues

Administration	0.005
Henry Leu Gardens and Museum	0.000

Fire Department

Fire Chief's Office	0.521
Operations Bureau	0.249
Administrative Services Bureau	0.009

Public Works.

Administration	11.104
Streets and Stormwater Services	5.831
Engineering Services	0.059
Parking	0.000
Capital Improvement	0.095
Wastewater	0.076
Transportation Engineering	0.005
Solid Waste	4.814

Police Department

Police Chief's Office	0.096
Investigative Services Bureau	0.000
Dept. Administration	0.000

Business and Financial Services

Facilities and Fleet Management	24.073
Procurement and Contacts	2.676
Chief Financial Officer	0.321
Technology Management	0.072
Real Estate Management	0.027
Management and Budget	0.019
Dept. Administration	0.000
Dubsdread Golf Course	0.000
Accounting and Control	0.000
Risk Management	0.000
Treasury Management	0.000

City Attorney's Office

City Attorney	0.739

Economic Development

Economic Development Administration	0.033
Business Development	0.000
City Planning	1.022
Code Enforcement	0.883
Community Redev. Agency	0.014
Downtown Dev. Board	3.932
Permitting Services	0.013
Transportation Planning	0.056

Housing and Community Development

Administration	0.006

Figure 8.4 City of Orlando organizational chart with functional units' betweenness centrality scores

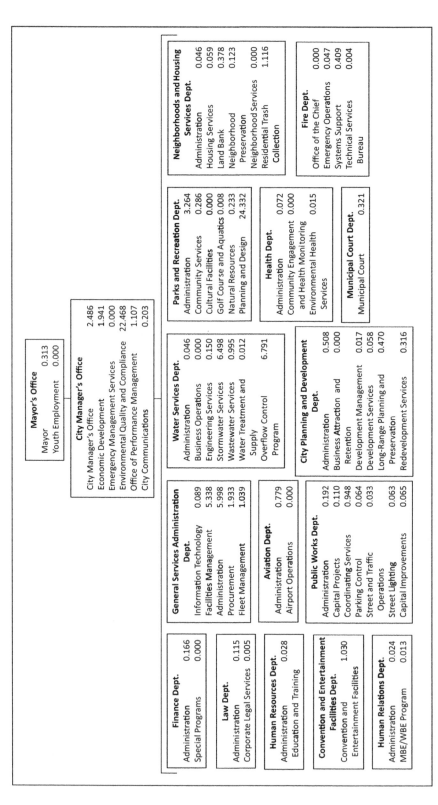

Mayor's Office

Mayor	0.313
Youth Employment	0.000

City Manager's Office

City Manager's Office	2.486
Economic Development	1.941
Emergency Management Services	0.000
Environmental Quality and Compliance	22.468
Office of Performance Management	1.107
City Communications	0.203

Finance Dept.

Administration	0.166
Special Programs	0.000

Law Dept.

Administration	0.115
Corporate Legal Services	0.005

Human Resources Dept.

Administration	0.028
Education and Training	

Convention and Entertainment Facilities Dept.

Convention and Entertainment Facilities	1.030

Human Relations Dept.

Administration	0.024
MBE/WBE Program	0.013

General Services Administration Dept.

Information Technology	0.089
Facilities Management	5.338
Administration	5.998
Procurement	1.933
Fleet Management	1.039

Aviation Dept.

Administration	0.779
Airport Operations	0.000

Public Works Dept.

Administration	0.192
Capital Projects	0.110
Coordinating Services	0.948
Parking Control	0.064
Street and Traffic Operations	0.033
Street Lighting	0.063
Capital Improvements	0.065

Water Services Dept.

Administration	0.046
Business Operations	0.000
Engineering Services	0.150
Stormwater Services	6.498
Wastewater Services	0.995
Water Treatment and Supply	0.012
Overflow Control Program	6.791

City Planning and Development Dept.

Administration	0.508
Business Attraction and Retention	0.000
Development Management	0.017
Development Services	0.058
Long-Range Planning and Preservation	0.470
Redevelopment Services	0.316

Parks and Recreation Dept.

Administration	3.264
Community Services	0.286
Cultural Facilities	0.000
Golf Course and Aquatics	0.008
Natural Resources	0.233
Planning and Design	24.332

Health Dept.

Administration	0.072
Community Engagement	0.000
Environmental Health and Health Monitoring Services	0.015

Municipal Court Dept.

Municipal Court	0.321

Neighborhoods and Housing Services Dept.

Administration	0.046
Housing Services	0.059
Land Bank	0.378
Neighborhood Preservation	0.123
Neighborhood Services	0.000
Residential Trash Collection	1.116

Fire Dept.

Office of the Chief	0.000
Emergency Operations	0.047
Systems Support	0.409
Technical Services Bureau	0.004

Figure 8.5 City of Kansas City organizational chart with functional units' betweenness centrality scores

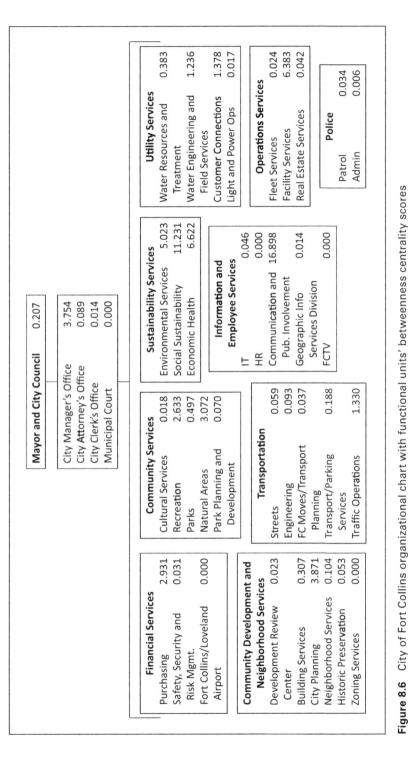

Mayor and City Council | 0.207

City Manager's Office | 3.754
City Attorney's Office | 0.089
City Clerk's Office | 0.014
Municipal Court | 0.000

Financial Services

Purchasing | 2.931
Safety, Security and Risk Mgmt. | 0.031
Fort Collins/Loveland Airport | 0.000

Community Development and Neighborhood Services

Development Review Center | 0.023
Building Services | 0.307
City Planning | 3.871
Neighborhood Services | 0.104
Historic Preservation | 0.053
Zoning Services | 0.000

Community Services

Cultural Services | 0.018
Recreation | 2.633
Parks | 0.497
Natural Areas | 3.072
Park Planning and Development | 0.070

Transportation

Streets | 0.059
Engineering | 0.093
FC Moves/Transport Planning | 0.037
Transport/Parking Services | 0.188
Traffic Operations | 1.330

Sustainability Services

Environmental Services | 5.023
Social Sustainability | 11.231
Economic Health | 6.622

Information and Employee Services

IT | 0.046
HR | 0.000
Communication and Pub. Involvement | 16.898
Geographic Info Services Division | 0.014
FCTV | 0.000

Utility Services

Water Resources and Treatment | 0.383
Water Engineering and Field Services | 1.236
Customer Connections | 1.378
Light and Power Ops | 0.017

Operations Services

Fleet Services | 0.024
Facility Services | 6.383
Real Estate Services | 0.042

Police

Patrol | 0.034
Admin | 0.006

Figure 8.6 City of Fort Collins organizational chart with functional units' betweenness centrality scores

Viewing the networks in their entirety, a first observation from the results is that all three exhibit relatively modest densities: 34 percent in Fort Collins and under 20 percent in Orlando and Kansas City. For comparison purposes, a network with 100 percent density indicates that every node has a direct tie to every other node in the network. While the density of the policy networks in each city may appear low compared to this potential, there are no comparable existing studies from which to benchmark the network densities observed in these analyses. Interaction is a prerequisite for collaboration; units that do not interact—and thus do not have network ties—are clearly not engaged in FCA with one another. The observed densities suggest that between approximately 66 percent and 82 percent of units in these cities *do not* interact with each other around sustainability. Despite this, our case study research shows that Fort Collins, Orlando, and Kansas City all have relatively high-achieving and well-integrated sustainability programs, suggesting that interdepartmental networks with this range of density can be highly functional.

A second observation pulled from the network analyses is that a city's overarching context—namely, how it has operationalized sustainability and the specific issues it prioritizes—influences which units play a dominant role relative to others. The calculation of two common egocentric centrality measures—degree centrality and betweenness centrality—provide empirical support for many of the conclusions drawn from the qualitative assessments. For example, in Orlando, energy efficiency is one of the most prominent sustainability policy issues. The Fleet and Facilities Management Division is responsible for preventative maintenance and repair services to city buildings and equipment, including converting the city's vehicle fleet to electric, natural gas, and other cleaner fuels. In conjunction with this division, the Public Works Department's Administrative Office, Solid Waste Management, and Streets and Stormwater Services divisions represent the functional units that were pointed to during the case study research as the primary implementers of energy efficiency initiatives. Along with Green Works Orlando, which was described in interviews as playing a consultant role to divisions, these units have the highest centrality scores in the policy network.

A similar dynamic is observed for Kansas City. As expected, the city government's sustainability policy network is centered around its designated lead, the Office of Environmental Quality. It is also centralized around the Planning and Design division, reflecting an alignment between the expertise in long-range planning for land use, parks and recreation, transportation, and overall quality-of-life improvements that come from urban redevelopment with green infrastructure best practices. Several units within the Water Services Department also have relatively high centrality measures, likely reflecting their roles in the city's ongoing implementation of its wide-reaching consent decree with the Environmental Protection Agency to resolve combined sewer overflow problems.

The lead agency in Fort Collins represents three functional units that have been administratively consolidated. They collectively represent the face of the city's sustainability efforts and, predictably, have emerged as focal actors in the network. Of them, the Social Sustainability department has the largest centrality scores. This would not necessarily have been predicted from the case study interviews, but likely reflects the embeddedness of social considerations in a broad range of functions and this unit's efforts to link to them. The high centrality scores for its Communication and Public Involvement Office is another noteworthy result from Fort Collins's network analysis that leverages the case studies and reflects the impact of context. Several of our interviewees described Fort Collins as having a "very demanding" public. Keeping them involved and appeased is a major and ongoing effort. This, plus the fact that communication and public engagement are generalist functions, which are equally relevant across all dimensions of sustainability, likely contributes to its wide reach.

A final observation from the network analyses is that, across all three cities, the chief executive—whether a mayor or city manager—appears to play a relatively minor role in linking functional units together around sustainability. In particular, the betweenness centrality scores for the mayors' and managers' offices, which indicate their positions as brokers bridging separate parts of the network, are low. A major finding from the case studies is the importance of having explicit support from the city's top leadership. In Chapter 9 we describe this explicit support as casting the shadow of authority, which enhances the lead unit's ability to achieve active cooperation on sustainability initiatives from other units across the organization. The fact that these shadow casters do not emerge as important players in the network suggests they are putting their weight behind the lead unit and are otherwise refraining from regular interaction with functional units on sustainability issues.

Conclusion

Exploring the efficacy of organizational arrangements for implementing sustainability policy and understanding how functional cleavages between administrative units can be overcome are the primary objectives of this book. In this chapter, we use networks as a framework and empirical tool to map the structure of units' interactions around sustainability. The ties represented by the networks in this chapter indicate that units had worked together on sustainability over the last year. This level of interaction is well below what is necessary for meaningful collaboration, but it is an important prerequisite. Network ties can thus be thought of as necessary but not sufficient to overcome FCA dilemmas.

By triangulating the network approach with the previously described quantitative and qualitative methodologies, we gain additional insights about FCA and policy integration. Although we were able to conduct network analyses for only three cities, representing two of the four overarching administrative arrangements, these analyses constitute a novel and value-added approach. Namely, the network analysis provides an empirical method to determine patterns of interactions and identify key actors. This strengthens and supports the case study findings. It also points to multiple opportunities for future research. First, the successful completion of similarly structured network analyses of city governments that are characterized as using decentralized network and relationship-and-bargaining-based approaches would allow for comparisons across all four administrative arrangements. Second, these networks—and indeed the entirety of the research in this book—consider a single period in time; the analyses offer a snapshot, and in the case of the networks, a baseline. It would be informative to replicate the network analyses in these three cities after some period of time to track how changes in sustainability-related personnel, priority issues, and/or administrative structure affect the structure of interactions that occur between functional units.

9

Key Themes and Findings at the Intersection of Cities, Sustainability, and Functional Collective Action

Several related observations motivated the research underlying this book. First, local governments increasingly tackle complex policy issues that extend far beyond their traditional core functions. These issues often do not fit within the administrative silos organized around function that characterize most local governments. Thus, in addition to resources and specialized technical expertise, their resolution requires the development of administrative structures and processes that integrate decision making to overcome collective action problems that arise as a result of authority fragmented across functional departments (Feiock et al. 2017). In the absence of such structures, policy decisions made by individual units can generate interagency spillover effects, lead to inefficient outcomes, and stymie larger citywide goals. A second observation is that, although functional coordination has long been a concern within public administration, these issues are not given adequate attention in contemporary policy theories. Thus, room remains for systematic thought and examination to add to general understanding about approaches to mitigate functional collective action (FCA) challenges. A third observation is that urban sustainability is an important and salient issue area that embodies the dynamics described above. Because it is a relatively new programmatic objective, there is considerable variation in how it is being administered across cities, providing fertile ground for study.

The book opens with the example of Kansas City, Missouri, and the city's response to a major combined sewer overflow problem. It illustrates how the city's choice to forgo the standard gray infrastructure fix and address it using a more comprehensively sustainable solution—that is, green infrastructure—introduced new logistical challenges as a result of it requiring the active participation of a larger number of semi-independent functional units across the government. The combination of a supportive city manager and city council, an organizational culture that increasingly values sustainability, and an influential lead agency to coordinate efforts has enabled progress around this challenging task. Numerous other examples of big-picture sustainability initiatives introduced throughout the book (e.g., climate protection in Fort Collins, equity through adaptation in Oakland) reinforce the importance of organizational arrangements able to facilitate interdepartmental cooperation around objectives that are shared by many but not wholly owned by any.

Although our focus is on the coordination, collaboration, and collective action challenges that occur intraorganizationally and must be overcome for local sustainability initiatives to be successful, this does not happen in a vacuum. Collaboration is often needed with a variety of external entities, including other governments, nonprofits, community groups, and business organizations. The limited attention we give to these external dynamics is not intended to suggest that they are in any way less important. In fact, up to this point, they have received far greater emphasis in the literature. This book's intentional focus on FCA and the intraorganizational arrangements to achieve it enable in-depth examination and theoretical development in this new area.

This chapter pulls together and highlights a sampling of the findings that were presented across the preceding eight chapters. In doing so it reiterates key points, identifies patterns, and draws new insights and conclusions. The next section offers a comparative overview of the different ways sustainability is operationalized by city governments and considers the implications it has on the necessary scope and likelihood of FCA. We then overview the administrative arrangements used by cities around FCA and discuss how findings from the qualitative case study research process shifted our original classifications of those cities. This is followed by a discussion of a handful of factors that emerged across administrative arrangements as particularly important to FCA resolution. We then provide select recommendations for future sustainability management and conclude with a discussion about the transferability of the findings presented to other functionally transboundary issues.

Different Operationalizations of Sustainability

The fact that sustainability is, by definition, a multidimensional objective is a primary reason we selected it as the issue lens through which to study

FCA. The idea that city governments operationalize what sustainability means in their communities in different ways and structure their initiatives accordingly was reinforced during the process of conducting this study. Although the differential operationalizations we observe are not unique (see Zeemering 2009) or altogether surprising, how they arise and the implications they have on FCA management warrant much-closer examination.

In Chapter 2 we describe the results of our nationwide Smart and Sustainable Cities Survey. We report that 88 percent of cities describe economic health as being a "high" or "very high" local sustainability priority. A similar prioritization for environment and social equity was reported by 60 percent and 45 percent of cities, respectively. The correlations between the stated prioritization of these different dimensions are positive but modest: 0.50 between the environment and social equity, 0.24 between social equity and the economy, and 0.14 between the environment and economy. The case studies, which employ interviews and document research as described in Chapters 4 through 7, provide more-nuanced insight into how these dimensions are pursued in relation to each other.

Figure 9.1 presents our assessment of the relative emphasis that the eight case study cities place on each of the three dimensions of sustainability. As depicted, the sustainability efforts in Providence and Fort Collins reflect a relatively explicit engagement with all three dimensions. In Fort Collins somewhat more attention is directed to environmental initiatives, whereas in Providence efforts related to equity have slightly more weight. Kansas City operationalizes sustainability first as an environmental issue, with equity being a growing focus. Oakland considers sustainability to be first and foremost about social equity and pursues environmental improvements as a means to achieve it. Ann Arbor treats sustainability almost exclusively as an environmental issue, leaving the majority of its other dimensions to the county government. Finally, Orlando, El Paso, and Gainesville occupy different spaces along the environmental-economic spectrum.

Sustainability is a normative concept in that it connotes that environmental, economic, and social well-being *should* be balanced in a way that can be maintained long-term (Portney 2013). However, this balance does not necessarily extend to the goals and composition of initiatives of every city. In fact, an argument could be made that local sustainability initiatives should disproportionately focus on the dimension that is weakest in a community to move toward greater overall balance. Despite the decades-long effort in some academic and governmental circles to generate a single agreed-on definition of sustainability, its local customization is inevitable and desirable in many respects.

Drawing from our case study research, two considerations appear to shape how cities operationalize sustainability and how they develop

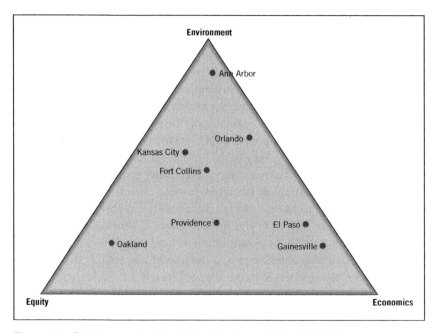

Figure 9.1 Relative emphasis of cities' treatment of sustainability

corresponding initiatives. The first is based on the recognition of a local weakness or underperformance around particular dimensions of sustainability. The second reflects an ability to garner political support by linking a particular framing of sustainability to a larger community value or priority. Sometimes these considerations are complementary and push sustainability in a single direction. For example, racial and economic inequality are large and historic problems in Oakland, and addressing them is a priority of the city's elected leaders. Thus, positioning sustainability as a means to address equity challenges reflects both of the above considerations. In other cases, such as with the cost-savings emphasis in Gainesville and the environmental orientation in Ann Arbor, sustainability's focus is not necessarily determined by greatest need but reflects local community and political values.

How a city operationalizes sustainability—as expressed by the relative emphasis its initiatives place on each dimension—shapes the type and extent of FCA that needs to occur among city departments to achieve it. In general, cities that embrace the challenge of actively pursuing sustainability improvements across all three dimensions face the greatest FCA dilemmas. This scenario involves both the largest number of distinct functional units as well as the most significant differences in professional orientation and technical background, which can challenge communication and cooperation efforts. In response to this, as described in Chapter 4, Fort Collins restructured its city government to create the Sustainability Services Area: a consolidated lead agency that brought together the individual units that were leading efforts toward environmental, economic, and social well-being. Providence, although also structuring local initiatives in a way that gives relatively balanced attention to all three dimensions, pursues them using a very different administrative arrangement: relationships and bargaining. Interestingly, no clear patterns emerge across the case study cities regarding how they operationalize sustainability and the general structure they use to administer it.

Characterizing Cities' Administrative Arrangements

In Chapter 3, we describe four general types of administrative arrangements that cities used to address FCA dilemmas around sustainability. These arrangements are based on two dimensions defined by institutional collective action (ICA) theory: the lead unit's scope of authority and the extent of decentralization characterizing the citywide effort (Feiock 2013; Feiock et al. 2017). The combination of these dimensions results in arrangements identified as lead agency consolidation (high authority, low decentralization), lead agency coordination (high authority, high decentralization), relationships and bargaining (low authority, low decentralization), and decentralized networks (low authority, high decentralization). In Chapters 4–7, we employ case study research to generate detailed illustrations of how these arrangements function, their development, and implications. Table 9.1 provides a comparative snapshot of the approaches the eight case study cities have used to implement their sustainability efforts. As can be seen, there is considerable variation both in the number of staff across them and in the lead unit's location within the city government.

The administrative arrangements reflect four fundamentally different ways of structuring organization-wide interactions to pursue a functionally transboundary objective. Although our original intent was to select and conduct case study research on two cities associated with each of the four administrative arrangements, their final distribution did not match our initial expectations. Why cities shifted from our original classification—which was based on a systematic although somewhat crude operationalization of authority and centralization—to their more nuanced post–case study placement is itself telling and offers insights worth highlighting.

Our selection of case study cities was aided by the responses we received from the Smart and Sustainable Cities Survey administered in late 2015 and early 2016 (and described in detail in Chapter 2). In it, respondents answered numerous questions about their city government's sustainability priorities and efforts, implementation leads and partner units, and overall

TABLE 9.1: SNAPSHOT OF CITIES' SUSTAINABILITY ARRANGEMENTS

City	Headquarters unit	Location in city organization	Number of staff
Lead agency consolidation			
Fort Collins, CO	Sustainability Services	One of seven core service areas in city	40
Lead agency coordination			
Kansas City, MO	Office of Environmental Quality	Unit in City Manager's Office	9
Orlando, FL	Green Works Orlando	Mayoral initiative/unit in Chief Administrator's Office	7
Relationships and bargaining			
Providence, RI	Office of Sustainability	Unit in Mayor's Office	3
Ann Arbor, MI	Systems Planning	Unit in Public Works Department	14
Oakland, CA	Sustainability Office	Unit in Public Work Department	2
Decentralized network			
El Paso, TX	N/A	In flux—informal coordination across line departments	1
Gainesville, FL	N/A	Informal coordination across line departments	0

collaborative culture. Using the data it generated, we operationalized "authority" as whether the sustainability lead is located in the executive branch (i.e., in the mayor or city manager's office) or as a line department; the hypothesis being that placement within the executive branch endows it with more authority. Decentralization was operationalized as the total number of different functional units involved in a city's sustainability efforts.

Upon completing the case study research, our classification of cities' administrative arrangements changed considerably. The case evidence demonstrated that simple operationalizations based on unit placement and partner count may not sufficiently capture the administrative arrangements' core dynamics. Although the theory-based classifications remain useful, different and more comprehensive proxies are necessary to more accurately identify cities' administrative arrangements using quantitative data. First, although having proximity to and the support of city leadership is important, a unit's "authority" (and as we discuss in more detail below, its "influ-

ence") is not consistently captured by an executive office versus line department distinction. While, in general, lead units located in the chief executive's office did benefit from additional clout by virtue of their proximity to
"the boss" (e.g., Orlando and Kansas City), this was not always the case (e.g.,
Providence). Moreover, certain line departments (e.g., the Sustainability
Services Area in Fort Collins) also emerged from the case studies as having high levels of access to and influence over citywide decisions, illustrat-
ing that executive placement is not a requisite for this.

In terms of systematically determining administrative arrangement
based on quantitative measures of decentralization, one challenge relates to
where, on a spectrum of decentralization, the line between the arrangements is best drawn. Our case study accounts reveal that decentralization is
not just a function of how many partners are involved but also how identifiable the lead unit is as a node that links them together. Figuring out how to
better capture this phenomenon with available quantitative city data is a
task for future research. In sum, the shift in our classification of several of
the case study cities before and after the qualitative research exposes substantively interesting limitations in our initial approach. An examination of
these limitations reveals new insights that can improve the operationalizations and proxy variables used in related statistical research.

Factors Affecting Functional Collective Action Resolution

The four administrative arrangements—lead agency consolidation, lead
agency coordination, relationships and bargaining, and decentralized
networks—are templates depicting four general ways that cities organize
and structure relationships to mitigate FCA dilemmas. Within each there is
room for considerable variation. Notably, all eight of the cities selected as
case studies are, to some degree, "high achievers" in that they had implemented more than the average number of sustainability activities defined in
the Smart and Sustainable Cities Survey. While this means we must be care-
ful not to generalize findings beyond these eight cities, their comparative
assessment provides insight into factors that appear to aid or inhibit successful integration around sustainability.

The case studies offer evidence that three of the four arrangements examined *can* work to achieve effective and durable integrated sustainability
initiatives. Fort Collins (lead agency consolidation), Orlando, Kansas City
(both lead agency coordination), Ann Arbor, and Oakland (both relationships and bargaining) serve as examples of where the different arrangements operate effectively. Providence (relationships and bargaining) struggles with citywide buy-in, but is making progress through its focus on small
wins. Both of the cities using the decentralized network arrangement (El

Paso and Gainesville) are having more trouble achieving and maintaining coordinated citywide action on a shared sustainability vision. Again, given the case study nature of this portion of the research, we are reticent to draw general conclusions that decentralized networks are less effective. Each city experienced some integrative success under a decentralized arrangement, yet it did not prove durable and weakened over time. The findings shed light on the potential practical challenges associated with not having a clearly designated lead. Several factors appear particularly important to FCA resolution and the successful implementation of sustainability objectives—namely, having a supportive organizational ethos, having an influential lead unit, being able to overcome the perceived "extraness" of sustainability, and having formal integration mechanisms in place that provide a scaffolding for informal efforts. The conclusion that some degree of focused coordination, particularly in decentralized settings, is necessary for robust local sustainability efforts has implications to larger studies of network management.

Programmatic Longevity and a Sustainability Ethos within the City Government

It is considerably easier to achieve FCA around sustainability in city governments where it is widely embraced by staff as an important value. Agreement about its worth does not eliminate logistical obstacles, competing priorities, fuzzy boundaries, or coordination challenges; however, it does remove an important source of potential resistance. The length of time that sustainability has been an explicit programmatic objective and the degree to which it has permeated the culture of a city government appear interrelated. Five of the city governments profiled in this book have had consistent and strong sustainability programs in place for well over a decade. In three of them (Ann Arbor, Oakland, and Fort Collins), a general sustainability or environmental ethos was prevalent among city staff prior to any programmatic formation. In Orlando and Kansas City, conversely, a culture of sustainability has arisen and grown within the city government over the years their programs have been in place. At the programs' start, not all staff understood or appreciated sustainability's place as a local objective, and subtle resistance was common. However, by virtue of its longevity as a priority and the relationships and successes built around it during that time, interviewees in both cities uniformly characterized sustainability as now being part of their "organizational culture."

The remaining three cities that we profiled have programmatically pursued sustainability either for a much shorter period (Providence) or with considerably less consistent or durable efforts (El Paso and Gainesville). In these locales, there is less consistency among city employees—both at the director and line levels—that local sustainability initiatives are warranted and/or are worth the extra effort. This makes attaining integration through FCA more difficult, particularly given the low-authority administrative arrangements that characterize sustainability implementation in these cities.

Influence of Lead Unit

As alluded to previously, whereas the formal authority of the sustainability lead is one of the dimensions determining the administrative arrangement cities use to overcome FCA challenges, its *influence* often appears more important in determining its actual success. Influence is a more complex and inclusive dynamic than authority. Whereas the latter can be determined by formal policies and chains of command, the former includes both formal and informal elements. Figure 9.2 depicts the factors that, on the basis of findings from the case study research, shape the overall degree of influence a lead unit has over the decisions of other units in a city government. Notably, formal authority is one of several factors that directly and positively associate with influence.

Having regular access to department heads is a second factor. The city governments in which sustainability officers have a regular seat at the table for department director meetings are also those that have exhibited the most meaningful shift toward sustainability. Interviewees from these cities—Fort Collins, Orlando, and Kansas City—noted that regular direct access to department directors has been essential to their ability to

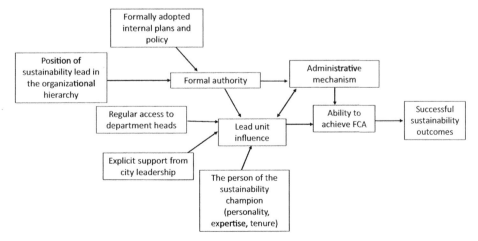

Figure 9.2 Factors shaping the influence of the lead unit for sustainability

successfully intervene on behalf of sustainability interests in the early stages of projects, when impact can be made with relative ease. This enables them to get ahead of the "too little, too late" dynamic that has characterized some sustainability efforts in other cities lacking this access pathway. Regular access to directors also aids in generating buy-in from departments across the city. By participating in directors' meetings, sustainability officers engage in repeated conversations with the city's key administrative decision makers. In doing so, they gain a better understanding of different departments' priorities and constraints and are able to build trust and establish general buy-in. Acceptance on the part of directors further has the effect of trickling down to line staff, building or reinforcing their commitments.

Having the explicit support of top city leadership is a third factor that increases lead unit influence. Even in the absence of formal authority, if an issue is a known priority of elected or appointed city leaders, their backing offers a shadow of authority that facilitates the lead unit's ability to engage in informal negotiations and coordination with other departments (Lam 2005; Scharpf 2018). In several case study cities, although perhaps most notably in Orlando and Fort Collins, interviewees suggested that the sustainability officer is viewed as almost an emissary from the city leadership; their requests are perceived as relaying what the mayor or city manager wants done. The three determinants of influence thus far described—formal authority, access to department heads, and explicit support from city leadership—represent distinct dynamics and are not necessarily linked, yet they tend to correlate with one another. Cities in which sustainability units have greatest support from leadership are also those that tend to have the most authority and access. Future work that explores interrelationships among these influence pathways in a quantitative setting holds great promise.

The fourth factor seen as directly shaping lead unit influence is different since it is embodied in the *person* of the sustainability champion. Most often this champion is the individual employed as the city's top sustainability officer, but his or her influence is based on much more than position. We characterize this personal influence as a function of the sustainability champion's personality, expertise, and tenure with the city. Although sustainability champions play an important role in bringing units together across all administrative arrangements, they appear most significant in cities using relationships-and-bargaining-based arrangements, wherein formal authority and access to department heads is systematically less.

Multiple interviewees described their sustainability officers as "outward focused" and "collaborative" and as being "connectors." These personality traits were stressed as important to the successful facilitation of interdepartmental collective action. The type of expertise the sustainability champion brings to the table is also linked to his or her personal influence. In this regard, being perceived as an expert who finds sustainability solutions that also help other departments advance their own goals is key. Our findings also point to the importance of there being a good match between the expertise of the sustainability champion and the city government's dominant professional orientation. Individuals holding sustainability officer positions come from a variety of professional and educational backgrounds, commonly including engineering, city planning, public administration, and landscape architecture. Although additional research is needed to more fully flesh out the dynamics and implications of a professional orientation match, our findings suggest that sustainability recommendations are better received when framed in a manner that reflects both the priorities and professional orientation of top city leadership. The respective professional backgrounds of the people in sustainability and city leadership can either facilitate this or make it more challenging. Finally, sustainability leaders who have a longer tenure in that role appear to have greater influence. This may reflect the time it takes to learn how to effectively maneuver an organization, build necessary trust relationships, and identify alignments of sustainability goals with agency interests.

In sum, the four factors indicated in Figure 9.2 together shape the degree of influence held by the lead unit, which in turn affects its ability to mitigate citywide FCA challenges around sustainability and achieve desired outcomes.

The Ability to Overcome the Perceived "Extraness" of Sustainability

Interviewees across the case study cities, even those in which sustainability is considered part of the local government's organizational culture, point to its perceived "extraness" as a primary barrier to robust collective action around it. That is, many employees see sustainability as additional to their core responsibilities. Participation in sustainability initiatives is often perceived as being akin to extra credit, in that it is valued and encouraged but not fundamental. As such, particularly when they are busy and/or when sustainability actions require extra time or involve a new way of doing things, staff may choose not to engage or do so in a superficial way.

Some of the organizational arrangements and integration mechanisms highlighted in the preceding chapters were able to mitigate, although not entirely eliminate, this dynamic. Notably, use of the lead agency consolidation administrative arrangement, which brings most sustainability functions together as part of a single unit, appears to be most successful on this front. Fort Collins's combination of Environmental Services, Social Sustainability, and Economic Health within a consolidated Sustainability Services

Area creates a structure that helps present their joint pursuit as a component of their core mission rather than extra. Certain discrete mechanisms can similarly have the effect of removing the extraness from sustainability. For example, by incorporating sustainability into its strategic plan, linking it to the budget, and identifying a goal team responsible for achieving it, El Paso has made sustainability a core consideration—at least for the set of identified goal team departments.

Formal Integration Mechanisms

El Paso's strategic plan is one example of a specific mechanism that provides a means to advance the integration of relevant units and functions around sustainability objectives. These mechanisms operate within the context of the larger administrative arrangements and their associated authority and decentralization dynamics. In the case study chapters, we divide the discussion of integration mechanisms to separately consider those that are formal (i.e., have been adopted or codified as part of the city's standard operating procedure) and informal (i.e., are tied to relationships, norms, and patterns of support). While both are important, here we focus on formal mechanisms that offer a metaphorical scaffolding around which FCA can be built. Many of the most impactful formal mechanisms are those that enable the development of relationships and other informal mechanisms (Park 2019).

A majority of the profiled cities use formal mechanisms that fall into three broad categories. First, the lead sustainability unit is itself viewed as a mechanism. In most of the case study cities, the lead unit and its staff act as the single most important component of the city government's larger sustainability system. They are charged with promoting the citywide vision and maintaining momentum for achieving it. The latter often involves directly confronting FCA challenges and finding context-specific solutions around them. Second, in every city profiled, the adopted plans serve as important integration mechanisms. Plans provide an agreed-on road map for action and give sustainability leaders something formal to point to when making requests of other city units. The city plans we reviewed as part of this research process—whether climate action plans, sustainability plans, strategic plans, or some other variant—generally follow best practices and contain goals, actionable strategies, and timelines. They also generally identify the units responsible for implementing each strategic action. Regardless of type, the plans with the most clout as integration mechanisms are in some way tied to the city's budget process. A third, albeit less consistently impactful, category of formal mechanisms contains the procedures that define venues for integration, such as standing meetings, reporting structures, and the like. These procedural mechanisms address FCA challenges indirectly by providing regular opportunity for communication, bargaining, and information exchange, which are prerequisites for integrated action.

The Future of Local Sustainability Management

Since its emergence as a local issue in the early 2000s, cities have used a variety of institutional arrangements to manage their sustainability initiatives. As Chapter 2 illustrates in more detail, U.S. cities demonstrate a considerable range in their basic administrative features. Moreover, although it is not uncommon for individual cities to have changed how they organize sustainability over time, there is no systematic evidence of their maturing or evolving in a particular direction. For example, between 2010 and 2015, the administrative location of the sustainability headquarters unit moved in 16 percent of U.S. cities but reveal no pattern or coalescence around a single best-practice type (Krause et al. 2019). While it is inevitable, and even desirable, that administrative arrangements be tailored to local context, the extent of the variation and its seemingly ad hoc nature reflects an overall lack of understanding about how different characteristics, structures, and capacities systematically shape the type and effectiveness of sustainability actions taken by cities.

The conceptual framing, classifications of administrative arrangements, factors identified as affecting collective action resolution, and formal and informal integration mechanisms discussed in this chapter have implications beyond political science and public administration and confront nexus problems for sustainability (e.g., the food-energy-water nexus or the climate-land-energy-water nexus). The study of nexus questions brings together engineering, climate science, planning, ecology and social science. FCA is arguably a type of nexus governance, since the challenges of integrating across human, engineered and natural systems in these settings share many characteristics of the challenges we examine in this book. Nexus problems are most salient in urban areas (Betsill and Rabe 2009; Artioli et al. 2017; Engstrom et al. 2017). Nevertheless, the literature on urban governance and institutional collective action has largely not been connected to nexus governance. The FCA concepts developed here offer a framing to facilitate the shift toward nexus governance more generally.

This book attempts to provide context, theory, and example to increase understanding about sustainability management and pave the way for its more thoughtful future treatment in research and practice. Throughout the chapters, we introduce and illustrate four general administrative arrangements that provide a menu of options for the basic ways city governments may organize to achieve collective action around functionally transboundary objectives. Perhaps to the chagrin of some readers, we do not recommend a single best approach. However, we do recommend the establishment of a clear headquarters unit having sufficient *influence* to effectively engage and obtain cooperation from other city departments. In making this recommendation, we simultaneously caution against the use of a decentralized network approach; having an influential lead unit consistently appears to matter. This is worth emphasizing, particularly because over the course of the case study interviews, several people made comments seemingly idealizing the decentralized network approach (for instance, "Hopefully at some point we'll work ourselves out of a job because sustainability will be a core part of every department's mission"). Although there is an appealing logic behind this aspiration, the importance of having a designated and influential champion—whether an individual or entire unit—is a primary takeaway point from this research. *Without someone keeping a spotlight on sustainability, there is a significant risk it will fall by the wayside and/or be overwhelmed by other priorities.* It is important to have a center of gravity when managing functionally transboundary issues.

Although lead agency consolidation and coordination arrangements offer some distinct advantages, we expect that relationships-and-bargaining-based approaches to sustainability management will be the most common going forward. This is because they require the smallest change from the status quo, while still having the potential to be effective. We saw this approach employed in Oakland, Ann Arbor, and Providence, whereby a small lead unit with little formal authority—typically embedded relatively deep within the organizational hierarchy—actively works to engage others throughout the city government. Shared values, goodwill, and mutually beneficial solutions ultimately motivate cooperation under this arrangement. The success of this approach is aided by the presence of a strong community or organizational culture around sustainability. In its absence, progress may be stymied or, as in Providence, largely limited to mutually beneficial small wins. In these situations, effectiveness can be enhanced by supportive formal mechanisms (e.g., plans linked to the budget process) or institutional adjustments that increase the lead unit's influence.

The Broader Applicability of Institutional Approaches for Functional Collective Action

"Different structures allocate responsibility differently" (Sinclair and Whitford 2012, 59). This statement is true for issues far beyond sustainability and organizations far beyond city governments. Similarly, FCA dilemmas are likely to be encountered as organizations address a wide range of responsibilities that do not conform to existing administrative silos. The lessons drawn from the governance of city sustainability may become increasingly relevant as modern policy problems grow in their complexity and require greater cooperation from multiple independent or semi-independent units within an organization.

As one salient example, universities are facing increasing pressure to actively address sexual misconduct on campus. Although, on its surface, this has nothing in common with local sustainability, the two issues confront similar FCA challenges. Whereas a city sustainability initiative may require participation from departments of community development, parks and recreations, and public works, a university initiative to prevent or respond to sexual misconduct may need the participation of the faculty, department heads, top administrators, the campus Title IX office, and campus police, among others. Although an important shared goal, sexual misconduct prevention is not the core responsibility of the majority of these units (Carlson et al. 2018). Meaningful collaboration may be difficult to acquire and maintain in the face of externalities and fuzzy boundaries. In the absence of a facilitating administrative structure, university responses are too often poorly handled. The four theoretically developed administrative arrangements presented in this book—lead agency consolidation, lead agency coordination, relationships and bargaining, and decentralized networks—are equally as applicable around this issue as they are for sustainability.

More research is needed to assess the functionality of these arrangements around different issues, but the parallel incentive structures they create give us reason to expect comparable dynamics. This book presents the first deep-dive exploring the idea of FCA, and developing and examining approaches able to achieve it. It also provides an in-depth study of the implementation of local sustainability initiatives, which moves well beyond the previous research that has largely focused on adoption. The eight cities that opened their doors to us are partners in the coproduction of knowledge. These cities shared their arrangements, mechanisms, and the approaches they use—inclusive of their strengths and shortcomings. In so doing, they contribute to advancing the implementation of local sustainability initiatives, as well as many other objectives that are similarly challenged as a result of being everyone's responsibility and no one's responsibility.

Appendix A

Survey Instrument

SUSTAINABLE AND SMART CITIES (AND TOWNS!) SURVEY

SUSTAINABILITY PRIORITIES

Sustainability encompasses a broad set of issues and services that do not always fit neatly into municipal governments' existing administrative structures.

1. To what extent are the following dimensions of sustainability a priority for your city/town?

	Not at all a priority	Low priority	Moderate priority	High priority	Very high priority
a. The environment	☐	☐	☐	☐	☐
b. The economy	☐	☐	☐	☐	☐
c. Social justice/equity	☐	☐	☐	☐	☐
d. Climate change mitigation	☐	☐	☐	☐	☐
e. Climate change adaptation	☐	☐	☐	☐	☐

RESPONDENT INFORMATION

2. In which unit of your city/town government do you work?

☐ Buildings unit	☐ Municipally owned local utility
☐ City Council or Commission	☐ Mayor's Office
☐ City/Town Manager or Chief Administrative Officer's (CAO) Office	☐ Parks and Recreation unit ☐ Planning unit
☐ Community Development unit	☐ Public Works unit
☐ Economic Development unit	☐ Streets or Transportation unit
☐ Energy or Sustainability unit	☐ Other: _____
☐ Environment or Environmental Services unit	

3. If applicable, indicate whether your unit is nested within a larger unit, such as the mayor's or city manager's office, or a larger independent line department.
   □ Part of the mayor's office
   □ Part of the city manager's or CAO's office
   □ Part of a larger line department (please indicate which) _____
   □ Not applicable—it is an independent line department

SUSTAINABILITY DESIGN

4. Compared to other units in your city/town government, which unit would you say has *primary* responsibility for *designing* sustainability initiatives?

□ Buildings unit	□ Municipally owned local utility
□ City Council or Commission	□ Mayor's Office
□ City/Town Manager or Chief Administrative Officer's (CAO) Office	□ Parks and Recreation unit □ Planning unit
□ Community Development unit	□ Public Works unit
□ Economic Development unit	□ Streets or Transportation unit
□ Energy or Sustainability unit	□ Other: _____
□ Environment or Environmental Services unit	

4a. Is this unit part of the mayor's office, city manager's office, or an independent line department?
   □ Part of the mayor's office
   □ Part of the city manager's or CAO's office
   □ Part of a larger line department (please indicate which) _____
   □ An independent line department

5. Compared to other government units, how much of the responsibility for *designing* the city/town's sustainability initiatives would you say this unit has?
   □ It is entirely responsible
   □ It has the bulk of the responsibility
   □ It has slightly more responsibility than other units
   □ It is one of several essentially equal players
   □ Don't know

SUSTAINABILITY MANAGEMENT AND IMPLEMENTATION

6. In your opinion, what unit has the *primary* responsibility for *coordinating/managing the implementation* of sustainability initiatives in your city/town?

□ Buildings unit	□ Municipally owned local utility
□ City Council or Commission	□ Mayor's Office
□ City/Town Manager or Chief Administrative Officer's (CAO) Office	□ Parks and Recreation unit □ Planning unit

☐ Community Development unit	☐ Public Works unit
☐ Economic Development unit	☐ Streets or Transportation unit
☐ Energy or Sustainability unit	☐ Other: _____
☐ Environment or Environmental Services unit	

6a. Is this unit part of the mayor's or city manager's office or an independent line department?
   ☐ Part of the mayor's office
   ☐ Part of the city manager's or CAO's office
   ☐ Part of a larger line department (please indicate which) _____
   ☐ An independent line department

7. Compared to other government units, how much of the responsibility for *coordinating/managing the implementation* of the city/town's sustainability initiatives does this unit have?
   ☐ It is entirely responsible
   ☐ It has the bulk of the responsibility
   ☐ It has slightly more responsibility than other units
   ☐ It is one of several essentially equal players
   ☐ Don't know

8. To the best of your knowledge, has this unit held *primary* responsibility for *managing the implementation* of sustainability initiatives since 2010?
   ☐ Yes→Go to question 9
   ☐ No

8a. If no, which unit previously held primary responsibility for managing the implementation of sustainability initiatives? (*select one*)

☐ Buildings unit	☐ Municipally owned local utility
☐ City Council or Commission	☐ Mayor's Office
☐ City/Town Manager or Chief Administrative Officer's (CAO) Office	☐ Parks and Recreation unit ☐ Planning unit
☐ Community Development unit	☐ Public Works unit
☐ Economic Development unit	☐ Streets or Transportation unit
☐ Energy or Sustainability unit	☐ Other: _____
☐ Environment or Environmental Services unit	

8b. If no, what is your *best estimate* of the year in which this change occurred?
   ☐ 2011
   ☐ 2012
   ☐ 2013
   ☐ 2014
   ☐ 2015

COOPERATION AND COLLABORATION WITHIN CITY GOVERNMENT

9. How often does this unit rely on each of the following to get cooperation from other city departments when implementing sustainability initiatives?

	Never	Infrequently	Sometimes	Frequently	Always
a. Informal communication with department directors	☐	☐	☐	☐	☐
b. Personal connections/relationships/favors	☐	☐	☐	☐	☐
c. Directives from mayor or manager	☐	☐	☐	☐	☐

10. Do you agree or disagree that the following statements describe this unit? This unit . . .

	Disagree	Somewhat disagree	Somewhat agree	Agree
a. Exercises a great deal of authority over other city units	☐	☐	☐	☐
b. Does *not* interact much with other units	☐	☐	☐	☐
c. Reports directly to the mayor or city administrator	☐	☐	☐	☐
d. Is effective in bargaining with other city units	☐	☐	☐	☐
e. Operates as a consolidated agency	☐	☐	☐	☐
f. Experienced turnover in leadership in last 5 years	☐	☐	☐	☐
g. Has limited influence on citywide strategies and goals	☐	☐	☐	☐
h. Is well funded relative to other units	☐	☐	☐	☐
i. Works with neighborhood associations	☐	☐	☐	☐

11. Aside from this unit, please indicate what other units have been involved and the extent to which they have influenced the *planning and design* of the city/town's sustainability programs.

	Not influenced	Somewhat influenced	Influenced	Greatly influenced
Buildings unit	☐	☐	☐	☐
City Council or Commission	☐	☐	☐	☐
City/Town Manager or Chief Administrative Officer's (CAO) Office	☐	☐	☐	☐

Community Development unit	☐	☐	☐	☐
Economic Development unit	☐	☐	☐	☐
Energy or Sustainability unit	☐	☐	☐	☐
Environment or Environmental Services unit	☐	☐	☐	☐
Local utility (municipally owned/ operated)	☐	☐	☐	☐
Mayor's Office	☐	☐	☐	☐
Parks and Recreation unit	☐	☐	☐	☐
Planning unit	☐	☐	☐	☐
Public Works unit	☐	☐	☐	☐
Streets or Transportation unit	☐	☐	☐	☐
Other 1: _____	☐	☐	☐	☐
Other 2: _____	☐	☐	☐	☐

☐ None

12. Which scenarios best describes your city/town's staffing on sustainability? (*select all that apply*)
    ☐ Dedicated staffing in the city/town manager's office or equivalent
    ☐ Dedicated staffing in the mayor's or council's office
    ☐ Dedicated staffing within a single line department
    ☐ Dedicated staffing spread across multiple departments
    ☐ A citywide task force, committee, or commission
    ☐ No dedicated staff working on sustainability

13. Does your city/town have a dedicated budget for sustainability work?
    ☐ Yes
    ☐ No

14. Please indicate the frequency with which departments in your city/town use the following to coordinate or collaborate on sustainability initiatives:

	Frequently used				Never used
	1	2	3	4	5
a. Ad hoc meetings	☐	☐	☐	☐	☐
b. Unplanned face-to-face interactions among staff	☐	☐	☐	☐	☐
c. Formal agreements that require consent of department managers	☐	☐	☐	☐	☐
d. Mandated collaboration by the manager or elected officials	☐	☐	☐	☐	☐

e. An appointed or standing task force	☐	☐	☐	☐	☐
f. Self-organized task force among departments	☐	☐	☐	☐	☐

15. Does your city/town government have rules in place to define how departments can collaborate or coordinate with each other?
    ☐ Yes
    ☐ No
    ☐ Don't know

15a. If yes, do these rules . . . (*check all that apply*)
    ☐ Coordinate actions with representatives from other city units?
    ☐ Specify roles and responsibilities among units?
    ☐ Create conditions for equal contributions among units?
    ☐ Address disagreements on priorities among units?
    ☐ Other _____

16. Does your city/town use interagency agreements among units to address sustainability issues in city government operations?
    ☐ Yes, they are used
    ☐ Yes, they exist on paper, but are not used
    ☐ No
    ☐ Don't know

17. To what extent do you agree or disagree that the following statements describe collaboration on sustainability among units in your city/town?

	Disagree	Somewhat disagree	Somewhat agree	Agree
a. Units fulfill commitments they make to one another	☐	☐	☐	☐
b. Representatives from different units trust one another	☐	☐	☐	☐
c. There is competition among city units	☐	☐	☐	☐
d. Unit heads are generally *unwilling* to take risks	☐	☐	☐	☐
e. Information is shared openly among units	☐	☐	☐	☐
f. Collaborating units agree about overarching sustainability goals	☐	☐	☐	☐
g. Collaborating units have difficulty agreeing on the distribution of the costs and benefits of collaboration	☐	☐	☐	☐
h. Monitoring the output of collaborative activities is difficult	☐	☐	☐	☐

COOPERATION AND COLLABORATION WITH ORGANIZATIONS OUTSIDE CITY GOVERNMENT

18. How frequently do elected city/town officials make requests or inquiries directly to agencies or departments about sustainability-related programs?
    - ☐ Never
    - ☐ Very infrequently
    - ☐ Occasionally
    - ☐ Frequently

19. To what extent have members of the political delegations representing your city/town provided assistance in implementing sustainability efforts?

	Not at all	Somewhat	To a great extent
a. State legislative delegation	☐	☐	☐
b. U.S. congressional delegation	☐	☐	☐

20. Is performance information collected on the outcomes of sustainability actions in your city/town?
    - ☐ No performance information is collected→Go to question 21
    - ☐ Performance information collected on some but less than half of sustainability actions
    - ☐ Performance information collected on most sustainability actions
    - ☐ Performance information collected on all sustainability actions

20a. If performance information is collected, do elected officials use performance measures in making decisions regarding sustainability policy?
    - ☐ Not at all
    - ☐ Infrequently
    - ☐ Frequently
    - ☐ All or almost all of the time

21. Has your city/town engaged in any of the following collaborative actions relating to sustainability, energy efficiency, or climate protection? (*check all that apply*)
    - ☐ Has worked with other agencies or local governments in activities such as an inventory of greenhouse gas (GHG) emissions
    - ☐ Has joined a collaborative partnership with other local entities
    - ☐ Has joined a regional partnership
    - ☐ Has entered into an *informal* agreement with one or more local governments on energy or sustainability issues
    - ☐ Has entered into a *formal* agreement with one or more local governments on energy or sustainability issues
    - ☐ Has jointly purchased energy services or equipment with another government
    - ☐ Other (please specify) _____
    - ☐ Has not engaged in any collaborative actions in these areas

22. How active is your city/town in the regional MPO (metropolitan planning organization)?
    - ☐ Not at all active
    - ☐ Somewhat active

☐ Active
☐ Very active

23. To what extent does your city/town work collaboratively on energy, sustainability, and climate issues with the following entities?

	Not at all				Great extent
	1	2	3	4	5
a. Other cities within your county	☐	☐	☐	☐	☐
b. Cities within the region or metro area that are not in your county	☐	☐	☐	☐	☐
c. County governments	☐	☐	☐	☐	☐
d. Universities	☐	☐	☐	☐	☐
e. State agencies	☐	☐	☐	☐	☐
f. Federal agencies	☐	☐	☐	☐	☐
g. Utility companies	☐	☐	☐	☐	☐
h. Private firms other than utilities	☐	☐	☐	☐	☐
i. Nonprofit organizations	☐	☐	☐	☐	☐
j. Regional organizations or partnerships	☐	☐	☐	☐	☐

24. To what extent do the following groups support or oppose climate protection efforts by your government?

	Strongly oppose	Moderately oppose	Neutral	Moderately support	Strongly support
a. General public	☐	☐	☐	☐	☐
b. Chamber of commerce/ business associations	☐	☐	☐	☐	☐
c. Neighborhood associations	☐	☐	☐	☐	☐
d. Environmental groups	☐	☐	☐	☐	☐

25. To what extent are each of the following an obstacle to your city/town's ability to achieve greater community sustainability?

	Not an obstacle				Substantial obstacle
	1	2	3	4	5
a. Cost/lack of funds	☐	☐	☐	☐	☐
b. Conflict with other budget priorities	☐	☐	☐	☐	☐
c. Lack of staff capacity or expertise	☐	☐	☐	☐	☐
d. Lack of informational resources	☐	☐	☐	☐	☐
e. Lack of "political will" in decision making	☐	☐	☐	☐	☐
f. Other _____	☐	☐	☐	☐	☐

LOCAL INITIATIVES

26. Has your city/town used regulations or financial incentives to encourage any of the following?

	Incentive	Regulation	Neither
a. Water conservation by city residents	☐	☐	☐
b. Green space or open space preservation	☐	☐	☐
c. Mixed-use development	☐	☐	☐
d. Brownfield site repurposing	☐	☐	☐
e. Reducing the use of plastic bags by grocery/ retail stores	☐	☐	☐

27. Indicate if, *during the last year,* your city/town government has offered residents or businesses *financial incentives* to take the following actions to reduce their energy consumption.

	Residential	Business/ commercial	Neither
a. Retrofit existing buildings	☐	☐	☐
b. Purchase energy-efficient appliances	☐	☐	☐
c. Upgrade heating or air-conditioning systems	☐	☐	☐
d. Install renewable energy infrastructure (e.g., solar panels)	☐	☐	☐
e. Conduct energy audits	☐	☐	☐

28. Has your city/town conducted an inventory of GHG emissions from *government operations*?
    ☐ No→Go to question 29
    ☐ Yes, less than 1 year ago
    ☐ Yes, between 1 and 3 years ago
    ☐ Yes, between 3 and 5 years ago
    ☐ Yes, over 5 years ago
    ☐ Don't know

28a. Does the city/town regularly update the *government operations* inventory to reflect current emissions?
    ☐ Yes, the GHG inventory is updated annually
    ☐ The GHG inventory is updated occasionally and is currently *up to date*
    ☐ The GHG inventory is updated occasionally but is currently *out of date*
    ☐ No, the GHG inventory has never been updated

28b. Have the results of the *government operations* GHG inventory resulted in changes to reduce emissions?
    ☐ No, the inventory had *no impact* on emissions reduction
    ☐ It was the basis for *minor* emissions reduction
    ☐ It was the basis for *modest* emissions reduction

☐ It was the basis for *significant* emissions reduction

☐ It was the basis for *major* emissions reduction

29. Has your city/town conducted an inventory of *community-wide* GHG emissions?

☐ No→Go to question 30

☐ Yes, less than 1 year ago

☐ Yes, between 1 and 3 years ago

☐ Yes, between 3 and 5 years ago

☐ Yes, over 5 years ago

☐ Don't know

29a. Does the city/town regularly update the inventory to reflect current *community-wide* emissions?

☐ Yes, the GHG inventory is updated annually

☐ The GHG inventory is updated occasionally and is currently *up to date*

☐ The GHG inventory is updated occasionally but is currently *out of date*

☐ No, the GHG inventory has never been updated

29b. Have the results of the community GHG inventory resulted in policy changes to reduce *community-wide* emissions?

☐ No, the inventory had *no impact* on emissions reduction

☐ It was the basis for *minor* emissions reduction

☐ It was the basis for *modest* emissions reduction

☐ It was the basis for *significant* emissions reduction

☐ It was the basis for *major* emissions reduction

30. Indicate which of the following your city/town does to support economic sustainability (*select all that apply*):

☐ Works with existing businesses, employers, or business associations to identify opportunities to "green" operations or services

☐ Provides financial incentives specifically targeted to support the renewable energy sector

☐ Has implemented "Buy Local" campaigns

☐ Provides property tax credit to any commercial building that achieves LEED certification

☐ Creates demand for green products through public procurement policies

31. Indicate which of the following your city does to support social sustainability (*select all that apply*):

☐ Provides supportive housing options for the elderly

☐ Provides citywide access to information technology for people without connection to the internet

☐ Supports a local farmers' market

☐ Provides funding for public health initiatives, such as home visitation programs for low-income and at-risk children and families

☐ Requires sidewalks in new developments

SUSTAINABILITY IMPACTS

32. Consider the outcome of your city/town's sustainability efforts over the past 5 years. What impact do you personally think they have had in the following areas?

	Large negative impact	Negative impact	No impact	Somewhat positive impact	Large positive impact
a. Environmental quality	☐	☐	☐	☐	☐
b. Social justice/equity	☐	☐	☐	☐	☐
c. Sustainable economic growth	☐	☐	☐	☐	☐
d. GHG emission reduction	☐	☐	☐	☐	☐

33. Based on your work, how would you define sustainability as practiced in your city or town?

_____

_____

_____

Would you like to receive the aggregate results of this survey?

☐ Yes
☐ No

Appendix B

Survey Invitation

Dear Mr./Ms. [Name],

Local governments address many complex policy issues that do not fit into traditional administrative silos. These issues often face special implementation and coordination challenges. Sustainability is one of these broad issues that many local governments—some more explicitly than others—are pursuing.

We invite you to participate in a study on the administration of sustainability activities by local governments, funded by the National Science Foundation's Science of Organizations. It is designed to be directly relevant to municipal officials interested in the effective implementation of sustainability-related efforts.

All cities, towns, and villages in the United States with populations over fifty thousand are being surveyed. To reach valid conclusions, it is essential to get as high a response rate as possible. Your response is very important. Kindly take approximately fifteen minutes out of your busy schedule and complete the questionnaire at the following link: [link to survey].

Individual responses will be kept confidential, but we are happy to share the aggregate results of the research with you when it is complete. Simply answer yes to the last question in the survey, which asks if you are interested in receiving this information.

This survey and related research has been approved by the University of Kansas Institutional Review Board process. Additional information is available as part of the following: [link to information statement]. If you have any questions about the survey, please contact Rachel Krause at [email address].

If you feel someone else in your city is better qualified to answer the questions asked, please either forward this email to them or let us know and we will send it to them directly.

Thank you for your time. Your response is important and your cooperation is appreciated!

Appendix C

*Template for Semistructured Interviews Conducted
in Case Study Cities*

INTRODUCTORY QUESTIONS

A. What are the major responsibilities of what [X unit] does as a unit or department?
B. What are the major roles and responsibilities of your job?

SUSTAINABILITY PRIORITIES

1. What would you identify as the city's two current sustainability priorities?
1a. How did these sustainability priorities rise to the top (e.g., political, legal, budgetary, policy champion influences)?
1b. Would you say that staff and elected officials share a similar understanding of what "sustainability" means for their city? Do they share a similar view of these priorities?

ADMINISTRATION AND INTERNAL COLLABORATION

2. Describe how responsibility for sustainability is currently organized in the city.
2a. What factors influenced your city to arrange/administer sustainability in the way that it did? (Political considerations? Personal initiatives? Personnel or budgetary reasons? Attempts to match actions with expertise?)
2b. What departments are involved or help with the sustainability initiatives that are currently ongoing in the city? In what capacity?
2c. To what degree do you think *different city departments* share a similar understanding of what "sustainability" means for your city? (Or even view it as an important goal?)
2d. What sorts of things were or are done to get buy-in (or cooperation) from these different departments? Are there any formal incentives for collaboration? Are there any information-sharing requirements?
2e. Does anything stand out as making collaboration between departments difficult?
2f. Are sustainability activities monitored? How? By whom? What is done with results?

ADMINISTRATIVE CHANGE OVER TIME

It appears that sustainability has been actively pursued in your city for about [X] years.

3. During this time, has its structure or administration meaningfully changed? If YES:
3a. What were the nature of these changes?
3b. What prompted them?
3c. How did this structural change affect how sustainability was coordinated and implemented in your city?

IMPACT OF THE ADMINISTRATIVE ARRANGEMENTS

You described your cities' organizational arrangement as [X].

4a. What do you think are the greatest *strengths* of this organizational arrangement?
4b. What do you think are the most significant *weaknesses* of this organizational arrangement?
4c. How would you describe the *degree of competition* (for resources, priorities, etc.) between city departments (in general)?
4d. In general, how open is the city government to taking risks/trying new things/being innovative?

INTERNAL COLLABORATION EXAMPLES

5a. Think of a sustainability issue for which there was some *difficulty* achieving cooperation or buy-in across different departments or individuals in the city. Describe this issue and what happened.
5b. Think of a sustainability issue for which achieving cooperation or buy-in from different city departments was *particularly easy*. Describe this issue. Why do you think this was the case?

EXTERNAL INFLUENCE

6a. Would you describe what role (support, influence) federal and state agency officials play in your city's sustainability design and implementation? MPOs? Nearby cities?
6b. How much influence do members of the public have on influencing your city's sustainability actions?
6c. Do any interest groups stand out as actively promoting or obstructing sustainability efforts?
6d. What other external organizations are involved in or influence your city's sustainability efforts? What roles do they play?
6e. How would you describe the local political climate in terms of sustainability as a general objective? What about climate protection?

IMPROVEMENT/FUTURE

7a. If you could make one change to how sustainability is done in the city, what would it be?
7b. In your opinion, what is the future of sustainability efforts in your city? In other words, where do you see sustainability activities in five, ten, or fifteen years in your city?

ENDING QUESTIONS

Is there anything I did not ask you about that is important for me to know?
May I contact you again for clarification?
Who else do you know who knows about this and might be able to help me under-
stand it?

Appendix D

Fort Collins, Colorado, City Profile

Situated at the northern end of Colorado's Front Range, the city of Fort Collins is the county seat of Larimer County and the fourth most populated city in Colorado. Its 2019 estimated population of 170,243 is 17.5 percent higher than it was in 2010 (144,879), which represents almost three times the national growth rate (U.S. Census Bureau 2019c). Home to Colorado State University and its approximately twenty-five thousand students, it embodies many college town characteristics, including a higher than average education rate (54.5 percent of residents over age twenty-five have a four-year college degree) and a younger-than-average population, with a median age of twenty-nine. Politically, it leans liberal, but is consistently described as a "purple" community. It is racially homogenous, with almost 89 percent of the population classified as non-Hispanic white. Median annual household income is approximately $62,000, which is just over the national average (U.S. Census Bureau 2019c).

One of Fort Collins's most defining features is its geographic location at the base of the Rocky Mountains. The city, which covers 56.8 square miles, boasts 40,000 acres of protected natural areas, 600 acres of parks, and 20 miles of off-street hiking and bicycle trails. Complementing its natural areas and recreational infrastructure are its urban activity centers. For example, Old Town Fort Collins, which abuts the city's downtown, is a nationally designated historic district that is also famously known to have served as the inspiration for the design of Disneyland's Main Street, USA (Visit Fort Collins 2016).

Fort Collins's primary economic drivers are a mix of health- and service-related industries. Educational services and the health care sector employ the largest proportion of the population (28.1 percent), followed by retail trade (13.1 percent) and scientific and professional occupations (12.8 percent). With over seven thousand employees, Colorado State University is the city's largest employer (Colorado State University 2016). The presence of the university has played a significant role in the decision of high-tech companies, including Hewlett-Packard and Intel, to locate their regional offices in Fort Collins

(Fort Collins Chamber of Commerce, n.d.). The city is also home to over twenty local and major breweries, which account for more than 70 percent of Colorado's craft beer production.

With its locational attributes, public amenities, and steady economic growth, the city frequently ranks high on various quality-of-life lists (e.g., tenth "Healthiest City in America," third "Best College Town to Live in Forever") published every year (Garcia 2015). However, the city's popularity has also contributed to the region's increased cost of living. While the city has been experiencing steady economic growth for the past several years, after adjusting for inflation, household income growth has not kept pace with rapidly rising housing costs in the area. The affordability gap has grown notably since 2000, and according to the city's 2013 Citizen Survey, affordable housing was the most significant challenge respondents identified as facing Fort Collins.

Fort Collins has a council-manager form of government and has benefited from relatively stable top leadership, including a city manager who has held that position since 2004. Its elected leadership consists of a six-person city council, with all members elected by district on a nonpartisan basis for staggered four-year terms. The mayor serves a two-year term and is elected at large (City of Fort Collins, n.d.b). The city government has approximately 1,200 full-time-equivalent employees and is organized around distinct service areas. Fort Collins has a municipally owned water and electric utility that has been recognized regionally for its innovative approach to renewable energy production. In 1998 it was the first utility in the state, and among one of the first in the nation, to provide its customers wind-powered energy. Likewise, the city's ambitious Climate Action Plan has received national and international recognition (Bloomberg Philanthropies 2017).

Appendix E

Kansas City, Missouri, City Profile

Kansas City, Missouri, sometimes called the "Heart of America" because of its location at the geographic center of the forty-eight contiguous states, is the anchor city of the Kansas City metropolitan area. With a 2019 population of 495,327, it is the largest city in the state of Missouri and the thirty-eighth largest in the United States. It has a relatively diverse racial makeup: 55.1 percent of residents are non-Hispanic white, 29.0 percent are black, 10.2 percent are Hispanic, and 2.7 percent are Asian (U.S. Census 2019e). Kansas City comprises 23 percent of the larger Kansas City metropolitan area population of over 2 million, which consists of 9 counties and 119 cities across the two states of Kansas and Missouri (Mid-America Regional Council, n.d.).

Geographically, Kansas City is large and sprawling. The 319 square miles that it encompasses are in part an artifact of history; Missouri was the first U.S. state to start building interstate freeways with its neighbor, Kansas, resulting in more freeway miles per capita than any other major metropolitan area and over 50 percent more than the average American metropolitan area (U.S. Department of Transportation 2018). While this extensive transportation network has enabled the city to become one of the nation's largest logistics hubs, it has also accelerated the city's excessive suburbanization. As Kansas City fleet administrator Samuel Sweangin noted in our interview, its large physical footprint is a noted challenge for achieving the city's ambitious sustainability and resource efficiency goals.

Kansas City has experienced many of the challenges that have plagued Rust Belt cities in the United States. White flight was a particular challenge for much of the latter half of the twentieth century. This population shift was particularly impactful between 1970 and 1990, when the city experienced a 15 percent net loss in residents. Although the population has since started to rebound, Kansas City remains one of the most racially segregated cities in the nation, with the majority of the black population living east of Troost Avenue, a historic dividing line in the city. Kansas City faces additional quality-of-life problems typical of many large U.S. cities, including crime, poverty, antiquated infrastructure, and an underperforming school system.

Despite these challenges, in recent years the city has witnessed a significant positive change in its trajectory. Targeted investment in the urban core has resulted in the building of a new streetcar system, the development of an arts and entertainment district, and a downtown residential population that has quadrupled in the last ten years. The city is home to a world-class art museum, several professional sports teams, and over two hundred urban parks. Its promotional slogan, "more boulevards than Paris and more fountains than Rome," characterizes much of the city's aesthetic charm.

Kansas City is one of ten regional headquarters for the U.S. government. Offices from more than 150 federal agencies—including the Internal Revenue Service, Federal Reserve Bank, General Services Administration, and the Social Security Administration—employ over thirty-eight thousand people. In addition, Kansas City has a strong private-sector manufacturing base, and several national companies, including Hallmark, Russell Stover Candies, and H&R Block, are headquartered in the city. There is also a burgeoning start-up community—Kansas City ranks fifteenth in start-up activity among all U.S. metropolitan areas (Kauffman Foundation 2017). Still, with a 2018 estimated median household income of $52,405 and per capita income of $31,143, earnings lag behind the metro region and the U.S. average (U.S. Census Bureau 2019e).

The city has an adapted council-manager form of government with thirteen elected officials: a mayor elected at large and twelve council members. Of the twelve council members, six are elected at large and six represent districts. The Kansas City government has approximately 4,300 employees, a total fiscal year 2017–2018 operating budget of $1.59 billion, and a general fund of $4.78 million. For the first time in several years, the 2017 budget did not include any sequesters or a reduction in staff (City of Kansas City 2017). Despite facing years of budget restrictions, the city government has also benefited from relative political and administrative consistency. The fact that Kansas City is a politically liberal city in a conservative state has caused tensions over a variety of policy matters and resulted in threats of state preemption when the city is perceived as overstepping its bounds.

Appendix F

Orlando, Florida, City Profile

With a 2019 population of 287,442, the city of Orlando is the fourth-largest city and municipal government in the state of Florida, behind Jacksonville (city-county consolidated government), Tampa, and Miami (U.S. Census Bureau 2019g). Orlando is a principal city within the Orlando-Kissimmee-Sanford metropolitan statistical area, which is commonly referred to as Central Florida. This region is a world-renowned tourist destination; it is home to the Walt Disney World Resort and the nation's second-largest convention center, both of which are located less than twenty miles from downtown Orlando. The Orlando area received 68 million visitors in 2016, infusing billions of dollars into the regional economy (Pedicini 2017). The tourism and hospitality industry thus represents an important economic base for the city. In addition, Orlando is home to several global technology and advanced manufacturing firms, including Lockheed Martin Corporation, Siemens Energy, and Mitsubishi Power Systems (Orlando Economic Partnership, n.d.).

Despite the presence of these companies, overdependence on the hospitality industry continues to be of significant concern to policy makers. The city has subsequently focused attention on entrepreneurship and business incubation with the aim of diversifying its economic base (City of Orlando 2014). Complementing these city-driven initiatives is the regional presence of the University of Central Florida and the thousand-plus-acre Central Florida Research Park, which houses more than 120 companies and employs close to ten thousand people, making it the nation's seventh largest research park. It is also among the nation's largest hubs of military training companies and simulation organizations for the U.S. Navy, Air Force, Marines, Army, and Coast Guard (Central Florida Research Park, n.d.).

The city of Orlando's natural environment, particularly its wetland system and natural freshwater springs, offers important wildlife habitat and recreational opportunities. To protect these amenities, in 1987 the city developed the 1,200-acre Orlando Wetlands

Park—the world's first large-scale man-made wetland treatment system—that naturally removes wastewater effluents before entering the St. Johns River, a primary source of drinking water in the region. The wetlands park provides habitats for wildlife as well as a wilderness park with public walking and bicycle trails (City of Orlando, n.d.b, n.d.c).

Despite these efforts, environmental degradation is a concern in the region. According to the 2017 Sunshine State Survey, the loss of natural land for wildlife was the top environmental concern, followed by water-related issues (Newborn 2017). There have also been growing debates over how to mitigate air pollution that disproportionally affects poor neighborhoods (Craven 2018). Among the most significant public investments to curtail air-quality issues, while also promoting development opportunities, has been the development of a regional commuter rail system that connects the suburbs of greater Orlando area (Florida Department of Transportation, n.d.).

Orlando's continued growth (nearly fifty thousand new residents since 2010) is largely the result of a growing Hispanic population. Approximately 31 percent of Orlando residents identify as Hispanic, 37 percent as non-Hispanic white, 25 percent as African American, and 4 percent as Asian. Although nearly 37 percent of the adult population has at least a four-year college degree, per capita income remains relatively low ($29,930), reflecting the prominence of the hospitality and tourism industry in the economy. Moreover, 18.2 percent of Orlando's population and 10.5 percent of all U.S. families live in poverty (U.S. Census Bureau 2019g).

The city of Orlando is governed by a strong mayor- council form of government. The city council comprises six elected commissioners, each representing one of the six districts located within the city's boundaries. In 2014, the city had 3,186 city employees, providing an employee-population ratio of 12.3 employees per 1,000 constituents (City of Orlando 2015).

Appendix G

Providence, Rhode Island, City Profile

Providence is the geographically compact and densely populated capital of Rhode Island. It is also one of oldest cities in the United States and serves as the regional hub of higher education and health services for the state. It is home to seven institutions of higher education, eight hospitals, and a sectional center facility—a regional hub for the U.S. Postal Service. It is a majority-minority city and has nearly 180,000 residents of diverse racial and ethnic backgrounds. Many of Providence's residents struggle economically: the city has a poverty rate of 26 percent, and the median household income is $42,158, which is notably lower than the national median of $60,293 (U.S. Census Bureau 2019h). The city of Providence has a mayor-council government structure with a strong mayor and fifteen council members, all elected by ward. The city employs slightly over five thousand people and had a 2017 budget of $716.8 million. The city government manages the school system, and a large portion of the total budget goes to support local schools.

Founded in 1636 and incorporated as a city in 1832, Providence was once the ninth-largest city in the United States (Bayles 1891). At the start of the twentieth century, it boasted some of the country's largest industries manufacturing textiles, steam engines, jewelry, and silverware (Kupperman 2005). Nicknamed the "Beehive of Industry" and the "Renaissance City," Providence was one of the wealthiest cities in the United States during this time. However, the Great Depression and postwar eras saw the beginning of the decline and dismantling of its industrial economic base. It has since struggled with challenges related to poverty and postindustrial pollution.

Being an old city, however, also brings some unique benefits and opportunities for sustainable development. Providence contains the country's largest contiguous area of pre–Revolutionary War buildings listed on the National Register of Historic Places (National Park Service 2020). Because it was already compactly built and populated before the advent of the automobile, its pedestrian-friendly streetscape has been in place since long before New Urbanist concepts emerged (Leinberger 2009). As a result, it is much less auto-dependent than most U.S. cities. According to the U.S. Census Bureau, of cities with populations over one hundred thousand, Providence has the eighth-highest share of pedestrian commuters ("List of U.S. Cities" 2020). Recent economic revival efforts promoting Providence as the "Creative Capital" emphasize its blending of historic character and modern urban lifestyle. Abandoned mills and industrial buildings in the city have become major targets for urban renewal. While steady economic growth has lagged behind similarly branded peer cities (see Nagle 2015), the city's efforts makes it a regular on the lists of top cities for live music, thrift shops, locally owned coffee shops, art shops, and small design shops (*Providence Journal* 2016). At the same time, however, revitalization efforts have fueled heated local debates over gentrification and the displacement of longtime residents and racial minorities (Jerzyk 2009). The city remains among the poorest in Rhode Island.

Appendix H

Ann Arbor, Michigan, City Profile

Located in southeast Michigan and on the banks of the Huron River, Ann Arbor has approximately 120,000 residents and is the sixth-most-populous city in Michigan. It is approximately forty-five miles from Detroit and is a part of the metropolitan area of Washtenaw County, which had a 2019 population of approximately 368,000 (U.S. Census Bureau 2019a). Ann Arbor is best known for being home to the University of Michigan, a major research university with almost forty-five thousand students. Since the university moved from Detroit to Ann Arbor in 1837, it has been the primary force shaping the city's economic and social landscape. The University of Michigan and the University of Michigan Health System are the city's first- and second-largest employers, respectively. In addition, the university estimates that it indirectly adds $100 million a year in local economic activity through student discretionary spending, sporting events, and university visitors (University of Michigan, n.d.). Despite Ann Arbor's economic reliance on the university, other notable economic sectors are active in the city including technology and media companies, pharmaceutical research facilities, and manufacturing.

As its "Tree Town" nickname suggests, the city is also known for its well-integrated natural environment that provides plenty of green space in its downtown and suburban areas. The city has a dense urban forest, with tens of thousands of trees along streets and residential areas. This plus over 79 miles of bike lanes and 400 miles of sidewalk enables city transportation to be decidedly multimodal (City of Ann Arbor, n.d.b). However, a steady influx of residents has also created challenges associated with sustainable land use and sprawl. In response, Ann Arbor approved a thirty-year tax in 2003 to fund a greenbelt plan, with the intention of protecting agricultural lands surrounding the city from development and to foster long-term preservation of natural areas (Stanton 2014). The Open Space and Parkland Preservation Millage generates more than $2 million annually (Stanton 2018).

Owing to the presence of the University of Michigan, residents of Ann Arbor have a high overall level of educational attainment: more than 75 percent of the adult population has obtained a bachelor's degree or higher, compared to the national average of 32 percent. The racial composition of city residents is approximately 71 percent white, 7 percent black, 17 percent Asian, and 5 percent Hispanic or Latino. The median household income in Ann Arbor is $63,956, which, along with the median home value ($298,400) and median rent ($1,213), exceeds the national average (U.S. Census Bureau 2019a). In the 1960s and 1970s, the city served as a locus for various forms of political activism and as an important hub for left-wing politics. The city's dominant liberal ideology continues to manifest in the enactment of progressive legislation, as well as in its political representation. Ann Arbor uses an adapted council-manager form of government in which its mayor and ten ward-based council members run on partisan ballots. For the past ten years, Democrats held all but one position on the ten-member city council and the mayoral office (City of Ann Arbor, n.d.a).

Appendix I

Oakland, California, City Profile

Oakland is the third-largest city in the San Francisco Bay Area and the eighth-largest city in California. As of the 2010 census, it had 390,724 residents, which grew to an estimated 433,031 by 2019 (U.S. Census Bureau 2019f). Oakland is recognized as one of the most ethnically diverse major cities in the United States (Ness 2001). It has roughly equal proportions of black, Hispanic/Latino, and non-Hispanic white residents, all hovering at slightly over 25 percent of the total population. Approximately 16 percent of Oakland's residents are Asian (U.S. Census Bureau 2019f).

Oakland experienced significant in-migration during the twentieth century as a result of burgeoning opportunities for high-paying jobs in the defense, shipbuilding, and manufacturing industries. During World War II, its port was home to many war-related industries. Such opportunities attracted migrants from other countries and from other regions of the United States, particularly the South. Black migration to Oakland was part of the Great Migration, in which African Americans left the South for the West from 1940 to 1970, drawn to the city for high-paying jobs in the defense and manufacturing industries (Lemann 1991).

Much of Oakland's recent history, particularly from the 1960s through the 1980s, has been characterized by racial tension tied to poor relations between black residents and a mostly white police force, which often used excessive force. The Black Panther Party was originally founded in Oakland in 1966 a means to protect black residents from police brutality (Duncan 2020). Although less than they once were, tensions between the police and the black community persist. Despite these adversities, Oakland houses a thriving black community that has helped shape black identity in the United States throughout the last five decades.

Affordability and income inequality are major challenges in Oakland. Its desirable location in the San Francisco Bay Area, proximity to Silicon Valley, and its own high-tech industries means that there is considerable wealth in the city. There is also considerable poverty and a large homelessness problem. Although the gap is not as large as in some other parts of the state, the California Budget and Poverty Center estimates that the top 1 percent of Oakland residents have twenty times the average income of the other 99 percent (Reidenbach et al. 2016). The median household income in Oakland is $68,442, more than the national average; however, the median single-family home price is nearly $628,000—more than triple the median home value across the United States (U.S. Census Bureau 2019f; City of Oakland 2017a). Affordable housing and preventing the displacement of long-term residents has become a significant policy concern in Oakland, culminating in the passage of a $600 million infrastructure and affordable housing bond in 2016 (City of Oakland 2017b).

Consistent with its name, Oakland has many parks and recreation centers, totaling nearly six thousand acres. It has a prominent art and music scene, gaining national and international recognition as a top travel destination. Its largest employment sectors are health care and transportation, with Kaiser Permanente and Southwest Airlines being the largest employers in each, respectively (City of Oakland 2017a). Since 1998, Oakland has operated as a mayor-council form of government, with a strong mayor. Its council is comprised of eight city council members—one elected at large and the other seven by ward. Approximately 4,300 full-time-equivalent employees work for the city government (City of Oakland 2017c).

Appendix J

El Paso, Texas, City Profile

ocated in the Chihuahuan Desert and at the southernmost tip of the Rocky Mountains, El Paso is positioned along the international border between the United States and Mexico. As of 2010, El Paso was home to 649,121 residents, growing to a population of 681,728 by 2019 (U.S. Census Bureau 2019b). Located at the intersection of three states, two in the United States (Texas and New Mexico) and one in Mexico (Chihuahua), El Paso is part of a combined international metropolitan area—along with Las Cruces, New Mexico, and Ciudad Juárez, Chihuahua—called Paso del Norte. With 2.9 million residents, this region constitutes the largest bilingual and binational workforce in the western hemisphere (Chamberlin 2007). Because of its proximity to Mexico, the population is majority Hispanic (80.9 percent), followed by non-Hispanic white (13.2 percent), black (3.8 percent), and Asian (1.4 percent). Nearly 70 percent of its residents speak a language other than English at home. El Paso has a median household income of $45,656, substantially lower than the national average (U.S. Census Bureau 2019b). Despite its relative poverty, border location, and proximity to the sometimes violent Ciudad Juárez, El Paso is notably safe. Its rate of violent crime has been lower than most other similarly sized U.S. cities for two decades (Federal Bureau of Investigation 2017).

El Paso was incorporated as a city in 1873 and its population boomed, drawing residents from other parts of Texas and Mexico, along with refugees fleeing the Mexican Revolution (City of El Paso, n.d.). Over the next century, El Paso became a major manufacturing, transportation, natural resources, and retail hub in the southwestern United States, benefiting from its economic relationship with Mexico. Its history of mining and manufacturing has also left a legacy of pollution in the region. Most notably the Asarco smelter, located in the middle of the city, processed copper for one hundred years. During that time, it released toxic fumes from its eight-hundred-foot smokestack and caused elevated blood lead levels in people living in surrounding neighborhoods and downwind in Mexico (Burnett 2010). When it closed in 1999, the city was left with a four-hundred-acre plot of contaminated land that has since been largely remediated as a Superfund site.

El Paso's local economy now includes international trade, military, government services, oil and gas, and health care, which contribute to a metro gross domestic product of over $29 billion (Bureau of Economic Analysis 2018). El Paso is home to U.S. Army Fort Bliss and several federal law enforcement operations, including U.S. Customs and Border Protection, U.S. Drug Enforcement Administration, and Joint Task Force North. The defense industry in El Paso employs over forty-one thousand residents and infuses $6 billion annually into the local economy (Ramirez 2013). The University of Texas at El Paso is the largest university in the region and the seventh-largest employer in the city.

Per the National Weather Service, the sun shines an average of 302 days per year in El Paso, giving it the apt nickname of "Sun City" ("El Paso," n.d.). El Paso gets approximately ten inches of rain annually, and the Rio Grande, which borders the city, often runs dry. Water conservation is a long-standing objective in the region. El Paso contains Franklin Mountains State Park, the largest urban park in the United States spanning twenty-four thousand acres. This park features the highest peak in the county: North Franklin Mountain at 7,192 feet (City of El Paso 2018).

El Paso operates under a home-rule charter and has had a council-manager government since 2004. The mayor is elected at large to a four-year term, while the eight council members are elected by district, also serving four-year terms. Both the mayor and council members are subject to term limits, serving no more than two four-year terms, or ten years. Over 69 percent of El Paso County residents voted Democrat in the 2016 general election and most elected officials representing El Paso are Democrats.

Appendix K

Gainesville, Florida, City Profile

Nested in north central Florida, the city of Gainesville is the county seat and largest city in Alachua County. Because of its proximity to the Gulf of Mexico, Gainesville's climate is characterized by warm summers and dry, mild winters, with rainfall averaging thirty-five inches per year. It is home to the University of Florida and, with a population of 133,997 residents, Gainesville serves as the cultural, educational, and commercial hub for the region. The city's population is diverse, with 56.9 percent of residents identifying as non-Hispanic white, 21.4 percent as black, 11.0 percent as Hispanic, and 7.2 percent as Asian (U.S. Census Bureau 2019d).

Colloquially, Gainesville is nicknamed "Hogtown," reflecting the name of a nineteenth-century Seminole village known for raising hogs, prior to acquisition of Florida by the United States (Grossman, Zavoyski, and Wetland Solutions 2012). By the 1850s, secessionist sentiments were strong in Gainesville, prompting white residents to organize a militia company called the Gainesville Minutemen, resulting in small-scale battles on two occasions during the Civil War (Hildreth and Cox 1981). Following the Civil War, the majority of Gainesville residents were African Americans, who were again disenfranchised by the 1890s alongside the rise of racially motivated violence by white supremacist groups, such as the Ku Klux Klan (Hildreth and Cox 1981).

By the end of World War II, Gainesville experienced rapid population growth, due in part to increased veteran enrollment at University of Florida, using G.I. Bill benefits after returning from war (Hildreth and Cox 1981). The University of Florida is the largest and oldest university in Florida. With over fifty-two thousand students, it is the fifth-largest university campus by enrollment in the United States. The university and its teaching hospital are two of the largest employers in Gainesville, employing 27,567 and 12,705 individuals, respectively (City of Gainesville 2017). Because of the university's presence, Gainesville residents are relatively well educated, with 44.6 percent of adults having a bachelor's degree or higher (U.S. Census Bureau 2019d).

The city is governed by a seven-member city commission, including four commissioners elected by district and two commissioners and the mayor elected at large (City of Gainesville, n.d.). While local elections are nonpartisan, the majority of Alachua County residents voted Democrat (59 percent) in the 2016 general election. Beginning in the 1990s, Gainesville has increasingly experienced suburban sprawl, prompting the city to undertake controversial revitalization efforts between the downtown areas and the University of Florida (Jewett 2007). Gainesville features strong preservation of historic buildings and the natural environment, along with numerous parks, lakes, and museums. The city also faces criticism for its criminalization of homelessness, including antipanhandling measures, meal limit ordinances, and prohibition of sleeping on outdoor property, resulting in it being ranked as the fifth-meanest city for the homeless population (National Law Center on Homelessness 2009).

The city of Gainesville owns a regional transit system, a municipal airport, a championship golf course, and a multiservice utility that provides electricity, natural gas, water, wastewater treatment, and telecommunication services (City of Gainesville 2017). The city strongly supported solar power by creating the first feed-in tariff in the United States, allowing small businesses and homeowners to supply on-site-generated solar electricity to the municipal power grid (McDermott 2009). The feed-in tariff program ended in 2013; however, Gainesville remains a global leader in solar power in terms of solar installations per capita (Curry 2013).

Appendix L

Betweenness and Degree Centrality Scores for All Functional Units in Orlando, Kansas City, and Fort Collins City Governments

TABLE L.1: CITY OF ORLANDO, FLORIDA

Functional unit	Betweenness*	Degree
Business and Financial Services		
Administration	0	3
Chief Financial Officer	.321	13
Dubsdread Golf Course	0	3
Facilities and Fleet Management	24.073	40
Procurement and Contracts	2.676	21
Real Estate Management	.027	8
Technology Management	.072	1
City Attorney's Office		
Office of City Attorney	.739	15
Economic Development Department		
Administration (ED)	.033	7
Business Development	0	5
City Planning	1.022	5
Code Enforcement	.883	15
Community Redevelopment Agency	.014	6
Downtown Development Board	3.932	27
Permitting Services	.013	6

(continued)

TABLE L.1 (CONTINUED)

Functional unit	Betweenness*	Degree
Families, Parks and Recreation		
FPR Director's Office	.635	11
Parks	.178	11
Recreation	1.155	14
Fire Department		
Fire Chief's Office	.521	10
Housing and Community Development		
Housing and Community Development	.006	5
Office of Chief Administrative Officer		
Office of Chief Administrative Officer	2.117	20
Green Works Orlando	27.316	45
Office of Mayor and City Council		
Office of City Commissioners	.008	7
Office of Community Affairs and Human Relations	.482	9
Office of Communications and Neighborhood Relations	.050	7
Office of the City Clerk	0	1
Office of the Mayor	.492	14
Orlando Venues		
Gardens, Galleries, and Museums—Harry P. Leu Gardens	0	3
Orlando Venues	.005	8
Public Works Department		
Administration	11.104	35
Capital Improvement/Infrastructure	.095	8
Parking	0	5
Solid Waste Management	4.814	26
Streets and Stormwater Services	5.831	23
Transportation Engineering	.005	7
Wastewater	.076	9
Police		
Police Chief's Staff	.096	4

* Normalized betweenness centrality score.

TABLE L.2: CITY OF KANSAS CITY, MISSOURI

Functional Units	Betweenness*	Degree
Office of the Mayor and City Council		
Mayor	.313	12
Youth Employment	0	1
City Manager's Office		
City Manager's Office	2.486	19
Economic Development	1.941	18
Emergency Management Services	0	3
Office of Environmental Quality	22.468	48
Office of Performance Management	1.107	17
City Communications	.203	8
Finance Department		
Finance Department/Administration	.166	7
Special Programs	0	1
Law Department		
Law Department/Administration	.115	7
Corporate Legal Services	.005	3
Human Resources Department		
Human Resources Administration, Education and Training	.028	3
General Services Department		
Information Technology	.089	5
Facilities Management	5.338	24
Administration	5.998	20
Procurement	1.933	17
Fleet Management	1.039	15
Aviation Department		
Administration	.779	12
Airport Operations	0	2
City Planning and Development Department		
City Planning and Development Administration	.508	15
Business Attraction and Retention	0	3
Development Management	.017	5
Development Services	.058	8
Long-Range Planning and Preservation	.47	14
Redevelopment Services	.316	13

(*continued*)

TABLE L.2 (*CONTINUED*)

Functional Units	Betweenness*	Degree
Health Department		
Administration	.072	6
Community Engagement and Health Monitoring	0	4
Environmental Health Services	.015	5
Water Services Department		
Administration	.918	16
Business Operations	0	3
Engineering Services	.15	11
Stormwater Services	6.498	29
Wastewater Services	.995	12
Water Treatment and Supply	.012	5
Overflow Control Program	6.791	32
Neighborhoods and Housing Services Department		
Administration	.046	6
Housing Services	.059	9
Land Bank	.378	12
Neighborhood Preservation	.123	9
Neighborhood Services	0	4
Residential Trash Collection	1.116	15
Convention and Entertainment Facilities Department		
Convention and Entertainment Facilities	1.03	16
Parks and Recreation Department		
Parks and Rec Administration	3.264	24
Community Services	.286	9
Cultural Facilities	0	2
Golf Course Operations (and Aquatics)	.008	4
Natural Resources	.233	9
Planning and Design	24.332	49
Human Relations Department		
Human Relations Department/Administration	.024	4
MBE/WBE Program	.013	3
Public Works Department		
Administration	.192	9
Capital Projects	.110	10
Coordinating Services	.948	17

Functional Units	Betweenness*	Degree
Parking Control	.064	6
Street and Traffic Operations	.033	7
Street Lighting	.063	7
Capital Improvements	.065	7
Fire Department		
Office of the Fire Chief	0	1
Communications	—	—
Emergency Operations	.047	2
Systems Support	.409	7
Technical Services Bureau	.004	3
Municipal Court		
Municipal Court	.321	9

* Normalized betweenness centrality score.

TABLE L.3: CITY OF FORT COLLINS, COLORADO

Functional unit	Betweenness*	Degree
Mayor and City Council	.207	14
City Attorney's Office	.089	13
City Clerk's Office	.014	6
City Manager's Office	3.754	27
Municipal Court	0	3
Police Services		
Police Administrative Services	.006	4
Patrol Services	.034	4
Financial Services Administration		
Purchasing	2.931	22
Safety, Security and Risk management	.031	6
Fort Collins/Loveland Airport	0	2
Information and Employee Services		
Information Technology	.046	10
Human Resources	0	5
Communications and Public Involvement	16.898	39
Geographic Information Services Division	.014	8
FCTV	0	5

(*continued*)

TABLE L.3 (*CONTINUED*)

Functional unit	Betweenness*	Degree
Utilities		
Water Resources and Treatment	.383	15
Water Engineering and Field Services	1.236	19
Customer Connections	1.378	21
Light and Power Operations	.017	9
Sustainability Services		
Economic Health	6.622	30
Environmental Services	5.023	30
Social Sustainability	11.231	35
Community and Operations Services		
Natural Areas	3.072	22
Recreation	2.633	20
Cultural Services	.018	8
Parks	.497	16
Park Planning and Development	.070	11
Operations Services (C&OS)		
Fleet Services	.024	8
Facility Services	6.383	28
Real Estate Services	.042	9
Community Development and Neighborhood Services (Planning, Development and Transportation)		
Development Review Center	.023	8
Building Services	.307	11
City Planning	3.871	27
Neighborhood Services	.104	8
Historic Preservation	.053	6
Zoning Services	0	7
Transportation (PD&T)		
Streets	.059	9
Engineering	.093	11
FC Moves/Transportation Planning	.037	9
Transport/Parking Services	.188	10
Traffic Operations	1.33	15

* Normalized betweenness centrality score.

References

Agranoff, Robert, and Michael McGuire. 2004. *Collaborative Public Management: New Strategies for Local Governments*. Washington, DC: Georgetown University Press.

Aldenderfer, Mark S., and Roger K. Blashfield. 1984. *Cluster Analysis*. Newbury Park, CA: Sage.

Anderson, James. 2008. *Public Policymaking*. Boston: Houghton Mifflin.

Anderson, Mickie. 2016. "GRU, Biomass Plant Gets Uglier." *Gainesville Sun*, July 30. https://www.gainesville.com/news/20160730/gru-biomass-plant-battle-gets-uglier.

Andrew, Simon A., and James M. Kendra. 2009. "Regional Integration through Agreements: Does Multiplexity in Urban Service Deliveries Matter?" Paper presented at the Workshop on the Workshop 4, Indiana University, Bloomington, June 3–6.

Artioli, Francesca, Michele Acuto, and Jenny Mcarthur. 2017. "The Water-Energy-Food Nexus: An Integration Agenda and Implications for Urban Governance." *Political Geography* 61:215–223

Bae, Jungah, and Richard C. Feiock. 2013. "Forms of Government and Climate Change Policies in US Cities." *Urban Studies* 50 (4): 776–788.

Bayles, Richard M. 1891. *History of Providence County, Rhode Island*. Vol. 1. New York: W. W. Preston.

Betsill, Michele M., and Harriet Bulkeley. 2006. "Cities and the Multilevel Governance of Global Climate Change." *Global Governance: A Review of Multilateralism and International Organizations* 12 (2): 141–160.

Betsill, Michele M., and Barry G. Rabe. 2009. "Climate Change and Multilevel Governance." In *Toward Sustainable Communities: Transition and Transformations in Environmental Policy*, edited by D. Mazmanian and M. Kraft, 201–225. Cambridge, MA: MIT Press.

Bienenstock, Elisa Jayne, and Phillip Bonacich. 2003. "Balancing Efficiency and Vulnerability in Social Networks." In *Dynamic Social Network Modeling and Analysis:*

Workshop Summary and Papers, 253–264. Washington, DC: National Academies Press.

Birchall, Jeff S. 2014. "Termination Theory and National Climate Change Mitigation Programs: The Case of New Zealand." *Review of Policy Research* 31 (1): 38–59.

Bloomberg Philanthropies. 2017. "C40 Cities Bloomberg Philanthropies Awards Celebrate 10 Best Cities for Climate Action in 2017." December 5. https://www.bloomberg .org/press/releases/c40-cities-bloomberg-philanthropies-awards-celebrate-10-best -cities-climate-action-2017/.

Brierly, Allen. 2004. "Annexation as a Form of Consolidation: An Analysis of Central Core City Boundary Expansion in the United States during the Twentieth Century." In *City-County Consolidation and Its Alternatives: Reshaping the Local Government Landscape*, edited by Jered B. Carr and Richard C. Feiock, 55–86. New York: M. E. Sharpe.

Brody, Samuel D., Sammy Zahran, Himanshu Grover, and Arnold Vedlitz. 2008. "A Spatial Analysis of Local Climate Change Policy in the United States: Risk, Stress, and Opportunity." *Landscape and Urban Planning* 87 (1): 33–41.

Brundtland, Gru, Mansour Khalid, Susanna Agnelli, Sali Al-Athel, Bernard Chidzero, Lamina Fadika, Volker Hauff, et al. 1987. *Our Common Future*. Brussels: World Commission on Environment and Development.

Bulkeley, Kelly, and Michele M. Betsill. 2003. *Cities and Climate Change: Urban Sustainability and Global Environmental Governance*. London: Routledge.

Burch, Sarah. 2010. "In Pursuit of Resilient, Low Carbon Communities: An Examination of Barriers to Action in Three Canadian Cities." *Energy Policy* 38 (12): 7575–7585.

Bureau of Economic Analysis. 2018. "Gross Domestic Product by Metropolitan Area, 2017." https://www.bea.gov/system/files/2018-09/gdp_metro0918_0.pdf.

Burnett, John. 2010. "A Toxic Century: Mining Giant Must Clean Up Mess." *National Public Radio*, February 4. https://www.npr.org/templates/story/story.php?storyId= 122779177.

Burt, Ronald S. 1992. *Structural Holes: The Social Structure of Competition*. Cambridge, MA: Harvard University Press.

———. 2004. "Structural Holes and Good Ideas." *American Journal of Sociology* 110 (2): 349–399.

Caplan, Andrew. 2018. "Report: GREC Contract among Country's Worst." *Gainesville Sun*, October 24. https://www.gainesville.com/news/20181024/report-grec-contract -among-countrys-worst.

Carlson, Juliana, Marcy Quiason, Alesha Doan, and Natabhona Mabachi. 2018. "What Can Campuses Learn from Community Sexual Assault Response Teams? Literature Review of Teams' Purpose, Activities, Membership, and Challenges." *Trauma, Violence, and Abuse*, July 25. https://doi.org/10.1177/1524838018789157.

Carr, Jered B. 2015. "What Have We Learned about the Performance of Council-Manager Government? A Review and Synthesis of the Research." *Public Administration Review* 75 (5): 673–689.

Carr, Jered B., and Richard C. Feiock. 2004. *City-County Consolidation and Its Alternatives: Reshaping the Local Government Landscape*. Armonk, NY: M. E. Sharpe.

Central Florida Research Park. n.d. "About Central Florida Research Park." Accessed June 17, 2020. http://cfrp.org/about-cfrp/.

Chamberlin, Lisa. 2007. "2 Cities and 4 Bridges Where Commerce Flows." *New York Times*, March 28. https://nyti.ms/2tuCyhr.

Chavez, Abel, and Anu Ramaswami. 2013. "Articulating a Trans-Boundary Infrastructure Supply Chain Greenhouse Gas Emission Footprint for Cities: Mathematical Relationships and Policy Relevance." *Energy Policy* 54:376–384.

City of Ann Arbor. n.d.a. "City Council." Accessed March 1, 2019. https://www.a2gov.org/departments/city-council/Pages/Home.aspx.

———. n.d.b. "Street, Bridge and Sidewalk Millage." Accessed March 1, 2019. https://www.a2gov.org/departments/engineering/pages/street-and-sidewalk-millage.aspx.

———. n.d.c. "Sustainability Framework." Accessed February 1, 2019. https://www.a2gov.org/departments/systems-planning/planning-areas/climate-sustainability/sustainability/Pages/SustainabilityFramework.aspx.

———. 2012. "Climate Action Plan." https://www.a2gov.org/departments/systems-planning/planning-areas/energy/Documents/CityofAnnArborClimateActionPlan_low%20res_12_17_12.pdf.

City of El Paso. n.d. "Downtown El Paso History." Accessed March 1, 2019. https://web.archive.org/web/20090705114058/http://www.elpasotexas.gov/downtown/history.htm#1_5.

———. 2009. "Livable City Sustainability Plan." https://icma.org/sites/default/files/301399_El%20Paso%20Sustainability%20Plan.pdf.

———. 2013. "Sustainability Report, 2012." http://legacy.elpasotexas.gov/muni_clerk/_documents/sccm/old_attachments/sccm0516131000/05161302%20Final%205132013.pdf.

———. 2017a. "Comprehensive Annual Financial Report for the Fiscal Year Ended August 31, 2017." https://www.elpasotexas.gov/~/media/files/coep/comptroller/financial%20reports/previous%20cafrs/cafr%202017.ashx.

———. 2017b. "2018 Budget." https://www.elpasotexas.gov/~/media/files/coep/office%20of%20management%20and%20budget/fy18%20budget/fy18%20adopted%20budget%20book.ashx?la=en.

———. 2018. "Resilient El Paso." https://www.100resilientcities.org/wp-content/uploads/2018/02/El-Paso-Resilience-Strategy-PDF.pdf.

———. 2019. "Strategic Plan 2019: 25 by 2025." https://www.elpasotexas.gov/~/media/files/coep/community%20information/strategic%20plan%202025%20-%20booklet%20-%20updated.pdf.

City of Fort Collins. n.d.a. "Budgeting for Outcomes." Accessed June 18, 2020. https://www.fcgov.com/bfo/.

———. n.d.b. "Mayor and Council." Accessed December 20, 2017. https://www.fcgov.com/council/.

———. 2015a. "Fort Collins 2015 Climate Action Plan Framework." https://www.fcgov.com/environmentalservices/pdf/cap-framework-2015.pdf.

———. 2015b. "2015–2019 Affordable Housing Strategic Plan." https://www.fcgov.com/sustainability/pdf/AHSPFinal.pdf.

———. 2016. "City Council Work Session Item." March 10. http://citydocs.fcgov.com/?cmd=convert&vid=72&docid=2666502&dt=AGENDA+ITEM&doc_download_date=MAR-10-2016&ITEM_NUMBER=01.

———. 2017. "2017–2018 Biennial Budget." https://www.fcgov.com/citymanager/pdf/budget-2017-2018.pdf?1490039113.

City of Gainesville. n.d.a. "City Commission." Accessed June 18, 2020. http://www.cityofgainesville.org/CityCommission.aspx.

———. n.d.b. "Department of Doing." Accessed August 2, 2020. http://www.cityofgainesville.org/DepartmentofDoing.aspx.

———. 2012. "One Community's Strategy to Reduce Climate Change." https://www.gru
.com/Portals/0/Legacy/Pdf/Final%20Climate%20Change.pdf.

———. 2015. "FY16 Adopted Budget." https://www.cityofgainesville.org/Portals/0/bf/
FY16%20Final%20BIB.pdf.

———. 2016. "The Gainesville Question." https://www.cityofgainesville.org/portals/0/
clerk/CityComm/blueribbonreport.pdf.

———. 2017. "Comprehensive Annual Financial Report: Fiscal Year Ended September 30, 2017." http://www.cityofgainesville.org/Portals/0/bf/2017%20City%20of%20
Gainesville%20CAFR.pdf.

———. 2019. "City Manager's Proposed Budget in Brief." http://www.cityofgainesville
.org/LinkClick.aspx?fileticket=j3Vb-pMvZkU%3d&portalid=0.

City of Kansas City. 2011. "Green Solutions and Sustainability." AR 5-5. August 15. In
the authors' possession.

———. 2015. "Energy Empowerment Ordinance." http://bomakc.org/downloads/2015
_06_09_kcmo_energy_empowerment_ordinance_one_page_summary.pdf.

———. 2017. "FY2016–17 Adopted Budget." https://drive.google.com/file/d/1O1vFjZc
FwwllWegXaPZ43oAkKuGVil6Y/view.

City of Kansas City, City Manager's Office. n.d. "Office of Environmental Quality."
Accessed September 22, 2020. https://www.kcmo.gov/city-hall/departments/city
-manager-s-office/office-of-environmental-quality.

———. 2019. "Environmental Management Commission." https://www.kcmo.gov/city
-hall/departments/city-manager-s-office/office-of-environmental-quality/envi
ronmental-management-commission.

City of Kansas City Finance Department. 2014. "Citywide Business Plan, 2014–2019."
In the authors' possession.

City of Kansas City Office of Environmental Quality. 2013. "Sustainability in Kansas
City." In the authors' possession.

City of Oakland. n.d.a. "Race and Equity." Accessed February 7, 2019. https://www
.oaklandca.gov/departments/race-and-equity.

———. n.d.b. "Transportation." Accessed February 7, 2019. https://www.oaklandca.gov/
departments/transportation.

———. 2012. "Energy and Climate Action Plan." http://www2.oaklandnet.com/oakca1/
groups/pwa/documents/report/oak039056.pdf.

———. 2017a. "Fiscal Year 2017–19 Adopted Policy Budget." http://www2.oaklandnet
.com/oakca1/groups/cityadministrator/documents/policy/oak067556.pdf.

———. 2017b. "Measure KK Funds Put Oakland on Path to 17K/17K Goal." December 22. https://www.oaklandca.gov/news/2017/measure-kk-funds-put-oakland-on
-path-to-17k-17k-goal.

———. 2017c. "Quarterly Economic Dashboard, Q2 2017." http://www2.oaklandnet
.com/n/OAK067405.

———. 2018a. "Energy and Climate Action Plan (Updated March 2018)." https://cao
-94612.s3.amazonaws.com/documents/oak069942.pdf.

———. 2018b. "2015 Greenhouse Gas Emissions Inventory Report." https://cao-94612
.s3.amazonaws.com/documents/Oakland-2018-GHG-Emissions-Inventory-Report
.pdf.

City of Orlando. n.d.a. "BEWES FAQ." Accessed May 1, 2018. http://www.cityoforlando
.net/greenworks/bewes-faq/.

———. n.d.b. "Orlando Wetlands Park." Accessed September 22, 2020. https://www
.orlando.gov/Parks-the-Environment/Directory/Wetlands-Park.

——. n.d.c. "Park History." Accessed June 18, 2020. http://www.cityoforlando.net/wetlands/history/.

——. 2012. "Green Works 2012: Municipal Operations Sustainability Plan." http://www.cityoforlando.net/wp-content/uploads/sites/9/2014/05/municipaloperationsplan2012.pdf.

——. 2013. "Green Works Orlando: 2013 Community Action Plan." http://www.cityoforlando.net/greenworks/wp-content/uploads/sites/9/2017/06/GreenWorksOrlando_CommunityActionPlan.pdf.

——. 2014. "City of Orlando Business Development Guide." http://www.cityoforlando.net/greenworks/wp-content/uploads/sites/26/2014/03/BusinessDevelopmentGuide_WEB.pdf.

——. 2015. "Annual budget: 2016/2017." http://www.cityoforlando.net/Archive2016/BudgetBook16-17FINAL.pdf.

——. 2016. "Progress Report: Municipal Operations Sustainability Plan." http://www.cityoforlando.net/greenworks/wp-content/uploads/sites/9/2017/02/GreenWorks_MunicipalSustainabilityPlan_ProgressReport_highres.pdf.

City of Providence. n.d.a. "Environmental Sustainability Task Force." Accessed March 23, 2018. https://www.providenceri.gov/sustainability/environmental-sustainability-task-force.

——. n.d.b. "Equity in Sustainability." Accessed June 18, 2020. https://www.providenceri.gov/sustainability/equity.

——. n.d.c. "SustainPVD Newsletter." Accessed February 17, 2018. https://www.providenceri.gov/sustainability/sustainability-newsletter.

——. 2008. "Greenprint: Providence." http://www.gcpvd.org/images/reports/2008-10-greenprint.pdf.

——. 2014. "Sustainable Providence." https://www.providenceri.gov/wp-content/uploads/2017/02/Sustainability-Providence.pdf.

Clark, William C. 2003. "Urban Environments: Battlegrounds for Global Sustainability." *Environment* 45 (7): 1.

Climate Mayors. 2019. "Paris Climate Agreement." http://climatemayors.org/actions/paris-climate-agreement/.

Clingermayer, James C., and Richard C. Feiock. 2001. *Institutional Constraints and Policy Choice: An Exploration of Local Governance.* Albany, NY: SUNY Press.

Cobb, Roger William, and Charles Elder. 1972. *Participation in American politics: The Dynamics of Agenda-Building.* Baltimore, MD: Johns Hopkins University Press.

Cohen, Darryl T. 2015. "Population Trends in Incorporated Places: 2000 to 2013." https://www.census.gov/content/dam/Census/library/publications/2015/demo/p25-1142.pdf.

Colorado State University. 2016. *Colorado State University Fact Book, 2015–2016.* Fort Collins, CO: Office of Institutional Research, Planning, and Effectiveness.

Craven, Julia. 2018. "Even Breathing Is a Risk in One of Orlando's Poorest Neighborhoods." *Huffington Post*, January 23. https://www.huffingtonpost.com/entry/florida-poor-black-neighborhood-air-pollution_us_5a663a67e4b0e5630072746e.

Crowder, David. 2014. "Shuffling the Deck at City Hall." *El Paso Inc.*, December 8. http://www.elpasoinc.com/news/local_news/shuffling-the-deck-at-city-hall/article_cc4657d0-7ef1-11e4-b727-8b622cbb6185.html.

Curry, Christopher. 2013. "City Commission Will Not Add to Feed-In Tariff in 2014." *Gainesville Sun*, December 19. https://www.gainesville.com/news/20131219/city-commission-will-not-add-to-feed-in-tariff-in-2014.

Dillman, Don A., Jolene D. Smyth, and Leah Melani Christian. 2014. *Internet, Phone, Mail, and Mixed-Mode Surveys: The Tailored Design Method.* Hoboken, NJ: Wiley.

Dillon, Karen. 2006. "Kansas City Taking First Environmental Steps." *Kansas City Star,* February 15, p. 3.

Duggan, Kevin. 2015. "Fort Collins Boosts Goals for Cutting Greenhouse Gases." *The Coloradoan,* March 3. http://www.coloradoan.com/story/news/2015/03/04/council-boosts-greenhouse-gas-goals/24358179/.

Duncan, Garrett A. 2020. "Black Panther Party." *Encyclopedia Britannica,* April 2. https://www.britannica.com/topic/Black-Panther-Party.

Dyer, Buddy. 2017. "City of Orlando Advances New 'Smart ORL' Initiative, Aims to Become Prototype City for Smart Cities Technologies." Brookings, May 19. https://www.brookings.edu/blog/the-avenue/2017/05/19/city-of-orlando-advances-new-smart-orl-initiative-aims-to-become-prototype-city-for-smart-cities-technologies/.

Ellinger, Alexander E., Scott B. Keller, and Andrea D. Ellinger. 2000. "Developing Interdepartmental Integration: An Evaluation of Three Strategic Approaches for Performance Improvement." *Performance Improvement Quarterly* 13 (3): 41–59.

"El Paso, Texas." n.d. *Familypedia.* Accessed September 22, 2020. https://familypedia.wikia.org/wiki/El_Paso,_Texas.

Engström, Rebecka Ericsdotter, Mark Howells, Georgia Destouni, Vatsal Bhatt, Morgan Bazilian, and Hans-Holger Rogner. 2017. "Connecting the Resource Nexus to Basic Urban Service Provision—with a Focus on Water-Energy Interactions in New York City." *Sustainable Cities and Society* 31:83–94.

Everitt, Brian. S. 1993. *Cluster Analysis.* 3rd ed. London: E. Arnold.

Federal Bureau of Investigation. 2017. "FBI Uniform Crime Report, 2017." https://ucr.fbi.gov/crime-in-the-u.s/2017/crime-in-the-u.s.-2017.

Feiock, Richard C. 2009. "Metropolitan Governance and Institutional Collective Action." *Urban Affairs Review* 44 (3): 356–377.

———. 2013. "The Institutional Collective Action Framework." *Policy Studies Journal* 41 (3): 397–425.

Feiock, Richard C., and Christopher Coutts. 2013. "Guest Editors' Introduction: Governing the Sustainable City." *Cityscape* 15 (1): 1–7.

Feiock, Richard C., Rachel M. Krause, and Christopher V. Hawkins. 2017. "The Impact of Administrative Structure on the Ability of City Governments to Overcome Functional Collective Action Dilemmas: A Climate and Energy Perspective." *Journal of Public Administration Research and Theory* 27 (4): 615–628.

Feiock, Richard C., Rachel M. Krause, Christopher V. Hawkins, and Cali Curley. 2014. "The Integrated City Sustainability Database." *Urban Affairs Review* 50 (4): 577–589.

Feiock, Richard C., Kent E. Portney, Jungah Bae, and Jeffrey M. Berry. 2014. "Governing Local Sustainability." *Urban Affairs Review* 50 (2): 157–179.

Feiock, Richard C., and John T. Scholz, eds. 2010. *Self-Organizing Federalism: Collaborative Mechanisms to Mitigate Institutional Collective Action Dilemmas.* Cambridge: Cambridge University Press.

Feiock, Richard C., António F. Tavares, and Mark Lubell. 2008. "Policy Instrument Choices for Growth Management and Land Use Regulation." *Policy Studies Journal* 36 (3): 461–480.

Ferrier, Pat. 2015. "Retired Hendee Still Taking Fort Collins to New Places." *The Coloradoan,* March 27. http://www.coloradoan.com/story/life/2015/03/26/bruce-hendee-fort-collins-development-sustainability/70491576/.

Fleischmann, Arnold, and Gary P. Green. 1991. "Organizing Local Agencies to Promote Economic Development." *American Review of Public Administration* 21 (1): 1–15.

Floater, Graham, Catarina Heeckt, Matthew Ulterino, Lisa Mackie, Phillipp Rode, Ankit Bhardwaj, Maria Carvalho, Darren Gill, Thomas Bailey, and Rachel Huxley. 2016. "Co-benefits of Urban Climate Action: A Framework for Cities." http://www.c40.org/researches/c40-lse-cobenefits.

Florida, Richard. 2002. *The Rise of the Creative Class: And How It's Transforming Work, Leisure, Community and Everyday Life.* New York: Basic Books.

Florida Department of Transportation. n.d. "SunRail: Media Information." Accessed April 26, 2018. http://corporate.sunrail.com/media-info/.

Fort Collins Area Chamber of Commerce. n.d. "Major Employers." Accessed April 24, 2018. https://fortcollinschamber.com/jobs/major-employers/.

Frederickson, H. George. 2016. *The Adapted City: Institutional Dynamics and Structural Change.* New York: Routledge.

Freeman, Linton C. 1978. "Centrality in Social Networks Conceptual Clarification." *Social Networks* 1 (3): 215–239.

Gainesville Regional Utilities. n.d. "Biomass Generation." Accessed April 27, 2018. https://www.gru.com/OurCommunity/Content/BiomassGeneration.aspx.

Garcia, Adrian D. 2015. "Fort Collins Is on Another Top 10 List: Should I Care?" *The Coloradoan*, October 23. https://www.coloradoan.com/story/news/2015/10/23/fort-collins-best-lists/74458484/.

Gonçalves, Bruno, Nicola Perra, and Alessandro Vespignani. 2011. "Modeling Users' Activity on Twitter Networks: Validation of Dunbar's Number." *PLoS One* 6 (8). https://journals.plos.org/plosone/article?id=10.1371/journal.pone.0022656.

Gordon, I. J., K. Bawa, G. Bammer, C. Boone, J. Dunne, D. Hart, J. Hellmann, A. Miller, M. New, J. Ometto, et al. 2019. "Forging Future Organizational Leaders for Sustainability Science." *Nature Sustainability* 2 (8): 647–649.

Granovetter, Mark. 1985. "Economic Action and Social Structure: The Problem of Embeddedness." *American Journal of Sociology* 91 (3): 481–510.

Grossman, Amy, Beth Zavoyski, and Wetland Solutions. 2012. "Glen Springs Restoration Plan." October. https://floridaspringsinstitute.org/wp-content/uploads/2018/07/Glen-Spring-Restoration-Plan-Final.pdf.

Hanf, Kenneth, and Fritz Wilhelm Scharpf. 1978. *Interorganizational Policy Making: Limits to Coordination and Central Control.* Vol. 1. Thousand Oaks, CA: Sage.

Hanson, Susan, and Robert W. Lake. 2000. "Needed: Geographic Research on Urban Sustainability." *Economic Geography* 76 (1): 1–3.

Hawkins, Christopher V., Rachel M. Krause, Richard C. Feiock, and Cali Curley. 2015. "Making Meaningful Commitments: Accounting for Variation in Cities' Investments of Staff and Fiscal Resources to Sustainability." *Urban Studies* 53 (9): 1902–1924.

Hawkins, Christopher V., Sung-Wook Kwon, and Jungah Bae. 2016. "Balance between Local Economic Development and Environmental Sustainability: A Multi-level Governance Perspective." *International Journal of Public Administration* 39 (11): 803–811.

Hawkins, Christopher V., and XiaoHu Wang. 2013. "Policy Integration for Sustainable Development and the Benefits of Local Adoption." *Cityscape* 15 (1): 63–82.

Heath, Yuko, and Robert Gifford. 2006. "Free-Market Ideology and Environmental Degradation: The Case of Belief in Global Climate Change." *Environment and Behavior* 38 (1): 48–71.

Hildreth, Charles, and Merlin Cox. 1981. *History of Gainesville, Florida, 1854–1979.* Gainesville, FL: Alachua County Historical Society.

Homsy, George C. 2018. "Size, Sustainability, and Urban Climate Planning in a Multilevel Governance Framework." In *Climate Change in Cities,* edited by S. Hughes, E. Chu, and S. Mason, 19–38. Cham, Switzerland: Springer.

Homsy, George C., and Mildred E. Warner. 2013. "Climate Change and the Co-production of Knowledge and Policy in Rural USA Communities." *Sociologia Ruralis* 53 (3): 291–310.

———. 2015. "Cities and Sustainability." *Urban Affairs Review* 51 (1): 46–73.

Horn, Murray. 1995. *The Political Economy of Public Administration: Institutional Choice in the Public Sector.* New York: Cambridge University Press.

Horsley, Lynn. 2017. "As Water/Sewer Bills Skyrocket, Kansas City Searches for Solutions." *Kansas City Star,* May 8. http://www.kansascity.com/news/politics-govern ment/article149321554.html.

Hultquist, Andy, Robert S. Wood, and Rebecca J. Romsdahl. 2017. "The Relationship between Climate Change Policy and Socioeconomic Changes in the U.S. Great Plains." *Urban Affairs Review* 53 (1): 138–174.

Hunter, Yvonne. 2009. "The Co-benefits of Sustainability Strategies." *Western City,* September. https://icma.org/sites/default/files/100057_Sept.%2009%20Sustainable %20Cities.pdf.

ICMA (International City/County Management Association). 2010. "Local Government Sustainability Practices and Programs, 2010." https://icma.org/sites/default/files/ 301646_ICMA%202010%20Sustainability%20Survey%20Summary.pdf.

———. 2016. "Local Government Sustainability Practices, 2015: Summary Report." https://icma.org/sites/default/files/308135_2015%20Sustainability%20Survey %20Report%20Final.pdf.

Isett, Kimberley R., Michael Sparer, Sherry A. M. Glied, and Lawrence D. Brown. 2011. "Aligning Ideologies and Institutions: Reorganization in the HIV/AIDS Services Administration of New York City." *Public Administration Review* 71 (2): 243–252.

Jennings, Edward. 1994. "Building Bridges in the Intergovernmental Arena: Coordinating Employment and Training Programs in the American States." *Public Administration Review* 54 (1): 52–60.

Jennings, Edward, and Jo Ann G. Ewalt. 1998. "Interorganizational Coordination, Administrative Consolidation, and Policy Performance." *Public Administration Review* 58 (5): 417–428.

Jerzyk, Matthew. 2009. "Gentrification's Third Way: An Analysis of Housing Policy and Gentrification in Providence." *Harvard Law and Policy Review* 3 (2): 413–430.

Jewett, Randy. 2007. "City Shouldn't Pay for University Corners." *Independent Florida Alligator,* December 5. https://www.alligator.org/opinion/letters_to_the_editor/ article_beac9169-4faf-5979-b991-439ad4b073ee.html.

Jimenez, Benedict S. 2014. "Separate, Unequal, and Ignored? Interjurisdictional Competition and the Budgetary Choices of Poor and Affluent Municipalities." *Public Administration Review* 74 (2): 246–257.

Kahn, Kenneth B. 1996. "Interdepartmental Integration: A Definition with Implications for Product Development Performance." *Journal of Product Innovation Management* 13 (2): 137–151.

Kauffman Foundation. 2017. "The Kauffman Index: Startup Activity; Metropolitan Area and City Trends." https://www.kauffman.org/wp-content/uploads/2019/09/2017 _Kauffman_Index_Startup_Activity_Metro_Report_Final.pdf.

Kaufman, Herbert. 1960. *The Forest Ranger: A Study in Administrative Behavior.* Baltimore, MD: Johns Hopkins University Press.

KCStat. 2017. "Neighborhoods and Healthy Communities." February 7. https://www.kcmo.gov/home/showdocument?id=240.

Keen, Meg, Sango Mahanty, and Justin Sauvage. 2006. "Sustainability Assessment and Local Government: Achieving Innovation through Practitioner Networks." *Local Environment* 11 (2): 201–216.

Kenis, Patrick, and Volker Schneider. 1991. "Policy Networks and Policy Analysis: Scrutinizing a New Analytical Toolbox." In *Policy Networks: Empirical Evidence and Theoretical Considerations,* edited by Bernd Marin and Renate Mayntz, 25–59. Boulder, CO: Westview Press.

Kettl, Donald F. 2002. *The Transformation of Governance: Public Administration for Twenty-First Century America.* Baltimore, MD: Johns Hopkins University Press.

———. 2011. *Sharing Power: Public Governance and Private Markets.* Washington, DC: Brookings Institution.

Kim, Serena Y., William L. Swann, Christopher M. Weible, Thomas Bolognesi, Rachel M. Krause, Angela Y. S. Park, Tian Tang, Kiernan Maletsky, and Richard C. Feiock. 2020. "Updating the Institutional Collective Action Framework." *Policy Studies Journal,* May 16. https://doi.org/10.1111/psj.12392.

Kim, Soonhee, and Hyangsoo Lee. 2006. "The Impact of Organizational Context and Information Technology on Employee Knowledge-Sharing Capabilities." *Public Administration Review* 66 (3): 370–385.

Knoke, David, and Song Yang. 2008. *Social Network Analysis.* Thousand Oaks, CA: Sage.

Kousky, Carolyn, and Stephen H. Schneider. 2003. "Global Climate Policy: Will Cities Lead the Way?" *Climate Policy* 3 (4): 359–372.

Kozak Thiel, Jackie. 2015. "In the City: Where the City's Climate Action Plan Stands." *The Coloradoan,* September 11. http://www.coloradoan.com/story/opinion/2015/09/12/fort-collins-city-column/72034358/.

Krause, George A. 1999. *A Two-Way street: The Institutional Dynamics of the Modern Administrative State.* Pittsburgh, PA: University of Pittsburgh Press.

Krause, George A., and James W. Douglas. 2004. "Institutional Design versus Reputational Effects on Bureaucratic Performance: Evidence from U.S. Government Macroeconomic and Fiscal Projections." *Journal of Public Administration Research and Theory* 15 (2): 281–306.

Krause, Rachel M. 2010. "Policy Innovation, Intergovernmental Relations, and the Adoption of Climate Protection Initiatives by U.S. Cities." *Journal of Urban Affairs* 33 (1): 45–60.

———. 2011a. "An Assessment of the Greenhouse Gas Reducing Activities Being Implemented in US Cities." *Local Environment* 16 (2): 193–211.

———. 2011b. "Symbolic or Substantive Policy? Measuring the Extent of Local Commitment to Climate Protection." *Environment and Planning C: Government and Policy* 29 (1): 46–62.

———. 2012. "Political Decision-Making and the Local Provision of Public Goods: The Case of Municipal Climate Protection in the US." *Urban Studies* 49 (11): 2399–2417.

———. 2013. "The Motivations behind Municipal Climate Engagement: An Empirical Assessment of How Local Objectives Shape the Production of a Public Good." *Cityscape* 15 (1): 125–141.

Krause, Rachel M., Richard C. Feiock, and Christopher V. Hawkins. 2016. "The Administrative Organization of Sustainability within Local Government." *Journal of Public Administration Research and Theory* 26 (1): 113–127.

Krause, Rachel M., and J. C. Martel. 2018. "Greenhouse Gas Management: A Case Study of a Typical American City." In *The Palgrave Handbook of Sustainability*, edited by R. Brinkmann and S. Garren, 119–138. Cham, Switzerland: Palgrave Macmillan.

Krause, Rachel M., Angela Park, Christopher V. Hawkins, and Richard C. Feiock. 2019. "The Effect of Administrative Form and Stability on Cities' Use of Greenhouse Gas Emissions Inventories as a Basis for Mitigation." *Journal of Environmental Policy and Planning* 21 (6): 826–840.

Krause, Rachel M., Hongtao Yi, and Richard C. Feiock. 2015. "Applying Policy Termination Theory to the Abandonment of Climate Protection Initiatives by U.S. Local Governments." *Policy Studies Journal* 44 (2): 176–195.

Kupperman, Karen Ordahl. 2005. *Providence Island, 1630–1641: The Other Puritan Colony*. New York: ACLS History E-Book Project.

Kwon, Sung-Wook, Richard C. Feiock, and Jungah Bae. 2014. "The Roles of Regional Organizations for Interlocal Resource Exchange: Complement or Substitute." *American Review of Public Administration* 44 (3): 339–357.

Kyle, Sarah. 2017. "Homeless Count: 16% of Fort Collins Homeless Are Minors." *The Coloradoan*, April 6. http://www.coloradoan.com/story/news/2017/04/06/2017-count-sheds-light-fort-collins-homeless-youth/99820986/.

Lam, Wai Fung. 2005. "Coordinating the Government Bureaucracy in Hong Kong: An Institutional Analysis." *Governance* 18 (4): 633–654.

Laughlin, J. 2013. "Seeing Green: Green Infrastructure Pilot Provides Valuable Lessons for KCMO." *WaterWorld* 29 (4). http://www.waterworld.com/articles/print/volume-29/issue-4/editorial-features/seeing-green-green-infrastructure-pilot-provides-valuable-lesson.html.

Laurian, Lucie, and Jan Crawford. 2016. "Organizational Factors of Environmental Sustainability Implementation: An Empirical Analysis of US Cities and Counties." *Journal of Environmental Policy and Planning* 18 (4): 482–506.

Lee, Taedong, and Chris Koski. 2015. "Multilevel Governance and Urban Climate Change Mitigation." *Environment and Planning C: Government and Policy* 33 (6): 1501–1517.

Leinberger, Christopher. 2009. *The Option of Urbanism*. Washington, DC: Island Press.

Lemann, Nicholas. 1991. *The Promised Land: The Great Black Migration and How It Changed America*. New York: Knopf.

Levesque, Vanessa R., Kathleen P. Bell, and Aram J. K. Calhoun. 2016. "Planning for Sustainability in Small Municipalities: The Influence of Interest Groups, Growth Patterns, and Institutional Characteristics." *Journal of Planning Education and Research* 37 (3): 322–333.

Lewis, David. 2003. *Presidents and the Politics of Agency Design*. Stanford, CA: Stanford University Press.

"List of U.S. Cities with Most Pedestrian Commuters." 2020. *Wikipedia*, March 18. https://en.wikipedia.org/wiki/List_of_U.S._cities_with_most_pedestrian_commuters.

Lubell, Mark. 2013. "Governing Institutional Complexity: The Ecology of Games Framework." *Policy Studies Journal* 41 (3): 537–559.

Lubell, Mark, Richard C. Feiock, and Edgar E. Ramírez de la Cruz. 2009. "Local Institutions and the Politics of Urban Growth." *American Journal of Political Science* 53 (3): 649–665.

Lubell, Mark, John Scholz, Ramiro Berardo, and Garry Robins. 2012. "Testing Policy Theory with Statistical Models of Networks." *Policy Studies Journal* 40 (3): 351–374.

March, James G., Martin Schulz, and Xueguang Zhou. 2000. *The Dynamics of Rules: Change in Written Organizational Codes.* Stanford, CA: Stanford University Press.

Marso, Andy. 2017. "Do You Live in One of the KC ZIP Codes Where Life Expectancy Is Going Down?" *Kansas City Star,* September 28. http://www.kansascity.com/living/health-fitness/article175312836.html.

McCabe, Barbara Coyle, and Richard C. Feiock. 2005. "Nested Levels of Institutions: State Rules and City Property Taxes." *Urban Affairs Review* 40 (5): 634–654.

McClurg, Scott D., and Joseph K. Young. 2011. "Political Networks: Editors' Introduction: A Relational Political Science." *PS: Political Science and Politics* 44 (1): 39–43.

McDermott, Mat. 2009. "Innovative Solar Power Program Approved in Gainesville, Fla." *Tree Hugger,* February 6.

Mendez, Michael Anthony. 2015. "Assessing Local Climate Action Plans for Public Health Co-benefits in Environmental Justice Communities." *Local Environment* 20 (6): 637–663.

Mid-America Regional Council. n.d. "Member Cities and Counties." Accessed June 18, 2020. http://www.marc.org/About-MARC/General-Information/Member-Cities-and-Counties.html.

Milward, Brinton H., and Keith G. Provan. 1998. "Measuring Network Structure." *Public Administration* 76 (2): 387–407.

Moe, Terry M. 1991. "Politics and the Theory of Organization." *Journal of Law, Economics, and Organization* 7:106–129.

Molotch, Harvey. 1976. "The City as a Growth Machine: Toward a Political Economy of Place." *American Journal of Sociology* 82 (2): 309–332.

Mori, Koichiro, and Tsuguta Yamashita. 2015. "Methodological Framework of Sustainability Assessment in City Sustainability Index (CSI): A Concept of Constraint and Maximisation Indicators." *Habitat International* 45:10–14.

Nagle, Kate. 2015. "Can Hipsters Save Providence?" *New Geography,* March 31. https://www.newgeography.com/content/004889-can-hipsters-save-providence.

National Alliance to End Homelessness. 2016. "The State of Homelessness in America, 2016." http://endhomelessness.org/wp-content/uploads/2016/10/2016-soh.pdf.

National Law Center on Homelessness and Poverty and National Coalition for the Homeless. 2009. "Homes Not Handcuffs: The Criminalization of Homelessness in U.S. Cities." July. http://www.nationalhomeless.org/publications/crimreport/CrimzReport_2009.pdf.

National League of Cities. 2010. "State of America's Cities: Sustainability." Previously available at https://www.nlc.org/sustainability-resources.

National Park Service. 2020. "National Register of Historic Places: Weekly List." June 12. https://www.nps.gov/subjects/nationalregister/weekly-list.htm.

Ness, Carol. 2001. "S.F.'s Diversity Comeuppance." *San Francisco Chronicle,* April 1. https://www.sfgate.com/news/article/S-F-s-Diversity-Comeuppance-2936391.php.

Newborn, Steve. 2017. "Environment One of Floridians' Top 5 Concerns." *WJCT,* October 23. https://news.wjct.org/post/environment-one-of-floridians-top-5-concerns.

North, Douglass Cecil. 1990. *Institutions, Institutional Change and Economic Performance.* New York: Cambridge University Press.

O'Leary, Rosemary, and Nidhi Vij. 2012. "Collaborative Public Management: Where Have We Been and Where Are We Going?" *American Review of Public Administration* 42 (5): 507–522.

Olson, Mancur, Jr. 1965. *The Logic of Collective Action: Public Goods and the Theory of Groups.* Cambridge, MA: Harvard University Press.

Orlando Economic Partnership. n.d. "Headquarters and Regional Operations." Accessed April 26, 2018. https://business.orlando.org/l/corporate-headquarters/.

Osgood, Jeffery L., Susan M. Opp, and Megan DeMasters. 2017. "Exploring the Intersection of Local Economic Development and Environmental Policy." *Journal of Urban Affairs* 39 (2): 260–276.

Ostrom, Elinor. 1990. *Governing the Commons.* New York: Cambridge University Press.

———. 2005. *Understanding Institutional Diversity.* Princeton, NJ: Princeton University Press.

———. 2007. "Institutional Rational Choice: An Assessment of the Institutional Analysis and Development Framework." In *Theories of the Policy Process,* 2nd ed., edited by P. A. Sabatier, 21–64. Cambridge, MA: Westview Press.

Ostrom, Vincent, Robert L. Bish, and Elinor Ostrom. 1988. *Local Government in the United States.* San Francisco: ICS Press.

Ostry, Jonathan, Andrew Berg, and Charalambos Tsangarides. 2014. "Redistribution, Inequality, and Growth." International Monetary Fund *Staff Discussion Note* 14 (2): 4.

Park, Jongsun, and Richard C. Feiock. 2012. "Stability and Change in County Economic Development Organizations." *Economic Development Quarterly* 26 (1): 3–12.

Park, Angela Y. S. 2019. "Beyond Adoption: The Influence of Local Institutional Arrangements on Sustainability Policy Implementation and Management." Ph.D. diss., University of Kansas.

Park, Angela Y. S., Rachel M. Krause, Richard Feiock, and Christopher V. Hawkins. 2018. "An Exploration of the Mechanisms Driving Collaboration in Local Sustainability Efforts: Assessing the Duality of Formal and Informal Drivers." Paper presented at the 2018 American Political Science Association annual conference, August 30–September 2, Boston.

Pedicini, Sandra. 2017. "Visit Orlando: Record 68 Million People Visited Last Year." *Orlando Sentinel,* May 11. https://www.orlandosentinel.com/business/tourism/os-visit-orlando-tourist-numbers-20170511-story.html.

Peters, B. Guy. 1992. "Government Reorganization: A Theoretical Analysis." *International Political Science Review* 13 (2): 199–217.

Peterson, Paul E. 1981. *City Limits.* Chicago: University of Chicago Press.

Pitt, Damian. 2010. "The Impact of Internal and External Characteristics on the Adoption of Climate Mitigation Policies by US Municipalities." *Environment and Planning C: Government and Policy* 28 (5): 851–871.

Portney, Kent E. 2013. *Taking Sustainable Cities Seriously: Economic Development, the Environment, and Quality of Life in American Cities.* Cambridge, MA: MIT Press.

Portney, Kent E., and Jeffery M. Berry. 2016. "The Impact of Local Environmental Advocacy Groups on City Sustainability Policies and Programs." *Policy Studies Journal* 44 (2): 196–214.

Prell, Christina, Hubacek Klaus, and Mark Reed. 2009. "Stakeholder Analysis and Social Network Analysis in Natural Resource Management." *Society and Natural Resources* 22 (6): 501–518.

Provan, Keith G., and Brinton H. Milward. 1995. "A Preliminary Theory of Interorganizational Network Effectiveness: A Comparative Study of Four Community Mental Health Systems." *Administrative Science Quarterly* 40 (1): 1–33.

Providence Journal. 2016. "Report Lists Providence as Seventh 'Most Hipster' City in United States." July 27. http://www.providencejournal.com/news/20160727/report -lists-providence-as-seventh-most-hipster-city-in-united-states.

Puppim de Oliveira, José A., Christopher N. H. Doll, Tonni Agustiono Kurniawan, Yong Geng, Manmohan Kapshe, and Donald Huisingh. 2013. "Promoting Win-Win Situations in Climate Change Mitigation, Local Environmental Quality and Development in Asian Cities through Co-benefits." *Journal of Cleaner Production* 58:1–6.

Queiroz, Alvaro, Fazil T. Najafi, and Pegeen Hanrahan. 2017. "Implementation and Results of Solar Feed-In-Tariff in Gainesville, Florida." *Journal of Energy Engineering* 143 (1). https://ascelibrary.org/doi/10.1061/%28ASCE%29EY.1943-7897.0000373.

Ramirez, Cindy. 2013. "Fort Bliss, Beaumont Infuse $6 Billion into El Paso Economy." *El Paso Times*, March 8. https://archive.is/20130825073153/http://www.elpasotimes .com/newupdated/ci_22747724/study-fort-bliss-beaumont-medical-center-infuse -6html.html.

Reidenbach, Luke, Mark Price, Estelle Sommeiller, and Ellis Wazeter. 2016. "Growth of Top Incomes across California." California Budget and Poverty Center, February. https://calbudgetcenter.org/wp-content/uploads/The-Growth-of-Top-Incomes -Across-California-02172016.pdf.

Rodgers, Randy. 2016. "In Kansas City, It's All about People." *IIMC News Digest*, August. https://www.iimc.com/ArchiveCenter/ViewFile/Item/463.

Ryan, Daniel. 2015. "From Commitment to Action: A Literature Review on Climate Policy Implementation at City Level." *Climatic Change* 131 (4): 519–529.

Satterthwaite, David. 2008. "Cities' Contribution to Global Warming: Notes on the Allocation of Greenhouse Gas Emissions." *Environment and Urbanization* 20 (2): 539–549.

Scharpf, Fritz W. 2018. *Games Real Actors Play: Actor-Centered Institutionalism in Policy Research.* New York: Routledge.

Schneider, Mark, John Scholz, Mark Lubell, Denisa Mindruta, and Matthew Edwardsen. 2003. "Building Consensual Institutions: Networks and the National Estuary Program." *American Journal of Political Science* 47 (1): 143–158.

Scott, Tyler A., and Craig W. Thomas. 2017. "Unpacking the Collaborative Toolbox: Why and When Do Public Managers Choose Collaborative Governance Strategies?" *Policy Studies Journal* 45 (1): 191–214.

Scott, Tyler A., and Nicola Ulibarri. 2019. "Taking Network Analysis Seriously: Methodological Improvements for Governance Network Scholarship." *Perspectives on Public Management and Governance* 2 (2): 89–101.

Seto, Karen C., Shobhakar Dhakal, Anthony Bigio, Hilda Blanco, Gian Carlo Delgado, David Dewar, Luxin Huang, et al. 2014. "Human Settlements, Infrastructure, and Spatial Planning." In *Climate Change, 2014: Mitigation of Climate Change*, edited by O. Edenhofer, R. Pichs-Madruga, Y. Sokona, E. Farahani, S. Kadner, K. Seyboth, A. Adler, et al., 923–1000. Cambridge: Cambridge University Press.

Sharp, Elaine B., Dorothy M. Daley, and Michael S. Lynch. 2011. "Understanding Local Adoption and Implementation of Climate Change Mitigation Policy." *Urban Affairs Review* 47 (3): 433–457.

Shrestha, Manoj, Ramiro Berardo, and Richard Feiock. 2014. "Solving Institutional Collective Action Problems in Multiplex Networks." *Complexity, Governance and Networks* 1 (1): 49–60.

Sinclair, Amber H., and Andrew B. Whitford. 2012. "Separation and Integration in Public Health: Evidence from Organizational Structure in the States." *Journal of Public Administration Research and Theory* 23 (1): 55–77.

Spencer, Benjamin, Josh Lawler, Celia Lowe, LuAnne Thompson, Tom Hinckley, Soo-Hyung Kim, Susan Bolton, Scott Meschke, Julian D. Olden, and Joachim Voss. 2017. "Case Studies in Co-benefits Approaches to Climate Change Mitigation and Adaptation." *Journal of Environmental Planning and Management* 60 (4): 647–667.

Stanton, Ryan. 2014. "Ann Arbor Greenbelt Turns 10: Thousands of Acres of Farmland Preserved." *M Live*, October 9. http://www.mlive.com/news/ann-arbor/2014/10/ann _arbor_greenbelt_program_10.html.

———. 2018. "$40M-Plus Spent, 5,200 Acres Protected under Ann Arbor Greenbelt." *M Live*, July 25. https://www.mlive.com/news/ann-arbor/2018/07/40m-plus_spent _5200_acres_prot.html.

STAR Communities. n.d. "Leading Indicators." Accessed March 14, 2017. http://www .starcommunities.org/get-started/leading-indicators/.

State of California. 2018. "State of California Sea Level Rise Guidance, 2018 Update." http://www.opc.ca.gov/webmaster/ftp/pdf/agenda_items/20180314/Item3_Exhibit-A _OPC_SLR_Guidance-rd3.pdf.

St. Louis Post-Dispatch. 1993. "State Threatens Action over Dump Near Stadium." December 14, p. 3C.

Swann, William L., and Aaron Deslatte. 2018. "What Do We Know about Urban Sustainability? A Research Synthesis and Nonparametric Assessment." *Urban Studies* 56 (9): 1729–1747.

Terman, Jessica N., and Richard C. Feiock. 2015. "Improving Outcomes in Fiscal Federalism: Local Political Leadership and Administrative Capacity." *Journal of Public Administration Research and Theory* 25 (4): 1059–1080.

Terman, Jessica, Richard C. Feiock, and Jisun Youm. 2020. "When Collaboration Is Risky Business: The Influence of Collaboration Risks on Formal and Informal Collaboration." *American Review of Public Administration* 51 (1): 33–44.

Thomson, Ann Marie, and James L. Perry. 2006. "Collaboration Processes: Inside the Black Box." *Public Administration Review* 66 (s1): 20–32.

University of Michigan. n.d. "Facts and Figures." Accessed March 1, 2019. http:// communityrelations.umich.edu/facts-figures/.

U.S. Census Bureau. 2019a. "Quick Facts: Ann Arbor City, Michigan." https://www .census.gov/quickfacts/fact/table/washtenawcountymichigan,annarborcitymichigan ,US/PST045219.

———. 2019b. "Quick Facts: El Paso City, Texas." https://www.census.gov/quickfacts/ table/PST045216/4824000,00.

———. 2019c. "Quick Facts: Fort Collins City, Colorado." https://www.census.gov/ quickfacts/fact/table/fortcollinscitycolorado,US/PST045219.

———. 2019d. "Quick Facts: Gainesville City, Florida." https://www.census.gov/ quickfacts/fact/table/gainesvillecityflorida,US/PST045219.

———. 2019e. "Quick Facts: Kansas City City, Kansas." https://www.census.gov/quickfacts/fact/table/kansascitycitymissouri,US/PST045219.

———. 2019f. "Quick Facts: Oakland City, California." https://www.census.gov/quickfacts/fact/table/oaklandcitycalifornia/PST045219.

———. 2019g. "Quick Facts: Orlando City, Florida." https://www.census.gov/quickfacts/fact/table/orlandocityflorida,US/PST045219.

———. 2019h. "Quick Facts: Providence City, Rhode Island." https://www.census.gov/quickfacts/fact/table/providencecityrhodeisland,US/PST045219.

U.S. Department of Energy. 2009. "Energy Efficiency and Conservation Block Grants." https://www.arc.gov/noindex/newsroom/ARRA/webinars/04-01-2009/DOE_Energy_Efficiency_and_Conservation_Block_Grants.pdf.

U.S. Department of Transportation. 2018. "State and Urbanized Area Statistics." March 29. https://www.fhwa.dot.gov/ohim/onh00/onh2p11.htm.

Visit Fort Collins. 2016. "Fort Collins Inspired Disneyland's Main Street U.S.A." July 29. https://www.visitftcollins.com/fort-collins-inspired-disneyland-main-street-u-s-a/.

Wang, XiaoHu, Christopher Hawkins, and Evan Berman. 2014. "Financing Sustainability and Stakeholder Engagement: Evidence from U.S. Cities." *Urban Affairs Review* 50 (6): 806–834.

Wang, XiaoHu, Christopher V. Hawkins, Nick Lebredo, and Evan M. Berman. 2012. "Capacity to Sustain Sustainability: A Study of U.S. Cities." *Public Administration Review* 72 (6): 841–853.

Wang, XiaoHu, Cheol Liu, and Christopher V. Hawkins. 2017. "Local Government Strategies for Financing Energy Efficiency Initiatives." *American Review of Public Administration* 47 (6): 672–686.

Wasserman, Stanley, and Katherine Faust. 1994. *Social Network Analysis: Methods and Applications*. Vol. 8. Cambridge: Cambridge University Press.

Whitley, Chris. 2010. "Kansas City, Mo., to spend $25 Billion to Cut Sewer Overflows." U.S. Environmental Protection Agency, May 18. https://www.epa.gov/enforcement/kansas-city-mo-spend-25-billion-cut-sewer-overflows.

Willem, Annick, and Marc Buelens. 2007. "Knowledge Sharing in Public Sector Organizations: The Effect of Organizational Characteristics on Interdepartmental Knowledge Sharing." *Journal of Public Administration Research and Theory* 17 (4): 581–606.

Wolch, Jennifer R., Jason Byrne, and Joshua P. Newell. 2014. "Urban Green Space, Public Health, and Environmental Justice: The Challenge of Making Cities 'Just Green Enough.'" *Landscape and Urban Planning* 125:234–244.

Yang, Tung-Mou, and Terrence A. Maxwell. 2011. "Information-Sharing in Public Organizations: A Literature Review of Interpersonal, Intra-organizational and Interorganizational Success Factors." *Government Information Quarterly* 28 (2): 164–175.

Zahran, Sammy, Samuel D. Brody, Arnold Vedlitz, Himanshu Grover, and Caitlyn Miller. 2008. "Vulnerability and Capacity: Explaining Local Commitment to Climate-Change Policy." *Environment and Planning C: Government and Policy* 26 (3): 544–562.

Zeemering, Eric S. 2009. "What Does Sustainability Mean to City Officials?" *Urban Affairs Review* 45 (2): 247–273.

———. 2017. "Sustainability Management, Strategy and Reform in Local Government." *Public Management Review* 20 (1): 136–153.

———. 2018. "Why Terminate? Exploring the End of Interlocal Contracts for Police Service in California Cities." *American Review of Public Administration* 48 (6): 596–609.

Index

Page numbers in italics indicate material in figures or tables.

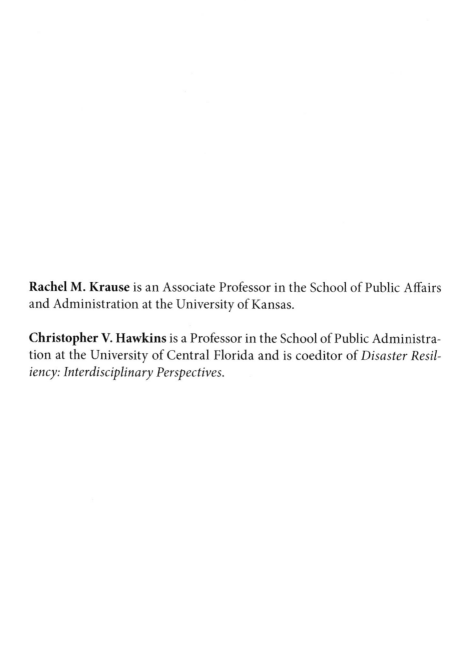

Rachel M. Krause is an Associate Professor in the School of Public Affairs and Administration at the University of Kansas.

Christopher V. Hawkins is a Professor in the School of Public Administration at the University of Central Florida and is coeditor of *Disaster Resiliency: Interdisciplinary Perspectives.*